VISIONS OF INNOVATION

Visions of Innovation

The Firm and Japan

MARTIN FRANSMAN

OXFORD

UNIVERSITY PRESS

OXFORD
UNIVERSITY PRESS

Oxford University Press, Great Clarendon Street, Oxford OX2 6DP

Oxford New York
Athens Auckland Bangkok Bogota Bombay
Buenos Aires Calcutta Cape Town Dar es Salaam
Delhi Florence Hong Kong Istanbul Karachi
Kuala Lumpur Madras Madrid Melbourne
Mexico City Nairobi Paris Singapore
Taipei Tokyo Toronto Warsaw
and associated companies in
Berlin Ibadan

Oxford is a registered trade mark of Oxford University Press

Published in the United States
by Oxford University Press Inc., New York

British Library Cataloguing in Publication Data
Data available

Library of Congress Cataloging in Publication Data
Fransman, Martin.
Visions of innovation: the firm and Japan / Martin Fransman.
p. cm.—(Japan business & economics)
Includes bibliographical references and index.
1. Technological innovations—Japan—Management. 2. Computer
industry—Technological innovations—Japan. 3. Telecommunication—
Technolgical innovations—Japan. 4. Organizational change—Japan.
I. Title. II. Series: Japan business and economics.
HD45.F7167 1999
658.4'063'0952—dc21 98-20647

ISBN 0–19–828935–9

1 3 5 7 9 10 8 6 4 2

Typeset by Best-set Typesetter Ltd., Hong Kong
Printed in Great Britain
on acid-free paper by
Biddles Limited, Guildford
and King's Lynn

For Judy, Karen and Jonathan

CONTENTS

Introduction

The Concept of Vision

'Vision' is the main theme of this book. This, however, immediately poses a question: what, precisely, is meant by vision? This question is all the more important as a result of the wide range of meanings that has been given to the term in popular discussion.

The first point to make in answering the question is that the concept of vision as used in this book is different in significant respects from that used popularly. In everyday discussion the term vision usually connotes creative foresight; a person with vision is one who knows what needs to be done and how to get it done. Most of all, a person with vision gets it right. To the popular mind vision is an indispensable aid in the modern world; presidents of both countries and companies therefore must have vision.

Vision and Beliefs

In this book the concept of vision is given a far more restricted meaning. At the most general level vision refers to beliefs about what the world is like, how it changes, and what it will be like with and without the believer's interventions. It is in the light of their beliefs that people act. Their beliefs allow them to envision the future, that is to 'see' the future by constructing mental pictures regarding the state of affairs that they intend through their actions to bring about. Beliefs, accordingly, provide the building blocks for the construction of visions.

The conceptualisation of vision in terms of belief, however, forces a break with the popular notion that vision implies foresight, that is an ability to know what is required in order to achieve the actor's objectives. The reason, simply, is that beliefs, as we all know, may turn out to be incorrect. Where this is the case, the visions which have been constructed on the basis of the incorrect beliefs will therefore also be incorrect. These cases will be referred to as instances of vision failure.

Since the notion of vision being offered here is dependent on the concept of belief it is necessary to explore this concept in more detail. In doing so two questions are crucial: How are beliefs constructed and how do they change?

One answer to both these questions has been given in terms of the further concept of information. In short, people are essentially information processors; their beliefs and hence their visions are the outcome of the information they have received and processed. (Received information includes the effects of experience and learning.) The receipt and processing of new information may result in a change in their beliefs and visions. This view has been put forward, for example, by the philosopher Dretske (1982). Dretske argues that 'information is that commodity capable of yielding knowledge' (p. 44). Knowledge, in turn, 'is identified with information-produced (or -sustained) belief' (p. 86). In other words, the processing of information by people results in their knowledge/belief.

In order to explore further this information-processing approach to beliefs it is useful to begin with an extreme assumption, namely that the actor possesses complete information. Complete information may be defined as the set of all information that is relevant to the issue or problem with which the actor is dealing. If this assumption is correct, then, following Dretske's definitions of information and knowledge/belief, it follows that the actor will be able to derive correct knowledge/beliefs (correct in the sense that the knowledge/beliefs will be compatible with and supported by the complete set of information).

To take an example, a bullion investor's knowledge/belief regarding yesterday's closing gold price might be based on processing a limited set of information provided in the Financial Times. Although there is always the possibility that this information contains an error that could have been made for numerous reasons, most investors most of the time will not be overly bothered by the possibility that they do not possess a complete information set. In cases such as these the argument that correct knowledge/beliefs are derived from the processing of complete information seems reasonable.

The complete information argument, however, is limited by possible problems. More specifically, in some cases it may not be possible to know when the set of information is complete in the sense that it contains all the relevant information. Might not some new information later become available which will turn out to be relevant to the problem at hand? How can the actor be sure that he/she possesses all the relevant information? But, to the extent that the actor cannot be sure, she/he will have to be to some extent tentative regarding the knowledge/beliefs which have been derived from the information set which has been obtained. And tentative knowledge/belief is, clearly, not the same as correct knowledge/belief. An actor acting on the basis of beliefs which are held to be tentative may act differently from one assuming that his/her beliefs are correct. In the case of tentative knowledge/belief the tight-coupling which in Dretske's view exists between information and knowledge/belief is necessarily loosened. This has important consequences which will be examined in more detail later.

Bounded Rationality and Interpretive Ambiguity

Two further cases are also worth exploring. The first case is where the set of relevant information in existence exceeds that which the actor is capable of acquiring and processing. The second case arises where the actor, rather than being unsure about being in possession of a complete information set, is sure that the set of information is incomplete.

The first case has been dealt with by Nobel Prize winner Herbert Simon in his celebrated notion of *bounded rationality*. Simon defines bounded rationality in the following way: 'the capacity of the human mind for formulating and solving complex problems is very small compared with the size of the problems whose solution is required for objectively rational behavior in the real world—or even for a reasonable approximation to such objective rationality' (quoted in Chapter 1 of this book). In this case the actor's rationality is bounded in the sense that, although his/her knowledge/beliefs are derived from the processing of information, the set of information acquired and processed by the actor is less than the total set of relevant information in existence. With the exclusion of some relevant information this implies that the actor's knowledge/beliefs might diverge from those that would have been derived had the actor possessed the complete set of relevant information. In this case too, Dretske's tight coupling between information and knowledge, the latter conceived of as justified true belief, breaks down. The actor's knowledge/beliefs, being based on a partial set of information, are not necessarily correct.

In the second case the problem arises, not from the great quantity of relevant information relative to the ability of the actor to process information as in the case of bounded rationality, but from the incompleteness of the existing information. To take an example bedevilling the British nation at the time of writing: is there sufficient information to justify the belief that BSE (bovine spongiform encephalopathy, so-called mad cow's disease) has spread to the human population in the form of CJD (Creutzfeldt–Jakob disease)? The existing set of relevant information includes data on the incidence of BSE and CJD. But at the current time this information set is incapable of yielding unambiguous knowledge/belief regarding the ability of BSE to spread via the food chain to the human population or the likely incidence amongst the human population if such spread is possible. In the light of incomplete information such as this, different actors can and do derive different, even contradictory, 'knowledge'/beliefs.

In the present book *interpretive ambiguity* is defined as existing when the current information set is capable of yielding inconsistent inferences regarding what should be believed. Under conditions of interpretive ambiguity, therefore, the information set is incomplete in the sense that it cannot generate unambiguous knowledge/belief.

How do actors act under conditions of interpretive ambiguity? My answer is that they make a 'leap' from the information which they have, information which is fuzzy in the sense that it does not allow clear and unambiguous beliefs to be derived, to a constructed set of more sharply defined beliefs. While this leap is not necessarily a leap in the dark, it is a movement from an incomplete set of information to a set of beliefs which are not wholly derived from the initial information. Under interpretive ambiguity, therefore, beliefs have an essential degree of autonomy from the information underlying them. In other words, there is under these conditions a loose coupling between information and belief. The function of this leap is to make the world appear to be more focused and therefore more understandable than it actually is in order to facilitate more decisive action. Otherwise, in a world of interpretive ambiguity, an actor might be immobilised by the absence of clear inferences.

The relative autonomy of belief from information, however, may present further problems. In the absence of a complete information set, existing beliefs may provide the basis for an interpretation of the incomplete information. Here the usual line of causality, namely from information acquired and processed to belief, will be reversed. In these circumstances it is possible that a disjuncture between information and belief will arise. An example, which is analysed in detail in Chapter 1, is what is referred to there as the IBM Paradox. In this case the beliefs of IBM, the information-processing company par excellence (i.e. beliefs until about 1991 in the ability of the mainframe computer to sustain the company's growth, size, and profitability) were increasingly inconsistent with information that the company had acquired regarding the rising competitiveness of smaller computers and the networks of these computers.

The discussion so far addresses one of the two questions posed earlier, namely how are beliefs constructed? To summarise, where there is complete information, beliefs are constructed from processed information (which may include past learning and experience). However, under conditions of interpretive ambiguity, constructed beliefs are relatively autonomous from the actor's set of (by definition incomplete) information. Beliefs under these conditions are partly derived from other factors which 'fill in' for the missing information, factors such as hunches, speculations, and suppositions which are not themselves derived from the possessed set of information. However, less has been said about the second question: how do beliefs change?

The Evolution of Beliefs

This discussion is also relevant in addressing the second question. The discussion suggests that in analysing the process of change in beliefs, or the evolution of beliefs, it is necessary to distinguish between two different circumstances. In the first circumstance there is a flow of new information which results in a new but complete set of information. In this case the beliefs which are held at time T will be revised at the later time T + 1 as a result of the new complete information which has been acquired and processed between T and T + 1. This case is the same, therefore, as the belief equals the processed information case, that is the case where there is a tight coupling between information and belief.

In the second circumstance, however, the information which is acquired and processed from T to T + 1 is incomplete in the sense defined earlier. As a result there is interpretive ambiguity regarding the revised beliefs that should replace the set of beliefs existing at time T. As always under conditions of interpretive ambiguity, an indeterminacy will be introduced between processed information and the beliefs which they inform. Different people, accordingly, may derive different beliefs from the same set of information at T + 1.

An example of the second circumstance is provided by the videophone. The idea of a telephone that will also show an image of the person with whom communication is taking place has a very long history. However, it was from the 1950s that experimentation with videotelephony began. In the late 1960s AT&T introduced a commercial videophone, forecasting a significant market for this new service. But the belief that there would be substantial demand for the videophone was contradicted by the sales information that accrued. In 1973 this information led AT&T to change its beliefs. Accordingly, the Picturephone was withdrawn by which time AT&T had spent an estimated half a billion dollars on the project.

However, while the information was unambiguous in its inference that there was not significant demand for the videophone at the price at which it was offered, the information set was incomplete regarding the precise reason for the low demand. Were potential adopters not forthcoming because the price was too high, because they were unaccustomed to seeing the people they were talking to on the phone, or because they did not want their privacy invaded? The information set and the interpretive ambiguity which it implied did not provide sufficient evidence to confirm or reject any of the sets of beliefs underlying these three hypotheses. And each of these hypotheses had very different implications regarding what telecommunications companies should do regarding the videophone. In 1992 AT&T reintroduced a videophone but again the market demand was disappointing. However, at present there are once more different schools of thought, based on inconsistent beliefs, regarding the future of the videophone. At the one extreme are the pessimists who believe that generally consumers will not want to purchase videophones under any likely conditions. On the other extreme are the optimists who believe that demand will increase significantly as price falls and familiarity with the videophone increases. All in all, a typical response under conditions of interpretive ambiguity.

This discussion allows us to make some generalisations regarding the
evolution of beliefs. An evolutionary path is generated by the interaction
of a process generating variety and a process which selects from the variety
that has been generated. In the case of the evolution of beliefs two important points emerge from our earlier discussion. The first is that interpretive
ambiguity contributes to the generation of variety since under these conditions different, even inconsistent, beliefs may be constructed from the
same incomplete set of information. The second point, shown clearly with
the videophone, is that even where a selection process is operating (e.g. the
negative feedback from the market regarding the belief in a high future
demand for the videophone), the continuing existence of interpretive ambiguity may mean that a variety of beliefs continues to be generated. While,
therefore, interpretive ambiguity injects a degree of indeterminacy and
unpredictability regarding the evolution of future beliefs, it at the same time
helps to generate the very variety that powers the evolutionary process.

Visions of the Firm

One of the implications of the last section is that in order to act, decision-
takers in firms will have to construct beliefs about the world in which
they are operating (including the internal world of their companies). To
the extent that they have complete information, there will be a tight-
coupling between the information they acquire and process, and the beliefs
and visions they construct. However, to the extent that they operate
under conditions of interpretive ambiguity, there will be a loose-coupling
between their information and the beliefs and visions they construct.
This is one sense in which the phrase, *Visions of the Firm*, should be
understood.

However, there is also a second sense to the book's title, namely the
visions of the firm which have been constructed by analysts of the firm. It
is these visions which constitute the object of analysis in Chapter 1.

As Edith Penrose has pointed out in a perceptive passage, the firm itself,
as an analytical object, in an ambiguous entity:

A 'firm' is by no means an unambiguous clear-cut entity; it is not an observable
object physically separable from other objects, and it is difficult to define except
with reference to what it does or what is done within it. Hence each analyst is free
to choose any characteristics of firms that he is interested in, to define firms in terms
of those characteristics, and to proceed thereafter to call the construction so defined
a 'firm'. Herein lies a potential source of confusion. (Quoted in Chapter 1.)

Given that the firm is an ambiguous entity, there is interpretive ambiguity attaching to its analysis. In Chapter 1 it is shown that, depending on their

interests and purposes, different analysts have given different answers to some fundamental questions regarding firms, for example: What is a firm? What do firms do? Why do firms exist? How do firms become and remain competitive? How do firms grow? In short, different analysts have constructed different beliefs and visions regarding the essential features of firms.

In Chapter 1 it is shown that some of the most prominent theories of the firm can be classified into one of two groups. The first group of theories sees the firm as a solution to information-related problems. These theories include visions of the firm which see the firm as a response to problems arising from bounded rationality; information-related costs of making market transactions; the need to monitor and control the activities of members of a jointly-producing team in order to prevent shirking; and the problem of possible misalignment of objectives of principals and agents. The authors examined in this group are Coase, Alchian and Demsetz, Jensen and Mechling, Simon, and Williamson.

The second group of theories sees the firm not as a response to information-related difficulties but as a repository of knowledge. According to this group of theories the firm is essentially a bundle of specific knowledge embodied in the firm's routines and competencies. It is this specific knowledge which leads not only to differences amongst firms (and hence to variety) but also to the earning of quasi-rents on the part of those firms which possess distinctive competencies which cannot be easily emulated by would-be competitors. As is shown in Chapter 1, this different vision of the firm leads its adherents to fundamentally different answers to the fundamental questions regarding the firm referred to above. The analysts in this group whose work is examined are Penrose, Chandler, Nelson and Winter, and Teece *et al*.

Visions and Routines

For the details regarding these theories of the firm the reader is referred to Chapter 1. However, since this introduction is concerned with the general concept of vision and since the concept of routines has become a central component in the second group of theories of the firm, a little more will be said here about the relationship between these two concepts.

In this introduction it has been argued that decision-makers have no option but to form beliefs regarding their world and to construct visions on the basis of these beliefs. Clearly, the process of belief and vision construction can be complex and can take a significant amount of time. Equally clearly, in making their decisions, decision-makers do not construct all of their beliefs and visions *ab initio*. Rather many of their beliefs and visions at any particular point in time become part of a set of starting assumptions about the circumstances in which the decision is being made, assumptions that are taken as given and are not re-examined or requestioned. To do otherwise would often be too costly in terms of time and other resources and may render the decision-making process inefficient.

The positive function performed by routinised behaviour is well understood. Most importantly, such behaviour allows the individual or organisation to respond quickly, short-circuiting the need to calculate the kind of response that is most appropriate in the circumstances. In the case of recurring events, routinised responses may be particularly efficient. However, where circumstances are changing and particularly where the changes are radical, there is a danger that the routinised response will be inappropriate. Organisational inertia results when an organisation is slow to change its responses. Inertia, and the success with which an organisation can overcome it, will play an important role in determining the outcome of an evolutionary selection process.

Routines, however, embody visions and beliefs as defined here, beliefs regarding the kinds of responses that are most appropriate in particular circumstances. This is evident at the time the decisions are made, explicitly or implicitly, to institute routinised responses. Over time, however, the visions and beliefs embodied in routines become submerged, disappearing from view. Indeed, for behaviour to become routinised the visions and beliefs embodied in the routines must become submerged. The reason is that, for routines to perform their economising function, the routinised responses must be made automatically, without reference to, and perhaps questioning of, the assumptions under which they have been formulated.

It may be concluded, therefore, that visions and routines are closely related, both in theory as well as in practice. An understanding of the one necessitates an understanding of the other.

Vision and the Evolution of Firms

The Paradox of Japanese Computer and Communications Firms

Chapters 2, 3, and 4 deal with the evolution of firms and include an analysis of the role of vision. In Chapter 2 a paradox relating to Japan's computer and communications companies is explained, companies such as NEC, Fujitsu, Hitachi, Toshiba, Mitsubishi Electric, and Oki: while these firms are amongst the global top ten in terms of size, they are dominant in very few markets outside Japan. They are therefore very different from the Japanese consumer electronics and motor car companies which in general are significantly more competitive outside Japan. (This issue is also dealt with in depth in the author's companion volume, *Japan's Computer and*

Communications Industry: The Evolution of Industrial Giants and Global Competitiveness, Oxford University Press, 1995.)

To be more specific, four out of the world's top ten computer companies are Japanese (Fujitsu, NEC, Hitachi, and Toshiba); two out of the top ten telecommunications equipment firms are Japanese (NEC and Fujitsu); and six out of the top ten semiconductor companies are Japanese (NEC, Toshiba, Hitachi, Fujitsu, Mitsubishi Electric, and Matsushita). However, while Japan's computer and communications companies have dominated global markets in areas such as memory semiconductors, optoelectronic semiconductors, microcontrollers, and liquid crystal displays, they have been significantly less successful outside Japan in crucial markets such as mainframe computers, workstations, servers, personal computers, microprocessors, packaged software, and complex telecommunications equipment. While the explanation of this paradox is complex and is provided in Chapter 2, more will be said here about the role played by vision.

To begin with, vision as defined earlier was a key determinant of the specific evolutionary path followed by each firm. One example, discussed in detail in Chapter 2, was the original decision of Fujitsu, now the world's second largest computer company, to enter the field of computers. Fujitsu was originally established as a joint venture between its parent, Fuji Electric, and Siemens to specialise in telecommunications equipment. After the Second World War, Fujitsu emerged as one of the four major suppliers of such equipment to the national telecommunications carrier, NTT. However, amongst the four suppliers it was NEC that was dominant and this constrained Fujitsu's opportunities for growth. Against this background, and in the light of emerging technical possibilities and market opportunities in the new field of computers, a belief was constructed by some of Fujitsu's younger technical staff that the company should make computers a key priority for future strategy. This belief, however, was strongly contested by the company's President and Board who, on the basis of the information available, constructed a contradictory set of beliefs. They argued that Fujitsu's priority should be restricted to telecommunications equipment since although the company was not the dominant supplier, the long-term relationship which it had forged with NTT guaranteed certain and steady growth. The field of computers, however, was characterised by significant entry costs and uncertainty and Western companies enjoyed a substantial lead. So strong was their conviction that it took a new President (whose accession to the position was somewhat fortuitous) for the belief in the importance of computers to become a central element in Fujitsu's corporate strategy.

However, it would be wrong to place too much emphasis on vision in the explanation of this paradox. Other factors such as the strength of Western competitors (including IBM, Intel, Microsoft, AT&T, Northern Telecom, and Ericsson), the *de facto* standards which emerged in Japan and which diverged particularly from US standards (in areas such as personal computers, software, and telecommunications equipment), and the rapid post-war growth rate in Japan which allowed these companies to prosper by serving Japanese markets, were crucial in limiting Japanese competitiveness in many information and communications markets outside Japan. While these factors were the outcome of the visions and actions of other agents, they appeared to the decision-makers in the Japanese computer and communications companies as the 'givens' within which they had to construct their own visions. To attempt to explain the paradox solely in terms of the visions of these Japanese companies would be to give too great a weight to subjective or voluntaristic factors.

AT&T, BT, and NTT: Similar Environments, Different Visions

The puzzle tackled in Chapter 3 is why firms in a similar changing environment sometimes construct fundamentally different visions regarding what they should be doing. The case examined is that of the major telecommunications carriers of the USA, Britain, and Japan, namely AT&T, BT, and NTT. In the mid-1980s these three companies faced similar radical changes in their environment. More specifically, all three lost their national monopoly status and faced competition from vigorous new entrants. Furthermore, they had to confront fundamental changes transforming the telecommunications industry. These included the maturation of their bread-and-butter service—the plain old telephone—the corresponding increasing importance of new services, and the globalisation of both telecoms services and equipment markets.

Given these changes, how should the firm play its cards? Significantly—as is shown in detail in Chapter 3—each of the firms answered this question in fundamentally different ways, constructing different beliefs and visions regarding what should be done. To summarise, after it was divested in 1984 and separated from the seven newly created 'Baby Bells', the big change for AT&T came in 1988 when Bob Allen assumed directorship of the company. He quickly introduced two major changes which set the course for the company until 1995 when it went through a further transformation. The first change (analysed in detail in Chapter 4) involved segmenting the company into some twenty business units, and decentralising substantially increased powers to these units.

The second change was based on Allen's twin beliefs, first, that AT&T's core competence lay in providing information solutions anywhere and anytime and, secondly, that this required in-house competences in three areas: network operation and development and service provision; telecommunications equipment; and computing. This second belief was derived from a further set of beliefs relating to the convergence of computer and communications technologies and the beneficial effects of synergies or economies of scope between the three areas. While the first two areas were part of AT&T's traditional business, the third was not. In order to acquire the competences in computing that according to Allen's beliefs were necessary, AT&T launched an ultimately successful hostile bid for the computer company NCR.

After its privatisation, BT, under Iain Vallence, went on to construct fundamentally different beliefs. Identifying BT's core competence as the 'running of telecommunications networks and the provision of services across them', Vallence publicly ridiculed Allen's belief in convergence. As he put it in 1990: 'What about "convergence"? Ten years ago that was the 'in' word. AT&T and IBM were going to clash in the battle of the titans. And I was going to wonder aloud whether AT&T had lost as much money in computers as IBM had in telecommunications'. Under Vallence, BT turned increasingly to the market to procure the equipment and computing inputs it required.

NTT occupied a position between the other two companies. While it refrained, as it always had done, from integrating 'backwards' into telecommunications equipment and computing, it believed that market forces could not be relied upon to deliver the advanced technologies and equipment that were needed at the right time. Accordingly, it continued its long-established practice of leading and working with a small group of suppliers in order to jointly develop advanced equipment. Increasingly, the small groups that were established to work on particular projects included major Western companies in additional to the traditional Japanese suppliers.

How have these inconsistent beliefs evolved into the second half of the 1990s? Taking the story beyond that provided in Chapter 3 and bringing it up-to-date, it is important to note that while BT and NTT have by and large maintained their beliefs in this area, a major change has taken place in AT&T. This occurred on 20 September 1995 when Bob Allen announced that AT&T would split itself into three separate companies, one offering telecoms services, one selling telecoms equipment, and one specialising in computers (the old NCR). Failing to specify for the benefit of his share-holders the precise changes that had occurred in his beliefs or the reason for these changes, Allen simply stated that 'We reached a time when the advantage of integration was outweighed by the disadvantage of complexity'. It was left to Business Week to summarise Allen's newly constructed beliefs: 'synergy is dead, and the concept of converging communications and computer markets, which drove the NCR deal, is an illusion'.

But is convergence dead? How about what is arguably the most important form of convergence yet, namely the convergence of cybernetworks (like the Internet) with the public switched telecommunications networks which will create competition between digital communications (including voice and video) provided over both sets of networks? Does this convergence mean that, finally, computer companies like IBM will come into head-to-head competitive rivalry with the telecommunications companies like AT&T, BT, and NTT? And what in-house competences will companies have to have in order to compete? As these questions imply, considerable interpretive ambiguity still surrounds these issues.

AT&T, IBM, and NEC: Resolving the Trade-off between Decentralisation and Cross-Business Coordination

In Chapter 4 one of the most important dilemmas facing the modern large computer and communications companies is analysed. This problem arises as a result of conflict between two contradictory organisational objectives. The first objective is to increase the decentralisation of the company in order to overcome the inefficiencies of large, centralised organisations. The second objective is to coordinate interdependent activities across the various decentralised units in order to realise the benefits arising from synergies and economies of scope. While decentralisation may provide important advantages by avoiding centralised decision-making, it at the same time increases the cost of coordination across relatively autonomous units.

For companies such as IBM, Siemens, Philips, Hitachi, Toshiba, NEC, and Fujitsu this dilemma assumes a particularly acute form since some of their most vigorous competitors are far more specialised than they are. For instance, in the field of computing companies like IBM, Fujitsu, Hitachi, NEC, and Siemens face strong competition from specialists such as Compaq, Dell, Microsoft, Intel, and Sun. In telecommunications equipment the 'all rounders'—like Siemens, NEC, and Fujitsu which produce telecoms equipment, computers, and semiconductors—confront specialists such as Ericsson, Northern Telecom, and Nokia. In semiconductors diversified firms including NEC, Toshiba, Siemens, Philips, Samsung, and Lucky Goldstar face the likes of Intel, Texas Instruments, Advanced Micro Devices, and Silicon Graphics.

To put the dilemma more starkly: would the value created by these diversified companies be greater if they were to split up into several smaller, independent, more specialised companies? In Chapter 4 the response of three companies to this dilemma is analysed, namely IBM, AT&T, and NEC. It is shown that all three companies, although at different times and in different ways, have constructed increasingly segmented forms of organisation—referred to in the chapter as S-form organisations. They have also developed different solutions to the problem of coordinating across relatively independent segmented units in order to realise the benefits of synergies and economies of scope. However, as mentioned earlier, in September 1995 AT&T came up with a far more radical solution to the dilemma when it decided to split itself up into three independent companies specialising in telecoms services, telecoms equipment, and computers. (This takes the AT&T story beyond the period covered in Chapter 4.) AT&T's move highlights the ongoing importance of this dilemma and, if anything, puts even more pressure on the diversified companies to clarify their beliefs regarding the benefits from integrating their wide range of activities. Once again, however, interpretive ambiguity bedevils any attempt to compare the benefits of specialisation with those of synergy and economies of scope.

Vision and Public Policy-Making

The remaining chapters—Chapters 5, 6, and 7—deal with the role of vision in public policy-making in Japan. Again there is a dual meaning attached to the phrase 'visions of policy-makers in Japan'. On the one hand, this phrase refers to the visions that the policy-makers have in mind when they formulate and implement their policies. On the other hand, however, the phrase also refers to a set of beliefs held by outside analysts regarding the significance of public policy-makers in Japan.

How Does the Japanese Innovation System Work?

To begin with the latter meaning, a reading of the literature on Japan makes it clear that there is considerable interpretive ambiguity regarding both the role and the effectiveness of public policy-makers in Japan. This interpretive ambiguity is manifest in the fundamentally different interpretations that have been given by different authors relating to the relative importance of 'government' and 'the market' in the explanation of the performance of the Japanese economy. For example, in a highly influential book, *MITI and the Japanese Miracle*, Chalmers Johnson has emphasised the important role played by the Japanese government and the Ministry of International Trade and Industry (MITI) in particular:

In states that were late to industrialize, the state itself led the industrialization drive, that is, it took on developmental functions. These two differing orientations toward private economic activities, the regulatory orientation and the developmental orientation, produced two different kinds of government-business relationships. The United States is a good example of a state in which the regulatory orientation predominates, whereas Japan is a good example of a state in which the developmental orientation predominates. A regulatory, or market-rational, state concerns itself with the forms and procedures—the rules, if you will—of economic competition, but it does not concern itself with substantive matters. . . . The developmental, or plan-rational, state, by contrast, has as its dominant feature precisely the setting of such substantive social and economic goals. (p. 19)

However, a fundamentally different vision of both the process and determinants of economic growth in Japan is to be found in the book, *Industrial Policy of Japan*, reporting on the outcome of a project involving some of Japan's leading economists and edited by Komiya, Okuno, and Suzumura. Regarding the question of 'the role of industrial policy in the rapid growth of postwar Japan' Okuno and Suzumura conclude:

All the participants in this project recognize that, excluding the brief period immediately after the end of the war, the foundation of rapid growth was competition operating through the price mechanism and a flourishing entrepreneurial spirit. In opposition to the 'Japan, Inc.' thesis, it can even be said that the course of the history of industrial policy in the principal postwar periods (in particular the 1950s and the 1960s) has often been that the initiative and vitality of the private sector undermined the plans of the government authorities to try to utilize direct intervention in the nature of 'controls'. Saying this does not mean that there were not industrial policy measures that should be favourably evaluated for their role in supplementing the price mechanism. (p. 553)

As these quotations from eminent scholars on Japan make clear, in the face of interpretive ambiguity, fundamentally different inferences and explanations may be constructed. (In this case, it is worth noting the incomplete information set, in terms of which interpretive ambiguity was earlier defined, is incomplete in the sense that it does not allow the derivation of unambiguous inferences regarding the cause and effect of market processes and government policies and interventions.) Precisely the same ambiguity is evident, for example, in debates (both intendedly positive and normative) about the role of government and the market in the 'Baby Tiger' economies of Korea, Taiwan, and Singapore. (For an attempt to resolve these ambiguities, an attempt that itself is riddled with ambiguity, see the World Bank's *The East Asian Miracle: Economic Growth and Public Policy*.) In the face of this interpretive ambiguity I attempt in Chapter 5 to produce my own vision of the way in which the 'Japanese Innovation System' works.

Does National Technology Policy Work in a Globalised World?

Chapter 6 deals with a major problem bedevilling policy-makers in the USA and Europe: can government play a positive role through the formulation and implementation of national industrial and technology policies? (In Japan, although there is currently a good deal of debate regarding the role of bureaucrats and their regulation of the economy, there is, as this and the following chapter show, more of a consensus regarding what government should be doing in the area of technology.)

More specifically, Chapter 6 begins with the argument that the effectiveness of national technology policy has been undermined by the globalisation of national economies through increasing international flows of knowledge, people, investment, and goods. But again interpretive ambiguity surrounds any attempt to answer this argument. This is apparent in the analysis of the implicit Japanese response to this argument which emerges from an examination of current national technology policy in Japan.

The Japanese vision of the role of technology policy is also the major concern of Chapter 7, researched and written with Shoko Tanaka. Here the question is far more specific: what should the Japanese government be doing to facilitate the growth of national competencies in a new technology area which it believes will become increasingly important for a wide range of industries, namely biotechnology? This question is all the more pressing since, for both historical and institutional reasons, Japan has been relatively weak in the life sciences. Chapter 7 contains a detailed description and analysis of the Japanese response to the advent of new biotechnology.

1

Visions of the Firm: A Critical Survey of Leading Approaches to the Firm

Economists have, of course, always recognized the dominant role that increasing knowledge plays in economic processes but have, for the most part, found the whole subject of knowledge too slippery too handle. (p. 77)

A 'firm' is by no means an unambiguous clear-cut entity; it is not an observable object physically separable from other objects, and it is difficult to define except with reference to what it does or what is done within it. Hence each analyst is free to choose any characteristics of firms that he is interested in, to define firms in terms of those characteristics, and to proceed thereafter to call the construction so defined a 'firm'. Herein lies a potential source of confusion. (p. 10)

Edith Penrose, The Theory of the Growth of the Firm, 1959

1.1 Overview

This chapter has the following purposes. The first purpose is to demonstrate that many of the best-known approaches to the firm in economics have in common a starting point which sees the firm as a response to information-related problems. The second is to review critically some of these approaches on the basis of the internal structure of their arguments. The third is to analyse some of the limitations of the 'information-related paradigm' in the light of the distinction which it is argued must be drawn between 'information' and 'knowledge'. Finally, the last purpose is to propose some additional approaches to the firm which merit further exploration.

This chapter was first published as 'Information, Knowledge, Vision and Theories of the Firm', *Industrial and Corporate Change*, 1994, 3(2), 1–45. The author would like to thank the following who gave comments on an earlier, longer version of the present chapter: Alfred Chandler, Edith Penrose, Brian Loasby, Richard Nelson, David Teece and Oliver Williamson. They are, however, not responsible for the contents of the present chapter.

1.2 Introduction

The firm as a response to information-related problems

Information may be defined as data relating to states of the world and the state-contingent consequences that follow from events in the world that are either naturally or socially caused. The total set of data is closed in that there is a closed set of states and consequences.

Several well-known approaches to the firm begin (implicitly) with this definition of information, plus the assumption that information is unevenly distributed amongst agents (that is, that there is asymmetric information). For example, as is shown in this chapter, Alchian and Demsetz's (1972) theory of the firm as joint team production, and Jensen and Meckling's (1976) theory of the firm as a nexus of contracts between principals and agents, are derived directly from this definition and assumption. Coase's approach to the firm, it is shown, is also essentially an approach based on information-related problems.

Williamson, however, challenges the view that asymmetric information *per se* presents problems. If people were honest they could be asked to 'tell the truth, the whole truth, and nothing but the truth'; and they would. In this way asymmetric information could become symmetrical. The problem is that people may become opportunistic. According to Williamson it is, therefore, opportunism rather than asymmetric information *per se* that presents problems. However, as argued later, asymmetric information is a necessary condition for opportunism: if information were symmetrically distributed, opportunism could not arise.

A further information-related problem which is given a central role in Williamson's approach is that of bounded rationality. In the present chapter this important concept is traced back to the original writings of Herbert Simon. For Simon, both human beings and their organisations are essentially information processors. It is this which links humans to computers and creates the basis for artificial intelligence, a field to which Simon has made important contributions.

It is shown later that according to a strict interpretation of Simon's most frequently quoted definition of bounded rationality, the problem arises where the quantity of relevant information is great relative to the ability of humans to deal with information (an ability, Simon stresses, which is not only physical, but is also psychologically and organisationally caused). Since humans often cannot deal with the entire set of relevant information, they have no alternative but to deal with only a subset. In this sense their decisions are 'bounded', based on the processing of only a subset of all the relevant information. (How 'rational' their decisions are is a question taken up in the later discussion on Simon.)

All the above-mentioned writers are united in their approach to the firm, and the economics of organisation more generally, by their concern with individual and organisational reponses to information-related problems.

The firm as a repository of knowledge

In the present paper a second approach to the firm is identified, namely an approach which sees the firm as a repository of knowledge. There is, however, a common starting-point between the second approach and the concerns of some in the first approach, namely the problem of bounded rationality. According to Nelson and Winter (1982) the routinisation of activities in the firm is largely a response to the quantity (including complexity) of information. However, although routines may be a response to information-related problems, attention in the Nelson and Winter approach to the firm shifts to the routines themselves. It is in its routines that a firm's organisational knowledge is stored. This is the source of *differences* amongst firms. And it is difference or variety which together with a selection mechanism drives the evolutionary process. At the same time it is the firm's routines which give Nelson and Winter a way of modelling the joint determination of the different behaviour patterns of different firms and market outcomes.

Although their particular purposes differ to some extent, it is shown that there is an important similarity between Nelson and Winter's approach and those of Penrose, Chandler, and Teece. For all of them the focus is on the firm as a repository of specific knowledge (including organisational and technological competence).

Information and knowledge

In all the above writings there is implicitly a 'tight coupling' between the concepts of 'information' and 'knowledge'. In view of this tight coupling none of the writers has felt it necessary to distinguish clearly between the two concepts. Following the philosopher Dretske (1982), the tight coupling may be expressed in the following way: information is a commodity that is capable of yielding knowledge; and knowledge is identified with information-produced (or sustained) belief. As this formulation makes clear, the line of causation is from information to knowledge. Knowledge is processed information.

There are, however, two major problems with this tight coupling of information and knowledge, both of which have important implications for the theory of the firm. The first is that under some circumstances a 'wedge' may be driven between information and knowledge with the result that they may become loosely coupled, or even uncoupled. Secondly, while information is a closed set, knowledge is essentially open (an insight that I owe to Brian Loasby). Following from the latter point, the process of knowledge-creation, a process central to all firms, cannot be analysed entirely in terms of the 'information-processing paradigm'. Both these problems require some elaboration.

To pursue the first problem, under conditions of *incomplete information* it will, by definition, be impossible to generate unambiguous knowledge from the information set used by the agent. Under such conditions the agent may derive alternative, even contradictory, 'knowledge' from the information set. Furthermore, different agents may derive different, even contradictory, 'knowledge' from the same set of information. Under these conditions a situation arises which may be referred to as one of *interpretive ambiguity*. It is intuitively obvious that situations of interpretive ambiguity will often arise. Under these conditions knowledge can only be loosely coupled to information and in the extreme case knowledge may become completely uncoupled. (Uncertainty regarding the future is a special case of incomplete information. Under conditions of uncertainty, information cannot be derived regarding future states and state-contingent consequences, including probabilistically-generated information. Under these conditions interpretive ambiguity will always exist.)

In the presence of interpretive ambiguity, the *beliefs* which comprise knowledge are not unambiguously sustained by the agent's information set. To go one step further, it may happen under these conditions that the agent's beliefs, which are relatively autonomous from the subjective information set, provide the basis for interpreting this set of information as well as new information. Under these circumstances the line of causation between information and knowledge will be reversed compared to the tight coupling case. Knowledge (belief) will be used to interpret the incomplete information (which cannot 'interpret itself' through the generation of unambiguous knowledge).

The second problem referred to above is somewhat different. Here the concern is not with the relationship between information and knowledge, as in the first problem, but with the different nature of information and knowledge. Information, as defined earlier, refers to data regarding states of the world and state-contingent consequences. Information refers inherently to a closed set of data. However, knowledge is essentially open-ended. Knowledge is always in a process of becoming, extending beyond itself. The firm's knowledge, therefore (that is the knowledge of its decision-makers including the knowledge of those who create the firm's knowledge) must be conceived of as being open-ended.

Implications for the theory of the firm

What are the implications for the theory of the firm of the present discussion of information and knowledge? In general, it is necessary to go beyond the 'information processing paradigm' in order to develop a more robust theory and understanding of the firm, while incorporating the important insights that this paradigm has provided. This requires two related conceptual advances.

First, knowledge (equated with belief) must be 'freed' from total dependence on processed information. While processed information may be an important input into the knowledge creation process, the creation of knowledge involves more than the processing of information. In order to analyse the process of knowledge-creation, a process central to most large firms, it is necessary to go beyond an analysis of information processing and treat knowledge on its own terms.

In the concluding section of this chapter the new concept of *vision* is developed for this purpose. While vision, which is based on a structure of beliefs, is influenced by processed information, it also embodies insight, creativity, and misconception. These are determinants of belief which, while drawing on processed information, go beyond it. The concept of vision is illustrated through a study of what is referred to as the 'IBM Paradox'. Here the paradox is examined whereby IBM, the information processing company *par excellence*, clung until 1991 to the mistaken belief in the ability of the mainframe computer to sustain its profitability, size, and growth. This belief was contradicted by information which IBM had processed regarding the increasing performance-cost of the microprocessor which resulted in the undermining of the mainframe.

Secondly, and closely following on the first point, a more sophisticated conceptualisation of the knowledge-creation process within firms must be developed. While this will require an understanding of the role of information processing, the conceptualisation must go further to treat knowledge on its own terms as an open-ended process.

1.3 The Firm as Response to Information-Related Problems

The authors included in the first approach have in common their view of the firm as a response to information-related problems. These include Alchian and Demsetz, Coase, Jensen and Meckling, Simon, and Williamson.

1.3.1 Asymmetrical Information

In elaborating on the information-related problems that are referred to by these authors we may begin with a few simplifying assumptions. Let it therefore be assumed that all possible states of affairs and state-contingent consequences relevant to a decision are common knowledge. Accordingly, there is a closed set of possibilities. Furthermore, let it be assumed that the state of affairs which actually pertains is unknown to one or more of the interactors. Under these conditions there is asymmetrical information, that is, some have information about the prevailing state of affairs that others do not have.

These conditions are sufficient, for both Alchian and Demsetz (1972) and Jensen and Meckling (1976), to explain the existence of the firm. But what, according to these authors, is a firm and what do firms do?

The firm as joint team production

For Alchian and Demsetz (1972) the firm is a specific form of organising co-operative productive activity, which they refer to as team production. The essential feature of team production is that it involves cooperation between the team members who together produce a joint output. However, the contribution to joint output made by each team member is not completely transparent. This creates the possibility of shirking. (Alchian and Demsetz actually go further than this and talk of an incentive to shirk.) To put it slightly differently, there is an asymmetrical distribution of information amongst the members of the team which prevents them all from knowing the precise contribution that has been made by each of them. Under these conditions it is not possible to fine-tune the alignment of contribution and reward, leading to the possibility of efficiency losses.

Furthermore, it is the information asymmetry and the resulting inability to align contributions and rewards that produces a need to monitor and control the activities or output of the team members. But who is to perform the monitoring and control function, and how is the monitor and controller to be monitored and controlled?

Alchian and Demsetz's answer to this question is that the team members have an incentive to consent to, and contractually-speaking in effect to appoint, a monitor and controller. This incentive arises from the greater productivity, the fruits of which will be enjoyed by all team members, that will follow from the reduction in shirking as a result of the advent of monitoring and controlling. (More specifically, it is assumed that the benefit of monitoring and controlling following from the greater productivity will exceed the cost of this activity.)

From the present discussion it is clear that Alchian and Demsetz's purpose is to examine the organisational implications of joint team production which takes place under conditions of asymmetrical information. This is apparent in the title of their paper, 'Production, Information Costs, and Economic Organisation'. This purpose leads them on to their answer to the twin questions, 'What is a firm? What do firms do?': 'the firm is the particular policing device utilized when joint team production is present' (ibid. 121). More generally, 'The problem of economic organization [is] the economical means of metering productivity and rewards' (113).

This view of what a firm is leads Alchian and Demsetz to dispute Coase's argument (that will be taken up again later) that the distinguishing feature of the firm is the allocation of resources by direction rather than by the price mechanism. As they put it:

> It is common to see the firm characterized by the power to settle issues by fiat, by authority, or by disciplinary action superior to that available in the conventional market. This is delusion. The firm does not own all its inputs. It has no power of fiat, no authority, no disciplinary action any different in the slightest degree from ordinary market contracting.... What then is the content of the presumed power to manage and assign workers to various tasks? ... To speak of managing, directing, or assigning workers to various tasks is a deceptive way of noting that the employer continually is involved in renegotiation of contracts on terms that must be acceptable to both parties. Telling an employee to type this letter rather than to file that document is like my telling a grocer to sell me this brand of tuna rather than that brand of bread. I have no contract to continue to purchase from the grocer and neither the employer nor the employee is bound by any contractual obligations to continue their relationship. Long-term contracts between employer and employee are not the essence of the organization we call a firm–(Alchian and Demsetz, 1972, 112).

The firm as a nexus of contracts between principals and agents

In approaching the firm, Jensen and Meckling's (1976) main purpose is to explore the significance of contracting relationships and of agency costs within these relationships. It is this purpose which leads them on to their answer to the two questions, 'What is a firm? What do firms do?', an answer that is significantly different from that proposed by Alchian and Demsetz (1972). According to Jensen and Meckling: 'Contractual relations are the essence of the firm, not only with employees but with suppliers, customers, creditors, etc. The problem of agency costs and monitoring exists for all of these contracts, independent of whether there is joint production in their [Alchian and Demsetz's] sense; i.e., joint production can explain only a small fraction of the behavior of individuals associated with a firm' (Jensen and Meckling 1976, 215).

Jensen and Meckling define the agency relationship as 'a contract under which one or more persons (the principal(s)) engage another person (the agent) to perform some service on their behalf which involves delegating some decision making authority to the agent' (ibid. 212). Agency costs arise from the fact that 'If both parties to the relationship are utility maximizers... the agent will not always act in the best interests of the principal' (212). Both principal and agent will normally attempt to accommodate such agency costs although they will be unable to eliminate them: 'The *principal* can limit divergences from his interest by establishing appropriate incentives for the agent and by incurring monitoring costs designed to limit the aberrant activities of the agent. In addition, in some situations it will pay the *agent* to expend resources (bonding costs) to guarantee that the principal will be compensated if he does take such actions. However, it is generally impossible for the principal or the agent at zero cost to ensure that the agent will make optimal decisions from the principal's viewpoint' (212).

What, therefore, is a firm? According to Jensen and Meckling, a firm is 'the nexus of a set of contracting relationships among individuals' (215). They continue, 'it makes little or no sense to try to distinguish those [contractual relationships] which are "inside" the firm (or any other organisation) from those . . . that are "outside" of it. There is in a very real sense only a multitude of complex relationships (i.e. contracts between the legal fiction (the firm) and the owners of labor, material and capital inputs and the consumers of output)' (215). In Jensen and Meckling's view, therefore, the firm is a form of market.

In commenting on Jensen and Meckling's view of the firm it must be noted that the problem of agency, which as we have seen is central to their view, is largely reducible to the problem of information asymmetry and the cost which arises in attempting to cope with the consequences of such asymmetry. If the principal possessed (and processed) the same information set as the agent, the 'agency problem' would be transformed since the principal would know if the agent's actions were inconsistent with his/her interests, even though he/she (the principal) would still have to decide how best to act in the light of this knowledge.

Ronald Coase and why firms exist

As Ronald Coase (1988) explains regarding his writings in the 1930s on the firm, 'my purpose . . . was to explain why there are firms' (Coase 1988, 38). It was this purpose that led him to focus on two puzzles.

The first puzzle that Coase defined and began to tackle in the early 1930s was the following: if specialisation is efficient, why does integration, a move away from specialisation, frequently take place? As early as 1932 Coase had defined integration as 'The bringing together under one control of different functions' (Coase 1988, 19). This puzzle was closely related to a second puzzle that Coase posed in his famous 1937 article, *The Nature of The Firm*: 'In view of the fact that, while economists treat the price mechanism as a co-ordinating instrument, they also admit the co-ordinating function of the "entrepreneur", it is surely important to enquire why co-ordination is the work of the price mechanism in one case and of the entrepreneur in another' (Coase 1937, 20).

It was these puzzles that led Coase to ask the question: why do firms exist? In order to deal with this question, however, Coase needed to deal with a logically prior question: what is a firm? Only by having a conception of what a firm is could he begin to explore why it existed.

Coase's answer to the question 'What is a firm?' emerges in his conceptualisation of an economy without any firms. In such an economy, he later explained, 'All transactions are carried out as a result of contracts between factors, with the services to be provided to each other specified in the contract and without any direction involved. . . . In such a system, the allocation of resources would respond directly to the structure of prices' (Coase 1988, 38).

While in the economy without firms economic activity is coordinated by contracts, within the firm it is coordinated by direction. Accordingly, the answer to the question 'What is a firm?' is that a firm is a form of coordination of economic activity by direction rather than by contract (although this did not rule out the possibility of some contracting within the firm). For Coase, therefore, a sharp boundary can be drawn between the firm and the market, unlike both Alchian and Demsetz (1972) and Jensen and Meckling (1976) for whom contracting is the main characteristic of the firm's activities.

With this conceptualisation of the firm in mind, Coase in his 1937 article went on to explain why firms exist: 'The main reason why it is profitable to establish a firm would seem to be that there is a cost of using the price mechanism' (38). In 1988 Coase summarised the main idea in his earlier contribution: 'The key idea in *The Nature of the Firm* [is] the comparison of the costs of coordinating the activities of factors of production within the firm with the costs of bringing about the same result by market transactions or by means of operations undertaken within some other firm' (38). Firms, therefore, exist where the costs of coordinating economic activities through the market exceed the costs of coordinating them within the firm. (In passing, it is worth noting Coase's insistence in the last quotation on a three-way comparison of coordination costs: within the market, within the firm, and within some other firm.)

What are the costs of using the price mechanism which Coase identified? Reference is made here to three of the costs analysed by Coase. First, 'The most obvious cost of "organizing" production through the price mechanism is that of discovering what the relevant prices are' (Coase 1937, 38). Second, 'The costs of negotiating and concluding a separate contract for each exchange transaction which takes place on a market must also be taken into account' (ibid. 38–9). Coase recognised that long term contracting might reduce some of the costs of concluding several shorter term contracts. But 'owing to the difficulty of forecasting, the longer the period of the contract is for the supply of the commodity or service, the less possible and, indeed, the less desirable it is for the person purchasing to specify what the other contracting party is expected to do' (ibid. 39–40).

Third, at the time that he wrote *The Nature of The Firm*, Coase was also aware of the problem now referred to as 'asset specificity'. In 1932 Coase discussed the following example of asset specificity in a letter to his colleague and friend, Fowler: 'Suppose the production of a particular product requires a large capital equipment which is, however, specialized insofar that it can only be used for the particular product concerned or can only be readapted at great cost. Then the firm producing such a product for one consumer finds itself faced with one great risk—that the consumer may transfer his demand elsewhere or that he may exercise his monopoly power to force down the price—the machinery has no supply price' (Coase 1988, 13).

What bearing does asymmetric information have on Coase's approach to the firm? As we saw earlier, asymmetric information was central to the approaches of Alchian and Demsetz (1972) and Jensen and Meckling (1976). Asymmetric information may significantly increase the costs of using the price mechanism. This is clear in the case of Coase's second cost, namely the cost of negotiating and concluding contracts. In the case of long term contracts, however, in addition to possible problems arising from the asymmetrical distribution of information regarding the states of affairs which currently pertain, there is a further problem. This is the problem of knowing what future states may pertain, or as Coase put it, the 'difficulty of forecasting'.

Similarly, asymmetric information may increase Coase's first cost, namely the cost of 'discovering what the relevant prices are'. In the case of Coase's third cost, asset specificity, the problem may arise from the difficulty of foreseeing how the purchaser might in the future change his mind regarding his demand for the output from the assets or the price he is willing to pay. Again, as in the case of long term contracting, this is a problem of forecasting future states. It may therefore be concluded that the availability and cost of information is a major determinant, from Coase's point of view, of the existence of firms.

1.3.2. Opportunism

The problem of asset specificity raises a further difficulty, namely the possibility of opportunistic behaviour. The owner of transaction-specific assets, in addition to confronting the possibility that the purchaser may change his/her mind, may also have to deal with the possibility that he/she will behave opportunistically (for example, with mal-intent, encouraging the seller to invest in specific assets only to exploit the seller's unavoidable commitment to the transaction later). Olive Williamson's development of the implications of opportunism adds a new dimension to the problems of information and contracting which have been discussed so far in this paper.

Indeed, contrary to what has been argued thus far, Williamson suggests that asymmetrical information does not provide an independent explanation for the existence and activities of the firm. Instead he proposes that opportunism is one of the key explanatory factors. The reason is simply that asymmetrical information is only a problem in the presence (or possible presence) of opportunism. Absent opportunism, Williamson argues, and the problems associated with asymmetrical information disappear. This follows since if there is no opportunism the principal or other team members can simply ask the agent or remaining team member to 'tell the truth, the whole truth, and nothing but the truth', to which they will get a truthful answer.

In this way, relevant information which may have been asymmetrically distributed in the first place can be made symmetrical. In other words, a further assumption has in fact been implicitly present in the discussion so far, namely the possibility of opportunism. When this assumption is made explicit, however, asymmetrical information disappears as a separate category explaining the existence and activities of the firm.

(In passing, it is worth noting that Williamson here implicitly assumes that the costs of asking that the truth be told, and getting an answer, are negligible. If these costs were not negligible then the request to tell the truth would only be worth making if the value of the answer at least compensated for the costs incurred. But if there is asymmetrical information to begin with, the requester may not be able to assess the value of the information he is requesting. The requester will then be unable to make a rational decision regarding whether or not to request the information. The only way he or she could make a rational decision would be to know the value of the information in advance of incurring the cost of obtaining it. But then the requester would have obtained the information without having paid for it and without having compensated the person from whom the information has been requested for the costs of providing the information. Under these conditions asymmetrical information would present problems even in the absence of opportunism.)

But, to return to the discussion, what is opportunism and where does it come from? Williamson defines opportunism as self-seeking with guile and argues that it is one of two key 'behavioral assumptions' characterising 'human nature' (Williamson 1985, 44). (Williamson's other behavioural assumption is bounded rationality which is brought into our discussion later.) These two behavioural assumptions are crucial because of the impact that they have on the cost of making transactions, and for Williamson 'the transaction is the basic unit of analysis' (ibid. 18). As will later become apparent, it is Williamson's focus on the transaction as the basic unit of analysis which leads on to his conception of what a firm is and what it does.

To take the present discussion of opportunism further, two points are worth noting. The first is that Coase explicitly considered the possibility of opportunism, or 'fraud' as he put it, in his discussion of the 'risk' facing the holder of specific assets. Around 1934 Coase addressed the question of the role of fraud in contracting. In this connection he referred to Marshall's observation that 'Money is more portable than a good reputation', which might provide an incentive for fraud. However, Coase 'concluded that the avoidance of fraud was not an important factor in promoting integration' of coordinated activities within the firm (Coase 1988, 31).

The second point is that, despite the centrality of the concept of opportunism in his approach to transactions in general and the firm in particular, Williamson's work begs the question regarding whether opportunism is a cause, as he generally argues, or a consequence of organisation.

On the one hand, Williamson insists that opportunism is an essential part of 'human nature', and it is for this reason that he incorporates it as a 'behavioral assumption' in his conceptual framework: 'Transaction cost economics characterizes human nature as we know it by reference to bounded rationality and opportunism' (Williamson 1985, 44).

On the other hand, Williamson notes that 'Both institutional and personal trust relations evolve. Thus the individuals who are responsible for adapting the interfaces have a personal as well as an organizational stake in what transpires. Where personal integrity is believed to be operative, individuals located at the interfaces may refuse to be part of opportunistic efforts to take advantage of (rely on) the letter of the contract when the spirit of the exchange is being emasculated. Such refusals can serve as a check upon organizational proclivities to behave opportunistically. Other things being equal, idiosyncratic exchange relations that feature personal trust will survive greater stress and will display greater adaptability.' (ibid. 62–3). In a footnote, Williamson, referring to Dore's 1983 article on 'goodwill and the spirit of market capitalism', notes that 'Ronald Dore's assessment of Japanese contracting practices also suggests that personal integrity matters' (ibid. 63).

However, Williamson cannot have it both ways, at least if he is to provide a consistent explanation of forms of organisation. In a causal explanation the cause must precede the effect. In the main thrust of Williamson's argument, the cause (opportunism, an inherent part of human nature) precedes the effect (forms of organisation designed to safeguard against opportunism). But elsewhere he reverses the argument: the cause becomes forms of organisation which precede (and produce) the effect, personal integrity and trust, thus contradicting the previous argument that opportunism is part of human nature. However, opportunism must be either a cause or a consequence of organisation, or, if in some cases it is the one and in other cases the other, a careful account is required of the reasons for the difference. This presents a significant dilemma for Williamson's theoretical schema which, as we have seen, is largely based on deduction from the twin behavioural assumptions of bounded rationality and opportunism.

This brings us to Williamson's second characteristic of 'human nature', namely bounded rationality.

1.3.3 Bounded Rationality

According to Williamson (1990), bounded rationality is the most important assumption on which the theory of contracting is based: 'Although frequently unexpressed, bounded rationality has become the operative behavioral assumption out of which the economics of contracting increasingly works' (ibid. 11). But what, precisely, is bounded rationality? To answer this question it is necessary to turn to Herbert Simon.

Herbert Simon and bounded rationality

Herbert Simon's purpose is to provide an intentional explanation for the existence and activities of organisations in general and the firm in particular.[1] According to this explanation, human action is oriented to the achievement of purposes or objectives. Human beings intend to act 'rationally' in the sense that they attempt to achieve their objectives to the greatest extent that they feel is possible under the circumstances as they see them.

However, it is in attempting to act rationally that human beings inevitably run into information-related problems. These problems arise because rational action in this sense requires information regarding both the alternative courses of action that are available to the actor, and the consequences of these actions. In some cases, but not necessarily all, the quantity of information required to make a rational decision is great relative to the ability of the individual to acquire, store, process, and recall that information.

These cases refer to what Simon calls bounded rationality, which he defines in the following way: 'the capacity of the human mind for formulating and solving complex problems is very small compared with the size of the problems whose solution is required for objectively rational behavior in the real world—or even for a reasonable approximation to such objective rationality' (Simon 1957, 198). Accordingly, under conditions of bounded rationality, 'human behavior is intendedly rational, but only limitedly so' (Simon 1961, xxiv).

But why is the capacity of the human mind 'very small' relative to the capacity that would be necessary for objectively rational behaviour? Simon makes it clear that the limitations of the human mind are not only or primarily physiological in nature, but are also psychological, social, and organisational:

'Administrative man is limited also by constraints that are part of his own psychological make-up—limited by the number of persons with whom he can communicate, the amount of information he can acquire and retain, and so forth. The fact that these limits are not physiological and fixed, but are instead largely determined by social and even organizational forces, creates problems of theory construction of great subtlety; and the fact that the possibilities of modifying and relaxing these limits may themselves become objects of rational calculation compounds the difficulties.' (Simon 1957, 199).[2]

Simon goes on to explain the existence of organisations (and also their activities) in terms of bounded rationality. This provides, in the case of the firm as a special kind of organisation, Simon's answer to the two questions, 'What is a firm? What do firms do?'. In short, firms provide a way for people, through cooperation, to pool the 'very small' capacities of their individual minds, their bounded rationalities, and in this way to achieve collectively what they cannot achieve individually. Simon notes, however, that collective achievements are dependent on the ability of the group to agree on goals, to communicate, and to cooperate. 'It is only because individual human beings are limited in knowledge, foresight, skill, and time that organisations are useful instruments for the achievement of human purpose; and it is only because organized groups of human beings are limited in ability to agree on goals, to communicate, and to cooperate that organizing becomes for them a "problem"' (Simon 1957, 199).

But how 'rational' is the behaviour that Simon analyses? In answering this question it is worth noting that bounded rational behaviour is even more limitedly rational than Simon suggests, or his followers imply[3]. This conclusion, as will now be demonstrated, follows logically from Simon's own analysis.

To begin with, bounded rational behaviour can be rational only with respect to the objectives that have been chosen. These objectives and their choice, therefore, lie outside the rationality process, even if individuals are consistent regarding the objectives they have chosen. Accordingly, the objectives themselves cannot be assumed to be rational.

Secondly, it may be deduced that it is impossible to rationally choose the information set upon which a decision or choice is made. At any point in time the boundedly rational individual has the choice whether or not to expand the information set at his/her disposal by acquiring and processing additional information. There is, however, a cost to the individual of so doing, at least in terms of the time taken to acquire and process information and the opportunity cost of that time.

How can a rational decision be made regarding whether or not to seek more information? In line with Simon's analysis, this decision can only be made on the basis of a calculation of the consequences of seeking or not seeking more information. However, since the individual does not yet possess the additional information, he/she will not be able to assess the consequences of having that information. He/she is therefore unable to calculate whether the benefit of having the additional information is sufficiently great to compensate for the associated costs. The only way of making the choice is to already possess the information, in which case the costs have been incurred in advance of an assessment of the benefits. In this case the decision to acquire the information could not have been rational. It is therefore possible that, *ex post*, the decision to acquire the information may turn out to be irrational.

Neither can a rational decision be salvaged by bringing expectations into the argument, that is by arguing that the rational decision regarding whether or not to seek more information will be made on the basis of the consequences that are expected. Since, *ex hypothesi*, the individual does not yet possess the information, there is no rational way of formulating expectations regarding the consequences of having the information. A rational decision, in the sense of a decision which enables the greatest achievement of the individual's objectives subject to the costs of information and decision-making—to use Jensen and Meckling's words quoted in the last footnote—therefore cannot be made. It is not possible, accordingly, to make a rational decision regarding whether or not to acquire more information. Bounded rationality, therefore, can only be rational with respect to a given and closed set of information.

Furthermore, there is no guarantee that under the conditions of bounded rationality postulated by Simon a decision will be 'intersubjectively rational', in the sense that two individuals will agree that the decision is rational. Indeed, the logic of Simon's own argument suggests that it is unlikely that a decision will be intersubjectively rational.

For Simon the essential assumption is that people are information processing organisms. But what is the 'information' that they process, how do they acquire it, and how do they process it? In answering these questions Simon makes it clear that it is necessary to distinguish the 'objective' information which exists 'out there' in the individual's environment from the information which 'enters' his faculties and is processed by them. The information which first enters his faculties is *selected* from the total set of objective information. This selection process follows from the individual's 'perception' and 'attention': 'Every human organism lives in an environment that generates millions of bits of new information each second, but the bottleneck of the perceptual apparatus certainly does not admit more than 1,000 bits per second, and probably much less' (Simon 1959, 273).

This perceptual bottleneck, however, cannot be thought of as a 'filter', but rather involves 'attention' which serves as an inclusion/exclusion mechanism. The selection from objective information based on perception and attention means that the information that first enters the individual's faculties is not necessarily 'representative' of the objective information which is out there. It is for this reason that Simon objects to the notion of the individual 'filtering' objective information:

Perception is sometimes referred to as a 'filter'. This term is as misleading as 'approximation', and for the same reason: it implies that what comes through into the nervous system is really quite a bit like what is 'out there'. In fact, the filtering is not merely a passive selection of some part of a presented whole, but an active process involving attention to a very small part of the whole and exclusion, from the outset, of almost all that is not within the scope of attention (Simon 1959, 272–3).

After the information, selected by the individual's perception and attention, first enters the individual's faculties, it is subjected to what we may refer to as a secondary selection process. This secondary selection process results from the problem-solving strategy which the individual has chosen. Accordingly, a subset of information will be selected, contingent on the problem-solving strategy which has been chosen, from the set of information which first enters the individual's faculties: 'there are hosts of inferences that might be drawn from the information stored in the brain that are not in fact drawn. The consequences implied by information in the memory become known only through active information-processing, and hence through active selection of particular problem-solving paths from the myriad that might have been followed' (ibid. 273). The information that the individual eventually ends up processing, therefore, is information which has gone through this double selection process. We may refer to this information as subjective information.

March and Simon (1958) acknowledge that both rounds of selection, involving perception and attention in the first round and choice of problem-solving path in the second, are influenced by psychological, sociological, and organisational determinants:

The theory of rational choice put forth here incorporates two fundamental characteristics: (1) choice is always exercised with respect to a limited, approximate, simplified 'model' of the real situation. . . . We call the chooser's model his 'definition of the situation'. (2) The elements of the definition of the situation are not 'given'— that is, we do not take these as data of our theory—but are themselves the outcome of psychological and sociological processes, including the chooser's own activities and the activities of others in his environment (March and Simon 1958, 12).

Because of the importance of what we have referred to here as subjective information, Simon argues that a theory of rational behaviour must also pay attention to the procedures that individuals use to choose their actions. This he calls *procedural rationality*:

[A] theory of rational behavior must be quite as much concerned with the characteristics of the rational actors—the means they use to cope with uncertainty and cognitive complexity—as with the characteristics of the objective environment in which they make their decisions. In such a world, we must give an account not only of substantive rationality—the extent to which appropriate courses of action are chosen—but also procedural rationality—the effectiveness, in light of human cognitive powers and limitations, of the procedures used to choose actions (Simon 1978, 8–9).

Returning to intersubjective rationality, it is clear from the present discussion that there is no inherent reason why different individuals in the same objective situation should end up with the same simplified 'model' of this situation, that is with the same 'definition of the situation'. Indeed, through his discussion of the importance of psychological factors, such as perception and attention, and social and organisational factors, Simon implies it is unlikely that different individuals will end up with the same definition of the situation. To the extent that their definitions of the situation differ, however, different individuals may disagree in any objective situation regarding what constitutes a rational decision. 'Rationality' is therefore dependent on the individual making the judgment. The possibility of different individuals arriving at different conclusions regarding what is a rational decision raises problems for explanations of firm behaviour based on rational calculation. A case in point, as we shall see later, is explanations based on transaction costs.

Similar objections confront 'intertemporal rationality', namely decisions that are assumed to remain rational over time. The reason is simply that perception, attention, and the other determinants of the decision-maker's definition of the situation are a function of time and are therefore likely to change over time. With a changing definition of the situation over time it is possible that a decision judged to be rational at time t will seem to be irrational at $t + 1$. By limiting rationality to a point-in-time judgment, however, further problems are posed for explanations couched in terms of rationality, since what is judged rational today may be judged irrational tomorrow.

[Intersubjective rationality may in fact be more common than is acknowledged in the present discussion based on Simon. While the unlikelihood of intersubjective rationality follows logically from Simon's focus on the decision-making *individual* as the appropriate unit of analysis, it may be that judgments regarding rationality are more of a *social* process, discussed, negotiated, and agreed *between* individuals. From the social point of view, decisions within organisations may be seen to be socially, rather than individually, made within the context of the processes of interpersonal dynamics, power relationships, etc that exist within the organisation. However, while Simon acknowledges that social determinants and the functioning of organisations influence factors such as perception and attention and therefore the decision-maker's definition of the situation, his focus remains at the individual rather than the social level. From the social point of view, it might be that 'intraorganisational rationality', involving shared judgments regarding what is rational within an organisation, is more likely than 'interorganisational rationality', that is shared judgments across different organisations. This, however, necessitates an explanation of the social processes which are responsible for the emergence of a social consensus regarding rationality and, on occasion, the emergence of social conflict. Such an examination requires the investigation of factors that go beyond Simon's writings.]

Simon's chess example

What Simon means by bounded rationality is made clearer by the example of chess to which he frequently refers. Indeed, according to Simon *et al.* (1992), 'Chess has become for cognitive science research [which for Simon includes both economics and artificial intelligence] what the Drosophila, the fruit fly, is for research in genetics. We need standard organisms so that we can accumulate knowledge. That's my excuse for talking so much about chess' (ibid. 29).

At this point let us return to the simplifying assumptions that were made at the beginning of this section. There it was assumed, first, that all possible states of affairs and state-contingent consequences relevant to a decision are common knowledge. There is, therefore, a closed set of possibilities. Secondly, it was assumed that the state of affairs which actually pertains is unknown to one or more of the interactors. It will be recalled that in analysing the implications of these assumptions the discussion went on to consider asymmetrical information and opportunism.

In the case of chess, however, only the first of these assumptions is necessary. A knowledge of the characteristics of the chess board and of the rules of the game provides knowledge of all possible states of affairs (configurations of chess pieces on the board) and state-contingent consequences (*if* a piece moves here, *then* . . .). What is the problem posed by chess that makes it suitable, according to Simon, as an 'ideal type' in cognitive science research? In the case of chess the significance of the information that is provided in the game is clear-cut and unambiguous (a point to which we shall later return). An opponent's move provides information regarding the new state of affairs which now pertains, information that is shared (once the move is made) with the other player. This indicates the set of options that now remain open (and also those that are foreclosed) to both players.

It is worth stressing that the problem which chess presents to other players has nothing to do with information asymmetry (at least once the move is made). Both players then have the same set of information. The difficulty, rather, arises from the lack of cognitive competence on the part of both players to compute, within the time allowed, all the possible moves that may be made, all the possible counter-moves, all the possible counter-counter-moves, etc. In other words, the problem arises from the *quantity* of information relative to the ability of the player to process it. The problem, therefore, is one of bounded rationality. Under these circumstances the player resorts to strategies or heuristics.

Bounded rationality, principals and agents, and joint team production

How does bounded rationality relate to our earlier discussion of the principal-agent and joint team production problems? The point to make here is that the latter two cases do not necessarily involve bounded rationality (although it is possible that bounded rationality could be a further complicating factor). In the principal-agent and joint team production cases the problem arises from the asymmetrical distribution of information plus, following Williamson, possibly the potential for opportunism. The great quantity of information relative to the ability of the individual to process this information, that is bounded rationality as strictly defined by Simon, is not necessarily a problem.

It is therefore possible to take issue with Williamson (1990) who, as quoted earlier, has suggested that 'bounded rationality has become the operative behavioral assumption out of which the economics of contracting increasingly works' (ibid. 11).

The firm as innovation economising on transaction cost

Having provided a critical analysis of the concept of bounded rationality, Williamson's approach to the firm will now be considered in more detail. Williamson's purpose is largely to examine the implications of transaction costs which he carefully distinguishes from production costs. As he defines it, 'Transaction cost economics characterizes human nature as we know it by reference to bounded rationality and opportunism' (Williamson 1985, 44). It is Williamson's concern with transaction costs that shapes his approach to the firm. According to Williamson, therefore, 'the modern corporation is mainly to be understood as the product of a series of organizational innovations that have had the purpose and effect of economizing on transaction costs' (ibid. 273). It is the attempt to do this which leads people to devise and select structures which appropriately govern the costs of transaction, that is, governance structures. As Williamson puts it, 'Transaction cost economics is principally concerned ... with the economizing consequences of assigning transactions to governance structures in a discriminating way' (46). Accordingly, 'the firm is (for many purposes at least) more usefully regarded as a governance structure' (13).

Based on this kind of reasoning, Williamson derives the 'organisational imperative that emerges in such circumstances ... : Organize transactions so as to economize on bounded rationality while simultaneously safeguarding them against the hazards of opportunism.' (emphasis removed). But what, precisely, does Williamson mean by 'economizing' and how consistent is this with other concepts which he employs? In *The Firm as a Nexus of Treaties* (1990) he stated that 'The new theories of the firm to which I refer [that is, the so-called New Institutional Economics which includes his own work] were initially regarded as rivals to the neoclassical theory. Increasingly, however, they are coming to be treated as complements' (ibid. 23). It is largely as a result of the common ground provided by 'economising' that this has been possible.

Williamson makes it clear that there is a close link between his concept of economising and Simon's concept of bounded rationality. According to Williamson, in both concepts a 'semistrong form of rationality' is posited. In both concepts people intend to act rationally (intend to economise) but because of the very small capacity of the human mind (to use Simon's words), they are able to do so only to a limited extent. As he puts it: 'Transaction cost economics acknowledges that rationality is bounded and maintains that both parts of the definition should be respected. An economizing orientation is elicited by the intended rationality part of the definition, while the study of institutions is encouraged by conceding that cognitive competence is limited' (Williamson 1987, 45).

As we have seen, Williamson's 'organisational imperative' is to economise on bounded rationality while safeguarding against opportunism. But when is the point reached where bounded rationality has been 'economised' and where opportunism has been 'safeguarded'? More specifically, from an *ex ante* point of view, how does the actor know that bounded rationality has been economised?

Following Simon's own logic underlying his concept of bounded rationality, a logic clearly spelled out earlier in this chapter, it can be argued that there is little reason for the actor to be sure that 'economisation' has been achieved, or for other actors to agree that this is the case. This conclusion follows from the complexity of the context that is likely to surround any attempt to economise on bounded rationality and safeguard against opportunism, including the unknowns and uncertainties involved. In these circumstances it is possible that the actor's 'definition of the situation', to use Simon's phrase, will differ in significant respects first from the objective situation, and secondly from the way in which other actors have defined the situation. In other words, under these circumstances economising itself is subjective, and intersubjective rationality and intertemporal rationality (in the senses defined earlier in the discussion on Simon) may not exist.

If this is accepted, however, the exhortation to economise on bounded rationality and safeguard against opportunism must be understood in a very different way from that implied by Williamson. In short, the notion of economising will have to be considerably watered down: do what you think will have the effect of economising on bounded rationality and safeguarding against opportunism. To the extent that this amended version of economising is accepted, however, the common ground with neoclassical economics is largely undermined.

1.4 The Firm as a Repository of Knowledge

The hallmark of the second approach to the firm identified in this paper is that the firm is seen, not only as a response to information-related difficulties as in the first approach, but also as a repository of knowledge.

In this section the work of five sets of authors will be examined: Nelson and Winter, Penrose, Chandler, Marshall, and Teece.

1.4.1 The Firm as Part of the Evolutionary
Process of Economic Change

The discussion of bounded rationality in the previous section of this chapter provides a direct link to the work of Nelson and Winter. Before this link can be explored further, however, it is necessary to examine their overall purpose since, as we shall see, it is this purpose which structures their approach to the firm.

Richard Nelson has clearly outlined the purpose which underlies Nelson and Winter (1982), *An Evolutionary Theory of Economic Change*:

The theory of the firm in conventional microeconomics (and conventional macro-economics) was developed as part of a theoretical structure whose central concern was to explain prices and quantities through the employment of the constructs of demand and supply curves. . . . Our central interests, at least in our book [i.e. Nelson and Winter 1982], were with economic growth fuelled by technical advance. So also, of course, are neoclassical growth theorists. Given their view of growth, the latter could work with 'a theory of the firm' essentially of the sort employed in conventional demand curve, supply curve, analysis. Given our view of technical advance, and of economic growth driven by changes in technology, Winter and I could not live with that kind of theory of the firm. We had to develop a theory of the firm in which 'firm differences matter' (Personal communication from Richard Nelson, August 17, 1992).

As this quotation makes clear, Nelson and Winter's 'theory of the firm', at least that theory of the firm explicit and implicit in their 1982 book, did not emerge from an attempt to understand the firm *per se*, but rather emerged in response to the need for a conceptual tool that would enable them to analyse the relationship between technical change and economic growth. The conceptual tool that they developed for this purpose, their 'theory of the firm', accordingly differed in significant respects from those developed by others in response to different purposes. For this reason Nelson and Winter's approach is to be distinguished from that, for example, of the behavioural writers such as Simon, Cyert, and March:

We diverge from the behavioral theorists in our interest in building an explicit theory of industrial behavior, as contrasted with individual firm behavior. This means on the one hand that our characterizations of individual firms are much simpler and more stylized than those employed by the behavioral theorists, and on the other hand that our models contain a considerable amount of apparatus linking together the behavior of collections of firms. Perhaps in the future it will become possible to build and comprehend models of industry evolution that are based on detailed and realistic models of individual firm behavior. If so, our work will at that point reconverge with the behavioralist tradition (Nelson and Winter 1982, 36).

I now go onto consider how Nelson and Winter develop a theory of the firm in which 'firm differences matter'.

Bounded rationality and routines

The starting point for Nelson and Winter's theory of the firm is the same information-excessive world (excessive relative to the ability of individuals to process that information) that Simon begins with. How do individuals, and the organisations within which they work, deal with this world?

In answer to this question Nelson and Winter draw directly on the ideas of March and Simon (1958) in which the importance of routinised behaviour is analysed: 'Activity (individual or organizational) can usually be traced back to an environmental stimulus of some sort, e.g. a customer order or a fire alarm.... The responses to stimuli are of various kinds. At one extreme, a stimulus evokes a response—sometimes very elaborate—that has been developed and learned at some previous time as an appropriate response for a stimulus of this class. This is the 'routinized' end of the continuum, where a stimulus calls forth a performance program almost instantaneously' (March and Simon 1958, 139).

As Nelson and Winter put it: 'Man's rationality is "bounded": real-life decision problems are too complex to comprehend and therefore firms cannot maximize over the set of all conceivable alternatives. Relatively simple decision rules and procedures [i.e. routines] are used to guide action; because of the bounded rationality problem, these rules and procedures cannot be too complicated' (Nelson and Winter 1982, 35).

Routines, therefore, refer to the 'regular and predictable' aspects of firm behaviour (ibid. 14). To explain the behaviour of the firm is to explain its routines: 'the behavior of firms can be explained by the routines that they employ.... Modeling the firm means modeling the routines and how they change over time' (128). In short, it is the firm's routines which render predictable and 'modelable' the response of the firm to its changing environment. 'The overall picture of an organization in routine operation can now be drawn. A flow of messages comes into the organization from the external environment and from clocks and calendars. The organization members receiving these messages interpret them as calling for the performance of routines from their repertoires... the performance of routines by each organization member generates a stream of messages to others', etc. (103). (In passing, it is worth noting that Nelson and Winter's emphasis on routines is in line with Simon's insistence (discussed above) on the importance of procedural rationality in addition to substantive rationality. This concern with procedural rationality, however, is not shared by Williamson in his approach to transaction cost economics[4].)

Routines and the firm as repository of knowledge

It is clear from the discussion so far that Nelson and Winter see routinised behaviour as both an individual and organisational response to complexity and uncertainty under conditions of bounded rationality. To this extent their routine-based theory of the firm shares with the other theories discussed above a view of the firm as a response to information-related difficulties.

However, in elaborating on the importance of routines, Nelson and Winter go beyond an approach which sees the firm primarily as a *response* to information-related problems. More specifically, the firm for Nelson and Winter itself becomes a *repository* of knowledge. And it is as a repository of knowledge, contingent on the firm's past history, that one firm differs from another. The focus accordingly shifts to the firm and the knowledge on which it is based. In turn this raises new questions that were not central in the theories examined above. This is evident in the following quotations from Winter (1988) which give his answer to the questions, 'What is a firm? What do firms do?': 'Fundamentally, business firms are organizations that know how to do things. Firms are repositories of productive knowledge. In fact . . . a particular firm at a particular time is a repository for a quite specific range of productive knowledge, a range that often involves idio-syncratic features that distinguish it even from superficially similar firms in the same line(s) of business' (175). However, 'it is necessary to unpack the metaphorical statement that 'organizations know how to do things' into an account of the processes by which productive knowledge is preserved in an organization while individual members come and go' (176).

It is in its routines that an organisation stores its knowledge: 'where and what is the memory of an organisation? We propose that the routinization of activity in an organisation constitutes the most important form of storage of the organization's specific operational knowledge' (Nelson and Winter 1982, 99).

As is clear from these quotations, the routine has a multipurpose use in Nelson and Winter's theory of the firm. First, it allows the firm to cope with complexity and uncertainty under the constraint of bounded rationality. At the same time, by linking bounded rationality and routines, Nelson and Winter are able to provide a realistic basis to their approach to the firm. This basis is superior to that of conventional economics with its demanding assumptions regarding the possession and cost of information.

Secondly, routinised behaviour allows Nelson and Winter to develop a theory in which firms differ, and in which the differences matter. This follows since there is no reason why different firms, even those in the same industry confronting similar complex and uncertain circumstances, should devise the same or even similar routines. Thirdly, routines provide a way of storing an organisation's accumulated knowledge. Fourthly, routinised behaviour provides a mechanism which allows Nelson and Winter to link, in both directions, market changes and firm responses. In this way they are also able to link technical changes and economic growth. Fifthly, routines, the source of a firm's distinctiveness, are also the source of it's competitiveness.

The firm in the evolutionary process

How does Nelson and Winter's routine-based theory allow them to analyse the evolutionary process of economic change which embodies the relationship between technical change and economic growth? Nelson and Winter (1982, 400) make it clear that there are three key concepts in their theory of evolutionary change: routine, search, and selection. The following is a summary of their understanding of the evolutionary process:

> The core concern of evolutionary theory is with the dynamic process by which firm behavior patterns and market outcomes are jointly determined over time. The typical logic of these evolutionary processes is as follows. At each point of time, the current operating characteristics [i.e. routines] of firms, and the magnitudes of their capital stocks and other state variables, determine input and output levels. Together with market supply and demand conditions that are exogenous to the firms in question, these firm decisions determine market prices of inputs and outputs. The profitability of each individual firm is thus determined. Profitability operates, through firm investment rules, as one major determinant of rates of expansion and contraction of individual firms. With firm sizes thus altered, the same operating characteristics would yield different input and output levels, hence different prices and profitability signals, and so on (ibid. 19).

Nelson and Winter continue, 'By this selection process, clearly, aggregate input and output and price levels for the industry would undergo dynamic change even if individual firm operating characteristics were constant. But operating characteristics, too, are subject to change, through the workings of the search rules of firms. Search and selection are simultaneous, interacting aspects of the evolutionary process: the same prices that provide selection feedback also influence the directions of search. Through the joint action of search and selection, the firms evolve over time, with the condition of the industry in each period bearing the seeds of its condition in the following period' (ibid. 19).

Search

Just as in the case of routines, Nelson and Winter draw on March and Simon (1958) for the idea of search. As the latter express it,

> At the other extreme [of the continuum beginning with routinised responses], a stimulus evokes a larger or smaller amount of problem-solving activity directed toward finding performance activities with which to complete the response. Such activity is distinguished by the fact that it can be dispensed with once the performance program has been learned. Problem-solving activities can generally be identified by the extent to which they involve *search*: search aimed at discovering

alternatives of action or consequences of action. 'Discovering' alternatives may involve inventing and elaborating whole performance programs where these are not already available in the problem solver's repertory (March and Simon 1958, 139–40).

For Nelson and Winter (1982, 247), the main features of search 'are irreversibility (what is found is found), its contingent character and dependency on what is 'out there' to be found, and its fundamental uncertainty'. Like routines, however, search according to Nelson and Winter is a rule-based activity. In the case of R&D, for example, the 'decision maker is viewed as having a set of decision-rules. . . . these rules determine the direction of "search". . . and may be termed a "search strategy". A strategy may be keyed to such variables as the size of the firm, its profitability, what competitors are doing, assessment of the payoff of R&D in general and of particular classes of projects in particular, evaluation of the ease or difficulty of achieving certain kinds of technological advances, and the particular complex of skills and experience that the firm possesses' (ibid. 249).

It is search which generates the *variety* which is, together with selection, the basis of evolutionary change. 'Our concept of search obviously is the counterpart of that of mutation in biological evolutionary theory. And our treatment of search as partly determined by the routines of the firm parallels the treatment in biological theory of mutation as being determined in part by the genetic makeup of the organism' (18).

Selection environment

The third key concept is that of the 'selection environment' of an organisation which 'is the ensemble of considerations which affect its well-being and hence the extent to which it expands or contracts' (401). However, it is important to realise that from an evolutionary perspective it is not the fate of individual firms that is of interest. 'Differential growth [of firms] plays much the same role in our theory as in biological theory; in particular, it is important to remember that it is ultimately the fates of populations or genotypes (routines) that are the focus of concern, not the fates of individuals (firms)' (401).

Routines, rules, and decision-making within the firm

The present discussion of Nelson and Winter (1982) has stressed that their 'theory of the firm' emerged from the need for a conceptual tool which would allow them to examine the co-relationship between the firm and market outcomes, and between technical change and economic growth. However, a conceptual tool fashioned for one purpose may not be well adapted for another. It is therefore necessary to ask how relevant their 'theory of the firm' is as a theory of the firm, that is as a conceptual tool for understanding the firm, even though it is acknowledged that this was not their purpose.

In answering this question it is clear that Nelson and Winter's approach to the firm has several particularly attractive features. Its grounding in an acceptance of complexity, uncertainty, and limited cognitive competence gives it a reality basis that, all other things equal, puts it ahead of theories which assume, explicitly or implicitly, that decision-makers know most of what there is to know and can acquire information at relatively little cost. It is these assumptions that usually underlie the conventional approach to the firm and its use of a production function. Similarly, the weight given to routines, including search as a routinised activity, and rule-driven behaviour is justified by the increasing amount of evidence which shows these to be important in both firms and organisations more generally (such as bureaucracies).

But, as an approach to the firm, an approach which in Nelson and Winter's own words is a 'simple and stylized' characterisation of individual firms, it is clear that there are important shortcomings. In this sense their conceptual tool, honed for one purpose, imposes significant costs when used for another purpose.

The main shortcoming stems from the need in Nelson and Winter's models for a mechanism that will allow them to co-relate changes in the market with firms' responses. This mechanism is provided, of course, by the firms' routines which mediate the interaction between market and firm, thus providing a deterministic outcome which in turn generates the model's results. While this mechanism may be appropriate for Nelson and Winter's purpose, as part of an attempt to understand the firm it has the cost of forcing the firm into a deterministic straitjacket, governed wholly by routine and rule. The point, however, is not that human beings never make or obey routines and rules; only that they may unpredictably change them. And this, surely, should be a feature of any attempt to theoriese the firm *per se*.

Following the same line of reasoning, it is worth commenting on the divergence between the approach to the firm taken in the more discursive parts of *An Evolutionary Theory of Economic Change* as well as in some of Nelson and Winter's other writings, and that taken in the formal sections. More specifically, the mechanistic nature of the firm's response to its environment through its routinised and search behaviour appears to be at variance with the conception of human (and firm) action and knowledge given elsewhere in the same book. This is evident, for example, in the authors' discussion of firm strategy: 'the economic world is far too complicated for a firm to understand perfectly; therefore the attempts of firms to do well must be understood as being conditioned by their subjective models or interpretations of economic reality. These interpretations tend to be associated with strategies that firms consciously devise to guide their actions. Such strategies differ from firm to firm, in part because of different interpretations of economic opportunities and constraints, and in part because different firms are good at different things' (Nelson and Winter 1982, 37).

Presumably, different subjective interpretations may also lead different individuals in the same firm to different conclusions regarding strategy, or the same individual to different conclusions at different points in time. To view the firm wholly in terms of routine- and rule-driven activities is to suppress an essential aspect of the way decisions are made under conditions of complexity, uncertainty regarding the future, and significant information costs.

Nelson and Winter (1977, 47) are surely nearer the mark when they state that 'Because of the uncertainty involved, different people, and different organizations, will disagree as to where to place their R&D chips, and on when to make their bets. Some will be proved right and some wrong. Explicit recognition of uncertainty is important...'. While the routine-based approach does not assume certainty, it does not deal adequately with the way in which uncertainty is confronted in decision-making in the firm. The very nature of routine abstracts from this process. The contrast with the notion of 'vision' discussed later in this chapter is worth noting.

1.4.2 Explaining the Growth of the Firm

Unlike any of the other writers discussed so far, the purpose of the next two authors, Edith Penrose and Alfred Chandler, is to explain the growth of the firm. More specifically, Penrose's purpose is to develop a theory of the growth of the firm, while Chandler's is to explain both the origin and the growth of the large, multiproduct and multidivisional firms which currently dominate both national economies and the international economy.

But what, for Penrose and Chandler, is a firm, and what do firms do? While the answer given by both writers to the first question is fundamentally the same, their answer to the second question is significantly different.

For Penrose (1959), the business firm is 'both an administrative organization and a collection of productive resources', both human and material (ibid. 31). However, echoing a distinction that others have drawn[5], Penrose is adamant that 'it is never *resources* themselves that are the "inputs" in the production process, but only the *services* that the resources can render' (25). These services are also a function of the experience and knowledge that have been accumulated within the firm. Services, according to Penrose, are to a significant extent firm-specific and therefore 'it is largely in this distinction [between resources and services] that we find the source of uniqueness of each individual firm' (25).

From Chandler's perspective the modern business firm may be seen as a collection of 'dynamic organizational capabilities' which are the source of the firm's competitiveness. Like Penrose's services, Chandler's organisational capabilities are accumulated in the course of carrying out the firms's activities, and 'depend on knowledge, skill, experience, and teamwork—on the organized human capabilities essential to exploit the potential of technological processes' (Chandler 1990a, 24).

It is in their view of what firms do, however, that a significant difference becomes apparent between Penrose's and Chandler's analysis of the firm. For Penrose 'the primary economic function of an industrial firm is to make use of productive resources for the purpose of supplying goods and services to the economy *in accordance with plans developed and put into effect within the firm*' (Penrose 1959, 15, emphasis added). The emphasis on the process of 'planning' within the firm in Penrose's conceptualisation of what firms do requires Penrose, as we shall see, to explore a number of difficult issues relating to information and knowledge. These are issues which Chandler, with a different view of what firms do, does not delve into. For him, firms and their managers are engaged in the pursuit of the 'dynamic logic of growth and competition' (Chandler 1990b, 133). This logic involves managers, within their hierarchically structured organisations, using their dynamic organisational capabilities (and in the process accumulating further capabilities) in order to reap competitive advantages from three primary sources: economies of scale, economies of scope, and reduced transaction costs between the operating units of the firm.

The firm as an information processor versus the firm as an image creator

How does Penrose theorise the planning process in firms, a process which is a central determinant of the growth of firms? In addition, I will consider how she views the firm's planners coming to grips with the problems of information and knowledge which are inherent in any planning process.

In answering the second point, it is illuminating to compare Penrose's approach with that of Simon, which has already been examined. For Simon the firm is essentially a form of organisation for the effective processing of information. Simon's view of the firm follows directly from his view of human beings. In an article significantly titled, 'Information Processing in Computer and Man', Simon argues that 'the thinking human being is also an information processor' (76) and that we can 'explain human thinking in terms of the organization of information processes' (this article, originally published in 1964, is contained in Simon 1992).

In contrast to Simon, Penrose makes it clear that she sees the firm's planners as 'image creators' rather than as 'information processors'. In other words, rather than beginning with the objective environment of the firm, and the information that this environment generates—in the form, for example, of market prices, market demands, the activities of competitors, etc—Penrose starts with the mental world of the planners who are situated within the context of their own firm and its specific productive services. These planners have to do at least two closely related things. First, they need to appraise the productive services at their disposal—their strengths and weaknesses, the uses to which they can and cannot be put, etc. Secondly, the planners must appraise the environment within which they find themselves. What are the opportunities and constraints that this environment presents?

In Penrose's words, 'the environment [of the firm] is treated... as an "image" in the entrepreneur's mind of the possibilities and restrictions with which he is confronted, for it is, after all, such an "image" which in fact determines a man's behaviour' (op. cit., 5). But where do the planners' images come from, if not from the processing of external information? Penrose makes it clear that in her view these images emerge from the experience and knowledge that is generated *within the firm*. Thus, 'I have placed emphasis on the significance of the resources with which a firm works and on the development of the experience and knowledge of a firm's personnel because these are the factors that will to a large extent determine the response of the firm to changes in the external world *and also determine what it "sees" in the external world.*' (79–80, emphasis added). She further elaborates: 'for an analysis of the growth of firms it is appropriate to start from an analysis of the firm rather than the environment and then proceed to a discussion of the effect of certain types of environmental conditions. If we can discover what determines entrepreneurial ideas about what the firm can and cannot do, that is what determines the nature and extent of the "subjective" productive opportunity of the firm, we can at least know where to look if we want to explain or predict the actions of particular firms' (42).

This way of dealing with the information and knowledge problems facing the firm leads on to what is probably Penrose's most important contribution to the theory of the firm, namely her concept of *productive opportunity*, which is a key determinant of the growth of the firm: 'The productive activities of... a firm are governed by what we shall call its "productive opportunity", which comprises all of the productive possibilities that its "entrepreneurs" see and can take advantage of. A theory of the growth of firms is essentially an examination of the changing productive opportunity of firms; in order to find a limit to the growth, or a restriction on the rate of growth, the productive opportunity of a firm must be shown to be limited in any period. It is clear that this opportunity will be restricted to the extent to which a firm does not see opportunities for expansion, is unwilling to act upon them, or is unable to respond to them' (Penrose 1959, 31–2).

The origin and growth of the large modern firm

The large modern firms which came to dominate the world economy first emerged in the 1880s in a number of industrial sectors. It may be appropriate now to consider why this enterprise appeared when it did.

Chandler's explanation rests on a chain of interlinked events. The first link in the chain was a cluster of interrelated innovations that together constituted a revolution in the field of transport and communications. These included the railroad and telegraph, steamship and cable. The significance of these innovations was that they facilitated a substantial increase in both volume and speed of output. This meant that for the first time, the enterprise could increase dramatically in size. At the same time this increased the ability of these firms to realise the 'dynamic logic of growth and competition' based on the economies of scale, scope, and transaction costs.

The potential for realising these economies, however, was not divided equally amongst all sectors. Accordingly, Chandler notes, 'In 1973, 289 (72.0%) of the 401 [of the world's largest industrial enterprises] were clustered in food, chemicals, petroleum, primary metals, and the three machinery groups—nonelectrical and electrical machinery and transportation equipment' (Chandler 1990a, 20).

The logic of economies of scale, scope, and transaction costs, however, was achieved neither automatically nor effortlessly. Rather, the realisation of the logic required, as a necessary precondition, the acquisition of dynamic organisational capabilities. In turn, these capabilities required investment, more specifically 'three pronged investment in production, distribution, and management'. Once in existence, however, how did the modern industrial enterprise grow? According to Chandler,

The first entrepreneurs to create such enterprises acquired powerful competitive advantages. Their industries quickly became oligopolistic. . . . These firms, along with the few challengers that subsequently entered the industry, no longer competed primarily on the basis of price. Instead they competed for market share and profits through functional and strategic effectiveness. They did so *functionally* by improving their product, their processes of production, their marketing, their purchasing, and their labor relations, and *strategically* by moving into growing markets more rapidly, and out of declining ones more quickly and effectively than did their competitors (Chandler 1990a, 8).

Chandler continues:

[R] ivalry for market share and profits honed the enterprise's functional and strategic capabilities. These organizational capabilities, in turn, provided an internal dynamic for the continuing growth of the enterprise. In particular, they stimulated its owners and managers to expand into more distant markets in their own country and then to become multinational by moving abroad. They also encouraged the firm to diversify by developing products competitive in markets other than the original one and so to become a multiproduct enterprise. . . . Salaried managers, not owners, came to make the decisions about current operating activities and long-term growth and investment (ibid. 8–9).

Bounded rationality, images, organisational capabilities and the growth of the firm

It is worth noting that the problems arising from bounded rationality are not dealt with explicitly in the writings of Penrose and Chandler. Penrose's company entrepreneurs are primarily preoccupied with the resources and services of their own company and it is these services and resources which shape what they see, and how they interpret what they see. Their problem, therefore, is not the Simonian bounded rationality problem of being condemned to attempt to make rational decisions by trying to take account of all the relevant information 'out there', while being unable to process it all. Rather, Penrose's entrepreneurs are led from 'in here'. It is their resources and competencies which they can and do know; bounded rationality does not prevent them from knowing them. And it is these resources and competencies which determine what they do (and should do, if they are to take advantage of the competence-led opportunities which they face).

Chandler's managers are also 'driven' by the capabilities they have accumulated in the past. However, unlike Penrose's, they also confront the problem of trying to grasp the logic of capitalist industrialisation based on economies of scale, scope, and transaction costs, and pursuing this logic once they have grasped it. For Chandler, therefore, the managers of large firms are not so much *ex ante* appraisers of the world as followers of the logic of industrial capitalism. As a result, they are not bedeviled by the problem of attempting to know in a world of complexity, uncertainty, and costly information. Chandler's account of the origin and growth of the firm, in marked contrast to Simon and Penrose, is therefore an *ex post* account, that is, an *ex post* explanation of why the firms originated when and where they did, why they grew as they did, etc. In this account, however, the problem of knowing in a complex, uncertain, and information costly world is absent, is abstracted from.

Corporate capabilities and the question of strategy

The discussion of Chandler's work, specifically the strategic implications of his analysis of the origins and growth of large industrial companies, raises by implication the minor role that has been allocated to the analysis of corporate strategy in the rest of the literature examined so far in this survey. This minor role is exemplified, for example, in Williamson's organisational imperative: 'economise on bounded rationality while safeguarding against opportunism'. This imperative, clearly, does not enable the analyst of the firm to address many of the wider strategic issues confronted by firms. Furthermore, it is probably fair to say that it is the absence of an applicable approach to corporate strategy in the economics literature on the firm, more than any other issue, which distinguishes the work of economists in this field from that of 'business analysts' (and has the unfortunate consequence of inhibiting intellectual communication between them).[6]

The question of strategy, however, is central in Teece and associates (1990), hereafter referred to as Teece (1990). This work is considered here primarily because it stems from the 'firm as repository of knowledge' approach. In Teece (1990) a 'dynamic capabilities approach' is proposed.

This, as Teece acknowledges, is best seen as an extension of the ideas developed by Penrose. As in Penrose, the firm is seen as a collection of capabilities which embody its knowledge. Following Penrose, causation runs from capabilities to strategy. While the firm's capabilities are the effect of learning, technological opportunities, and the selection process, at any point in time these capabilities are not only inherited from the past, they are also constrained by the past. In Teece's words, capabilities are 'sticky' in the sense that they cannot easily, quickly, and at low cost be acquired or passed on. Certainly, there is no well-oiled market in capabilities. It is this key fact of life, present also in Penrose, from which the rest of the Teece argument follows.

Since capabilities are sticky, they present the firm with its most important opportunity, the chance to become and remain competitive through its distinctiveness. Other potential competitors, constrained by their own capabilities, are not readily able to acquire a successful firm's distinctive capabilities. From this follows Teece's definition of the concept of core or distinctive competence: 'A core competence is a set of differentiated skills, complementary assets, and routines that provide the basis for a firm's competitive capacities and sustainable advantage in a particular business' (Teece 1990, 28).

The analysis of strategy follows logically from the analysis of capability or competence. Capability affects strategy in both a positive and a negative way. In a negative way, a firm's capability constrains the strategic possibilities which are open to it. As Teece puts it: 'Because of imperfect factor markets, or more precisely the non-tradeability of "soft" assets like values, culture, and organizational experience, these capabilities generally cannot be acquired; they must be built. This sometimes takes years—possibly decades. The capabilities approach accordingly sees definite limits on strategic options at least in the short run. Competitive success occurs in part because of policies pursued and experience obtained in earlier periods' (ibid. 30–1).

However, in a positive way, a firm can devise successful strategies by making use of its distinctive capabilities in order to earn an economic rent. On this basis, Teece, following Penrose directly, develops the following strategic imperative: 'the process of strategic formulation proceeds as follows: (1) identify your firm's unique resources; (2) decide in which markets those resources can earn the highest rents; and (3) decide whether the rents from those assets are most effectively utilized by (a) integrating into related market(s), (b) selling the relevant intermediate output to related firms, or (c) selling the assets themselves to a firm in a related business' (16).

Routines, resources and services, and strategic capabilities

At the beginning of this section we saw that in Nelson and Winter (1982) the routines of the firm serve the function of enabling the firm to deal with bounded rationality while at the same time acting as the firm's 'memory', as the place where its knowledge is stored. In this way the firm is both a response to information-related problems (specifically, bounded rationality), and a repository of knowledge. In Penrose, Chandler, and Teece, however, the firm is seen exclusively as a repository of knowledge and Nelson and Winter's concern with bounded rationality is left in the background.

Conceiving of the firm in terms of knowledge is by no means new. Indeed, according to Alfred Marshall (1969, 115), 'Capital consists in a great part of knowledge and organisation. . . . Knowledge is our most powerful engine of production; it enables us to subdue Nature and force her to satisfy our wants. Organisation aids knowledge'. It is worth noting in passing that Marshall's observation on the relationship between knowledge and organisation has not yet received the attention it deserves from economists. However, by viewing the firm as a repository of firm-specific knowledge— embodied in the firm's routines, services, and strategic capabilities—an approach to the firm is taken which differs significantly both from the approach in orthodox economics and that taken in the firm as response to information-related problems approach discussed in the previous section of this chapter.

As repositories of firm-specific knowledge, firms by definition differ from one another. Furthermore, firms are significantly constrained in what they know and what they can do. Moreover, it is their firm-specific capabilities which play a particularly important role in their competitiveness, and therefore in the process of competition more generally. Finally, the 'firm as repository of knowledge' approach leads logically on, as we have seen, to a detailed analysis of corporate strategy. By facilitating an analysis of corporate strategy, this approach also provides a spin-off benefit by creating an intellectual bridge to some of the work being done by business analysts of the firm.[7]

1.5 The IBM Paradox

In this section some of the implications of the IBM story will be examined for the theories of the firm discussed in this chapter. Particular attention will be paid to what will be called the IBM Paradox.

The information-processing paradigm

It is clear from the approaches to the firm examined critically in this paper that what may be referred to as an 'information processing paradigm' has exerted a significant conceptual influence. According to this paradigm the firm is seen as a form of organisation whose primary task is to acquire and process information, making decisions on the basis of the information so processed. The main characteristic of many of the theories of the firm examined here has been the identification of specific information-related problems, followed by an analysis of the way in which these problems are dealt with by the firm.

This line has also been followed by some of the proponents of what has been called the 'firm as repository of knowledge approach'. This is particularly clear in the case of Nelson and Winter whose concept of routine, as we have seen, is derived directly from information-related difficulties, although in the writings of Penrose, Chandler, and Teece there is less emphasis on information processing and more on the firm-specific competencies that are accumulated.

As pointed out in the introduction to this chapter, one of the most important features of the information processing paradigm is the 'tight coupling' that it implies between 'information' and 'knowledge'. In short, information is implicitly defined as a commodity that is capable of yielding knowledge; while knowledge is implicitly conceptualised as belief which is sustained by information. Accordingly, knowledge is equated with processed information: the firm knows what it knows because of the information it has acquired and processed.

The IBM story

The IBM experience should be of great interest to analysts of the firm. Not only is it the story of the unexpected downfall of a great company which was almost universally admired by analysts (corporate, financial, and academic), but also the significance of its demise has resulted in an unusual amount and quality of information about what happened inside the company. There are many lessons from the IBM story which have implications for the theories of the firm which have been examined in this paper. These include, for example, the shortcomings of the M-form (multidivisional form) of organisation. According to Williamson, the evolution of the M-form is to be explained in terms of its efficiency in the processing of information, which results in the economisation of bounded rationality at the same time as safeguarding against opportunism.

The IBM story, however, suggests that while the M-form might have provided information processing benefits, its main shortcoming lay in the conflicts that it generated between the contradictory interests of the different divisions. In the end it was the interests of the mainframe division which triumphed. These interests, however, became reactionary after the failure of the Future Systems project in the 1970s designed to produce a great leap forward in computer systems. The political interdependence of the divisions under the hegemony of the mainframe division resulted in

IBM's failure to take full advantage even of many of the breakthrough products and technologies which it had been the first to invent, such as the personal computer and RISC (reduced instruction set) microprocessor.

In order to deal with these problems (which had little to do with information processing *per se*) IBM in December 1991 followed the example which AT&T had set in 1988. In so doing, IBM transformed its M-form of organisation into what may be called an S-form, a segmented form of organisation based on thirteen relatively autonomous business and geographic units with significantly reduced powers for its headquarters. At the same time this radical reorganisation assigned a significantly enhanced role to internal market mechanisms in order to coordinate and control the activities of these units. This reversed significantly the tendency that Coase and Williamson had seen for activities to be increasingly integrated under the hierarchical control of the modern corporation. The S-form firm itself (as opposed to the networks of firms which surround it) is simultaneously *both* market *and* hierarchy, in a way the M-form firm never was.

The IBM paradox

Another lesson for the theory of the firm emerges from what will be called the IBM Paradox. This refers to the paradox arising from IBM, the information processing company *par excellence*, clinging until at least 1991[8] to a mistaken belief in the ability of the mainframe computer to sustain its profitability, growth, and size, *despite the information which it possessed (and processed) contradicting this belief*. The paradox, furthermore, extends beyond IBM itself to all those analysts in financial, academic and other institutions who were free to arrive at their own independent assessment of the information relating to the company, but who chose to interpret it in a similar way to IBM's directors (as is evident from IBM's share price movement up to the early 1990s). IBM's belief in the mainframe emerges clearly from the now-famous public forecast which it made in 1984 of revenue of $100 billion by 1990 and $185 billion by 1994. This compares with actual revenue of $69 billion in 1990, $64.77 billion in 1991, and $64.52 billion in 1992.

Was IBM's belief in the mainframe the result of the company's processing of information, as a tight coupling of information and knowledge/belief suggests? To answer this question let us examine some information which IBM undoubtedly possessed and had processed.

Increasing performance of microprocessors The first microprocessor ('computer on a chip'), the Intel 4004, was produced by Intel (now the world's largest semiconductor company) in 1971. As early as 1964 Gordon Moore, Chairman and co-founder of Intel, had noted that with the development of the planar transistor in 1959 the number of elements in advanced integrated circuits has been doubling each year. This observation led him to formulate the well-known Moore's Law, which states that the complexity of integrated circuits would double each year. Fig. 1.1 shows the evolution of Intel's microprocessors in accordance with Moore's Law. In terms of MIPS (millions of instructions per second), the standard measure of microprocessor performance, over the roughly twenty years that elapsed between the original Intel 4004 and the 80486 microprocessors, performance increased almost 280 times. By 1984, therefore, when IBM made its $100 billion revenue forecast, the evolutionary trend towards increasing microprocessor power was already very well established.

Increasing substitution of smaller computers for mainframes   One of the main implications of increasing microprocessor power was that smaller computers became increasingly powerful as well as cheap (in terms of cost of information unit processed). This meant that smaller computers, particularly personal computers and workstations, begain increasingly to substitute for mainframes, often in distributed networks. By 1984 the trend for PCs and workstations to win a larger share of the computer market was also well established. In Fig. 1.2, for example, data is presented on this trend for the European computer market, one of IBM's most important. By 1984 PCs and workstations made up more than 30% of the market.

IBM's beliefs regarding smaller computers   Furthermore, the information regarding the increasing power of microprocessors and the move towards 'downsizing' had been processed by IBM as early as the mid-1970s and the

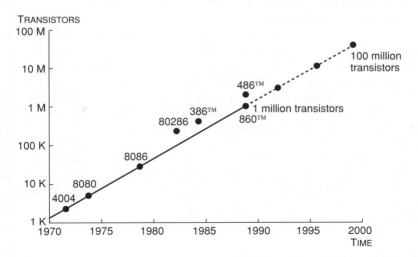

Fig. 1.1 Evolution of Moore's Law for Intel Microprocessors
Source: Molina (1992).

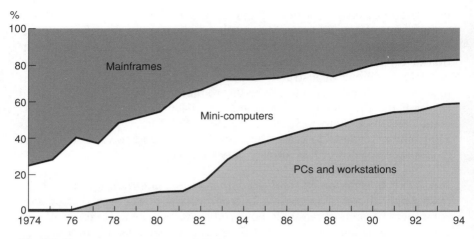

Fig. 1.2 European computer market share

Note: By product category.

Sources: Datastream and OTR Pedder.

implications distilled. This is evident in the commitment that Frank Cary, who became IBM's chief executive officer in 1972, made to personal computers. Cary had led IBM into minicomputers in the late 1960s and was convinced that the greatest growth in the computer industry would come from the smaller end. Indeed, in the 1960s IBM built the SCAMP, probably the world's first personal computer, and followed this with the 5,100 in the mid-1970s even though it made little progress in commercialising them (Ferguson and Morris 1993).

In the light of evidence such as this it is a puzzle that IBM's directors continued to believe until as late as 1991 in the ability of the mainframe to sustain its growth, profitability, and size. As expressed in one of the best of the current accounts of IBM's demise, 'it is more surprising that IBM's top management missed the straws swirling in the wind in the 1970s and 1980s that computing was undergoing fundamental change, that the 360/370 [IBM's major mainframe systems introduced in 1964 and 1970 respectively]—indeed, the whole mainframe principle—was heading for a dead end' (ibid. 16). Closer to the concerns of the present chapter, *The Economist* (1993) noted that 'Mr Akers [who became Chairman of IBM in 1985 and resigned in 1993] and his colleagues had access to more information about the industry than any of their rivals. . . . [However,] their flood of information did them little good'.

IBM, information, and knowledge

It is clear from the evidence presented here that during the 1980s there was a growing disjuncture in IBM between processed information (regarding the increasing performance-cost of microprocessors and substitutability of smaller computers and mainframes) and the company's knowledge-belief (in the sustaining power of the mainframe). It is possible, however, that in the early 1980s the information was still incomplete in the sense that ambiguity still surrounded the extent of the 'downsizing' that would occur. Under these conditions of 'interpretive ambiguity' it may still have been reasonable to interpret this information as suggesting that substitution would only take place at the fringes of the mainframe market, leaving largely intact IBM's market growth and profit margins on mainframes.

But as the decade progressed, IBM's belief in the mainframe remained unaltered while the information became less and less ambiguous. By 1991, however, under the weight not only of complete information but also of the feedback provided from IBM's selection environment in the form of falling revenues and profit margins on mainframes, the belief finally cracked. (It is worth noting, incidentally, that the disjuncture between information and belief had nothing to do with bounded rationality as strictly defined by Simon. That is, the problem was not the quantity of information relative to the company's ability to acquire and process information; the problem followed rather from the way in which the directors of the company chose to interpret the information available in the light of their belief in the mainframe.)

Two questions are raised by the IBM Paradox. The first (and for present purposes less important) question is the following: What caused this belief in IBM and how was it sustained in the face of growing information to the contrary? The second, more important, question is: What are the implications for the theory of the firm?

Although this is not the place for an exhaustive enquiry into the first question (and it may be that the evidence necessary to answer it is not yet available), the following three elements appear to be important parts of the answer. The first element was IBM's historical and spectacular experience of success with mainframes, particularly Systems 360 and 370 on which many of the company's directors in the 1980s cut their teeth. This experience coloured the beliefs of the directors. Secondly, the failure of the Future Systems project in the mid-1970s, which was intended to displace current computers with a quantum jump in computer technologies, was a blow to the confidence and morale of IBM's directors. This resulted in a regressive and defensive tendency to cling to past beliefs. The third element in the wake of the failed Future Systems project was the fear of encouraging products and technologies that might undermine what was believed to be the company's lifeblood—System 370 and its various incarnations. This further reinforced the hegemony of the mainframe division and its beliefs, at the expense of the other divisions producing smaller computers and technologies (such as RISC microprocessors) which it was feared might eat into the revenue from mainframes.

It is a fitting conclusion to this discussion of the IBM Paradox to lament with T. S. Eliot (1963), 'Where is the wisdom we have lost in knowledge, Where is the knowledge we have lost in information', a lament that is all the more pertinent in the so-called 'information age'.

1.6 Implications For the Theory of the Firm

The concept of vision

The IBM Paradox is a particularly dramatic example of a disjuncture between information and knowledge. However, interpretive ambiguity (which occurs whenever there is incomplete information, driving a 'wedge' between information and knowledge) and the tenacity of beliefs are sufficiently frequent occurrences to merit inclusion in the theory of the firm. The way to do so, I propose, is to distinguish information from knowledge. Information is defined, as above, as data relating to states of the world and the statecontingent consequences that follow from events in the world. Knowledge, on the other hand, is defined as belief. While belief may be influenced by information processed by the believer, belief is not necessarily wholly determined by processed information. In the formation of belief, accordingly, there is room for insight, creativity, and misconception. Furthermore, while information is a closed set, knowledge is essentially open-ended. Information and knowledge as thus defined, therefore, are loosely coupled.

The 'vision' of a firm is defined as the dominant set of beliefs in the firm regarding the firm's internal and external circumstances, the shape of things to come in the future, and, in the light of these, the way the firm should 'play its cards'. Since vision depends on the particular construction of particular beliefs, vision is by definition always bounded. 'Bounded vision' and the possibility of 'vision failure' are, therefore, logical implications of this conception of vision.

Routine, competence, and knowledge-creation

In the concept of vision, knowledge is treated on its own terms, as an open-ended process, and not merely as processed information. While the concept of vision relates primarily to the way in which the firm appraises its circumstances and decides on the actions it should take, it is suggested that the conception of knowledge which underlies the notion of vision should also be extended to the analysis of the firm's knowledge base.

While we agree with Marshall (1969) that 'Knowledge is our most powerful engine of production', and while it is acknowledged that this idea is embodied in the concepts of routine and competence exmined earlier in this paper, it is necessary to go beyond these *ex post* concepts to an analysis of the *knowledge-creation process* itself within the firm. This also requires treating knowledge on its own terms, as an open-ended process. This involves, *inter alia*: the integration of knowledge fragmented in various parts of the firm (confronting within the context of the firm Hayek's problem of utilising knowledge not known to anyone in its entirety); mobilising and combining tacit and explicit knowledge; understanding the learning process in all its manifestations; and understanding the process of creativity involved in all innovative activity, including research.

1.7 Conclusion

As Penrose notes in the quotation reproduced at the beginning of this chapter, knowledge is such a difficult concept with the result that most economists have found it 'too slippery to handle'. The recognition, however, of the 'dominant role that increasing knowledge plays in economic processes' leaves us with little option but to take this concept fully on board in the attempt to produce a more robust theory of the firm.

NOTES

1. Simon's intentional explanation of the existence, activities and organisation of the firm is to be contrasted with causal and functional explanations. See Elster's (1983) useful discussion of the distinction between these different types of explanation.
2. Williamson is therefore incorrect when he states that bounded rationality 'refers to neurophysiological limits on the one hand and language limits on the other' (1975, 9).
3. Williamson (1990) argues that 'Although it is sometimes believed that Simon's notion of bounded rationality is alien to the rationality tradition of economics, Simon actually enlarges rather than reduces the scope for rationality analysis' (ibid. 11). Similarly, Jensen and Meckling (1976) state that 'Unfortunately, Simon's work has often been misinterpreted as a denial of maximizing behavior, and misused, especially in the marketing and behavioral science literature. His later use of the term "satisficing"... has undoubtedly contributed to this confusion because it suggests rejection of maximizing behavior rather than maximizing subject to costs of information and decision-making' (Putterman 1986, 211).
4. As Williamson (1987) puts it: 'Economizing on bounded rationality takes two forms. One concerns decision processes, and the other involves governance structures. The use of heuristic problem-solving... is a decision process response.

Transaction cost economics is principally concerned, however, with the economizing consequence of assigning transactions to governance structures in a discriminating way. Confronted with the realities of bounded rationality, the costs of planning, adapting, and monitoring transactions need expressly to be considered. Which governance structures are more efficacious for which type of transaction? *Ceteris paribus*, modes that make large demands against cognitive competence are relatively disfavored' (ibid. 46).

Williamson's de-emphasis of 'decision process responses' to bounded rationality, like heuristic problem-solving, marks a significant point of departure between transaction cost economics and evolutionary economics of the kind proposed by Nelson and Winter which is based strongly on decision process responses such as routinised behaviour. In this respect Williamson also deviates from Simon who, as was shown earlier, insists that in a world of uncertainty and cognitive complexity—which is also Williamson's world—'we must give an account not only of *substantive rationality*—the extent to which appropriate courses of action are chosen—but also *procedural rationality*—the effectiveness, in light of human cognitive powers and limitations, of the *procedures* used to choose actions' (Simon 1978, 8–9).

5. Penrose's distinction between resources and services is similar to Marx's distinction between 'labour power', the commodity or resource which is bought on the market, and 'labour' which refers to the services which are extracted from the labourer. For Marx it is this inevitable distinction which requires that forms of organisation and control be developed within the firm to ensure that labour services will be satisfactorily obtained from the labour power that has been bought. Ironically, Marx's viewpoint is not too distant from Alchian and Demsetz's (1972) concern with the possibility of shirking in team production. This is ironic since Alchian and Demsetz, *contra* Marx, were also concerned to stress the symmetry in the relationship between employer and employee.

6. Increasing concern is being expressed regarding the opportunities that are being lost as a result of the absence of intellectual interaction between economists and 'business analysts' working on the firm. See, for example, John Kay, 'Economics and Business', *Economic Journal*, January 1991, and, in a more satirical vein, *The Economist*, 1991.

7. Examples of work being done by business analysts of the firm—where an intellectual bridge may be built connecting what has been referred to here as the 'firm as repository of knowledge' approach—include Prahalad and Hamel (1990) and Stalk, Evans, and Shulman (1992) whose articles appear in the *Harvard Business Review*. For both, the concept of competences or capabilities is central in deriving an appropriate strategy for the firm. The main difference between them is that while the former define 'competences' largely in terms of technology and products, the latter insist that 'capabilities' must refer to the entire value chain, thus including marketing, distribution, and consumer satisfaction.

8. The present author's interviews at IBM's headquarters at Armonk, New York in early 1993 indicate that it was only in 1991 that IBM's directors amended their belief in the mainframe.

2

A Vision of the Firm and the Evolution of Japanese Computer and Communications Firms

2.1 Introduction

In this chapter, a conceptualisation of the firm is developed in order to analyse the evolution of the major Japanese computer and communications companies, Fujitsu, NEC, Hitachi, Toshiba, Mitsubishi Electric, and Oki. Particular attention is paid to the paradox presented by these companies which feature strongly in the world's top ten in terms of total sales but which, unlike Japanese consumer electronics and automobile companies, are globally dominant in very few markets outside Japan.

According to this conceptualisation, a firm may be analysed in terms of four closely related dimensions: competences, organisation, vision, and selection environment. Competences, the firm's activities and knowledge, define what that firm knows and can do. Organisation determines how the firm's competences are coordinated and controlled in order to produce a competitive output. Vision refers to the set of beliefs which guide the firm's leaders in deciding what the firm should be doing and where it should be going. Selection environment is the sum total of factors external to the firm (and to the population of firms) which determine whether the firm will survive and prosper or not. This 'vision' of the firm has been implicitly compared and contrasted in Chapter 1 with other visions of the firm developed by some of the best-known analysts of the firm, showing the similarities and differences which exist.

2.2 Chapter Overview

This chapter begins with a brief analysis of the concepts of competence, organisation, vision, and selection environment, showing how they are interrelated. The paradox of the Japanese computer and communications companies is then outlined, showing that although these companies are amongst the largest in the world in this industry, they do not enjoy the same global competitiveness as their Japanese counterparts in the consumer electronics and automobile industries. To explain this paradox is one of the objectives of this chapter.

The evolution of the Japanese computer and communications companies and industry is then analysed. What were the major forces which shaped the evolution of this industry in Japan? It is shown that the telecommunications industry provided the initial incubator for the development of competences. A periodisation of the evolution of their competences is then provided, examining how, from a base in telecommunications, these companies moved into electronic devices such as transistors and integrated circuits, and into computers and related software.

The selection environment of the companies is analysed next. How important was the Japanese government in providing a conducive environment? This issue begins with an examination of the role of organs of the Japanese government in facilitating the initial emergence of these companies and fostering their early growth. Particular attention is given to the impact of 'controlled competition', a form of organisation developed by the Ministry of Communications in the 1920s and 1930s for the production of telecommunications equipment. It was controlled competition that was responsible for the emergence in Japan of *several* competing telecommunications equipment suppliers while in the USA there was only one, Western Electric (the subsidiary of AT&T). These Japanese companies went on to develop competences in *both* communications *and* computers, in contrast to their U.S. counterparts—such as AT&T and IBM—which accumulated competences in only one of these areas.

Other important influences in the selection environment are then examined including foreign sources of technology, strong competitive pressure in Japanese markets, and the role of Japanese financial institutions and practices.

What role was played by vision in the evolution of these Japanese companies? One illustration of the importance of vision is provided by the decision-making process in Fujitsu which led ultimately to this company becoming the largest in the Japanese computer industry and the second largest in the world. However, it is shown that this process in Fujitsu was hesitant and was accompanied by both controversy and conflict within the company.

The next section goes on to show how important the specific history of each of the companies has been in shaping its current competences, strengths and weaknesses. Although Fujitsu, NEC, Hitachi, Toshiba, Mitsubishi Electric, and Oki are all part of the same industry and share many similar 'Japanese' characteristics and management and organisational practices, they remain substantially different animals, shaped by different histories.

Why have the Japanese computer and communications companies not performed globally as well as Japanese consumer electronics and automobile companies? This question is tackled in the final section, through an analysis of the sources of global competitiveness of the consumer electronics and automobile companies. It is shown that in adapting successfully to the specificities of the markets for computers and communications equipment in Japan, the computer and communications companies have, ironically, failed to establish the same degree of international competitiveness of their counterparts in the other two industries.

2.3 Theory of the Firm

Following the idea of Occam's Razor, the more parsimonious a theory the better. It is suggested that there are four key interdependent concepts that can be used as the basis of a theory of the firm that is consistent with the above objectives.

2.3.1 Theories of the Firm

There are two major 'non-neoclassical' approaches to the theory of the firm that are dominant in the current economics literature. The first may be referred to as the 'firm as response to information problems' approach. The second may be called the 'firm as repository of knowledge' approach. The first approach is associated with writers such as Coase, Simon, Williamson, Mechling, Jensen, and Aoki. The second approach is derived from the work of writers such as Marshall, Penrose, Nelson, Winter, Chandler, and Teece. We outlined our approach to these theories of the firm in Chapter 1 (see also Fransman 1994b). Our aim in this chapter is to propose a conceptualisation of the firm that is consistent with the evolutionary approach to economic change and will serve to explain the growth of real firms. For this purpose, Nelson and Winter's classic, *An Evolutionary Theory Of Economic Change* (1982), will serve as the reference point for the evolutionary approach. As will become apparent, the present proposed conceptualisation draws heavily on the second approach to the firm.

2.3.2 The Four Key Concepts

Four key interrelated concepts are proposed. They are: competence, vision, organisation, and selection environment. These four concepts are depicted in Fig. 2.1.

SELECTION ENVIRONMENT

The 'Firm'

Fig. 2.1 Four key concepts for a theory of the firm

Competences

The concept of 'competences' may be found in Marshall's belief that 'knowledge is our most powerful engine of production', in Penrose's distinction between resources and services, in Nelson and Winter's notion of 'routines', in Chandler's view of organisational capability, and in Teece's idea of competences. Chapter 1 provides a broader outline of these terms. Competences may be defined here as that set of 'doings' and 'knowings' (activities and knowledge) which allow the firm to reproduce itself over time. This chapter is concerned with those cases where reproduction requires competitiveness. Competences apply to all the interrelated links in the value chain including sale, marketing, production, development, and research.

Competences define a firm's specificity. They are both difficult and costly to acquire and, for the firm as a whole, take a long time to accumulate—decades rather than years. It is in its competences that a firm carries its history. Furthermore, competences as a whole are difficult and costly for would-be competitors to acquire. There are no efficient spot-markets in competences. The reason is the complexity of the activities and knowledge which comprise competences.

The concept of competences as defined is closely linked to the performance of the firm. It can be used as part of the explanation of the firm's performance. Where this is attempted, however, it is necessary to avoid circularity. Although competences are those activities and knowledge which have allowed a firm to compete (*ex post*), and which are intended to allow it to compete in the future (*ex ante*), the activities and knowledge must be defined independently of their effect, that is the competitiveness, or lack of competitiveness, in which they result.

The link that the concept of competence provides with the performance of the firm is one of the major strengths of the concept. One of the main problems with the 'firm as a response to information problems' approach is that it does not provide a robust explanation of firm performance. All firms and their forms of organisation are seen as the result of attempts to deal with information-related difficulties; but not all firms perform equally well. The concept of competence, as will be seen, is capable of throwing light on the firm's forms of organisation as well as on its performance.

Vision

As the above discussion makes clear, at any point in time a firm's competences can be looked at from two points of view. First, from the *ex post* point of view, it is its competences which have allowed the firm to compete in the past. Second, from the *ex ante* point of view, it is its competences that are intended to allow the firm to compete in the future. The *ex ante* dimension, however, raises further problems (as always in economics). The reason is that *uncertainty* and *expectations* are unavoidably brought into the picture. It is not perfectly clear what competences the firm will need in order to allow it to compete in the future (and perform as well as its directors desire). The longer into the future the directors' time-horizon, the greater the lack of clarity.

The concept of vision is necessary in order to deal with the *ex ante* point of view. Vision may be defined as the set of *beliefs* regarding the firm's circumstances. It is these *beliefs* (rather than the firm's 'objective' circumstances) which shape the directors' views regarding the activities and knowledge which the firm should have to compete in the future. (We shall return later to the question of how these beliefs are determined, to the relationship between 'belief', 'information', and 'knowledge'.)

The concepts of competence and vision are, therefore, inextricably linked. This becomes manifestly apparent at those junctures in the firm's evolution when decisions have to be made regarding the competences that the firm will need for the future. These may be referred to as 'competence-creating moments'. These moments bring out the *ex ante* point of view regarding competences. They are to be contrasted with the notion of 'path-dependency', which points to the dependence at any point in time of a firm's current competences, as well as the competences which it can in the future create, on the competences which the firm has in the past created. The notion of path-dependency brings out the *ex post* point of view regarding competences.

It is therefore a firm's vision which orients and shapes the broad outline of its *strategies* and *tactics*.

Organisation

A firm's activities and knowledge must be organised for it to compete. Williamson is correct when he states that 'organization form matters' and when he laments the fact that 'Most recent treatments of the corporation [in economics] . . . accord scant attention to the architecture of the firm and focus entirely on incentive features instead' (Williamson 1985, 281).

The organisation of the firm may be defined as the forms of coordination which it chooses so that its activities and knowledge will result in competitiveness. As this definition makes clear, competence, vision, and organisation are interdependent concepts. Competences mush be organised. But there are different possible ways of organising competences. Which ways are preferable will depend on the beliefs, or visions, of those who have responsibility for deciding on forms of organisation. It is usually not possible to predict the effects of different forms of organisation—if it were, all competing firms would converge on the same, optimal, form of organisation. Choice of form of organisation (like choice of technology) is therefore an important source of variety amongst firms. And it is variety together with the selection process which drives the evolution of a population of firms.

A firm's forms of organisation will be a major determinant of the degree of success with which its activities and knowledge are transformed into competitiveness. The major task in the study of concrete forms of firm organisation—the organisational architecture of the firm—is to understand the effectiveness of different forms in facilitating the creation of competitiveness.

Selection environment

There is also interdependence between a firm's competences, vision, and organisation and its selection environment. The firm's selection environment may be defined as the set of external factors which together influence the ability of the firm (and the population of firms) to reproduce itself (themselves) and to grow.

A firm's competences, vision, and organisation must be appropriate for its selection environment. If they are inappropriate, if they do not allow the firm to adapt to its environment, then the firm will be unable to reproduce itself over time. Conversely, if they are well adapted to the selection environment, then the firm may be able to grow relative to the other firms in the population.

From the firm's point of view, the selection environment is best treated as subjective rather than objective. It is the firm's vision of its environment that will determine the opportunities and threats which it sees (a point emphasised by Edith Penrose). Like beauty, the selection environment is in the eye of the beholder.

The firm's selection environment, however, provides powerful feedback for the firm through its effect on indicators of firm performance such as profitability. A deterioration in a firm's performance provides a signal that the firm must change. And the firm, like other social organisms, has a greater degree of freedom in its ability to change than its biological counterparts. (In this sense, competences, vision, and organisation in the social organism that is the firm cannot be compared to the genes in the biological organism).

However, the relationship between the feedback provided by a firm's selection environment and the changes which the firm ultimately makes is not a deterministic one. Part of the reason has to do with the firm's vision, its beliefs regarding its circumstances and what it considers needs to be done. The relationship between selection environment and belief is not deterministic. Different people in the same selection environment may come to different beliefs regarding what should be done. There is often no 'objective' or 'rational' way of deciding who is right and who is wrong. (This has implications for the relationship between 'selection environment', 'information', 'knowledge', and 'belief' which will be considered shortly.)

The application of the concept of selection environment in empirical studies of firms, however, raises a number of difficulties. For example, how should the analyst proceed in categorising the main characteristics of the firm's selection environment? How can the effects of these characteristics, directly on the firm's competences, vision, and organisation, and indirectly on its performance, be analysed—or the effects on a population of firms? How can the different characteristics be weighted in terms of their effect on the firm/population? These problems are ultimately problems resulting from the complexity of interactions. They do not arise in the formal models of the evolutionary process which sidestep this complexity through their simplifying assumptions.

Information, knowledge, and belief*

The approach proposed here implies a specific conceptualisation of information and knowledge. This conceptualisation becomes apparent when we enquire further into the concepts of vision and competence.

Vision was defined earlier as the firm's set of beliefs (more specifically, the dominant beliefs of its leaders) regarding its circumstances. It is these beliefs, embodied in the firm's vision, which shape its views regarding what should be done. But where do these beliefs come from? In part the beliefs

---

* Readers who have read the introduction to this book may want to skip this section.

are derived from the information regarding the firm's circumstances (both internal and external to the firm) which has been processed by the firm's directors. To this extent, beliefs may be thought of as processed information. As we saw in Chapter 1, information may be defined as a set of data relating to states of the world and it is, by definition, a closed set.

The information processed by the firm's directors, however, is sometimes less than the total set of relevant information in existence. This may result from constraints on the information processing abilities of the directors. To the degree that beliefs are derived from the information processed, they will be constrained by this information. This is the essence of Herbert Simon's concept of bounded rationality (see Chapter 1 and Simon (1957)).

However, beliefs are not necessarily totally derived from processed information. Indeed, in some cases processed information cannot generate unambiguous belief and we may define this as incomplete information. These conditions will generate interpretive ambiguity, that is ambiguity regarding the beliefs that may justifiably be derived from the set of information processed.

Under these conditions of incomplete information, where there is interpretive ambiguity, there is necessarily a loose coupling of processed information and belief. It is accordingly necessary to distinguish between the two. In addition, a person's beliefs regarding his/her circumstances may be thought of as that person's knowledge. It follows that information and knowledge must also be distinguished and do not necessarily refer to the same thing.

Moreover, as was shown earlier, information refers essentially to a closed set of data relating to states of the world. On the other hand, knowledge, as a set of beliefs, is necessarily open-ended. The reason is that at any point in time beliefs can change, even when 'objective' circumstances and processed information remain constant, and beliefs often do. This may happen when there is incomplete information, and there-fore interpretive ambiguity. Under these conditions, different beliefs, even contradictory beliefs, may appear to be sustainable. Similarly, knowledge of the world, defined as beliefs about the world, may change over time (and does change over time), even though the 'objective world' remains constant. This is obvious from a reading of the history of scientific thought in any area. In this sense, therefore, knowledge/belief is necessarily open-ended. Knowledge is in a constant process of becoming other than what it is.

The present discussion of the concepts of information and knowledge has emerged from an analysis of the concept of vision. 'Knowledge', however, was also present in the concept of competence, defined earlier as 'that set of activities and knowledge which allow the firm to reproduce itself over time'. The same concept of knowledge is used by Nelson and Winter (1982) who see the firm as a repository of knowledge.

Knowledge embodied in vision and in competence   We turn now to the relationship between the 'knowledge' embodied in vision, and the 'knowledge' embodied in competences. The latter may be divided into two 'kinds' of knowledge: 'know-how' and 'know-why'. For example, a semiconductor firm may know how to produce memory semiconductors with a particular degree of integration, at particular levels of productivity and defect rates, etc. Know-how, however, does not imply know-why. A semiconductor firm that knows how may not know why it achieves the results it does. Know-how and know-why are, therefore, two different sets of knowledge. However, know-how may be an input into a process that leads to know-why: or vice versa.

In fact, we can see that the underlying concept of knowledge is the same in both vision and competences. Knowledge is equated with belief; and knowledge is inherently open-ended. Know-how and know-why can be thought of as sets of beliefs regarding how to achieve particular outcomes, in the first case, and why particular outcomes are achieved, in the second case. Furthermore, know-how and know-why are open-ended, as is evident to anyone who has examined their evolution over time in particular contexts. Beliefs regarding 'how to' and 'why' are in a constant process of change; the longer the time-period, the greater the change. Knowledge is constantly being created by means of knowledge. Know-how and know-why are *processes* rather than *states*, and are therefore essentially the same as the knowledge of circumstances embodied in vision. That is, the same concept of knowledge is implied in both cases.

Knowledge fragmentation-integration; and the problem of communicating knowledge   There are two further propositions regarding knowledge which have crucial implications for the competences and organisation of the firm. First—as a result of the division of labour, limitations on the ability of individuals to process information, and the process of the construction of beliefs—the stock of knowledge in any firm is always fragmented, that is divided amongst different individuals and groups of individuals. However, to a greater or lesser extent, depending on the firm's selection environment, fragmented knowledge must be integrated for the firm to be competitive. This raises within the context of the firm the problem that Hayek (1945) has analysed for society as a whole, namely the problem of utilising knowledge not known by anyone in its entirety.

Second, there are inherent problems in communicating whole sets of knowledge from one human mind to another. One problem arises from Polanyi's (1967) celebrated notion of tacit knowledge (which he defined as existing when we know more than we can tell). But the concept of knowledge proposed here suggests that the very process of the construction of knowledge as belief by individuals presents further (different) problems for the communication of knowledge. For example, even where there is no tacit knowledge, communication problems are likely to arise where different individuals, in the light of interpretive ambiguity, have constructed different beliefs on the basis of the same set of incomplete information. These two issues will not be pursued further here but see also Fransman (1994*c*).

2.4 Explaining the Performance of the Major Japanese Information and Communication Companies

2.4.1 The Paradox

The major Japanese information and communication (IC) companies— including NEC, Fujitsu, Hitachi, Toshiba, and Mitsubishi Electric—present an important paradox: although they feature strongly in the world's top ten (measured by total company sales) in the three key information and communication markets of computers, telecommunications equipment, and semiconductors, they are relatively weak in terms of global competitiveness. The aim of this section is to explain this paradox.

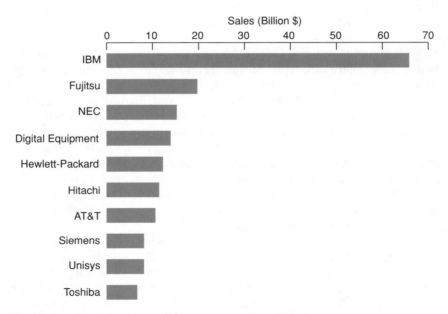

Fig. 2.2 Largest Information Technology suppliers (1992)
Source: Datamation.

As shown in Fig. 2.2, IBM dominates the computer market with sales of around $65 billion. However, Japanese companies feature strongly with Fujitsu second, NEC third, Hitachi sixth and Toshiba tenth. In the case of telecommunications equipment, as indicated in Fig. 2.3, while Alcatel and AT&T hold the first and second positions, NEC and Fujitsu are in fifth and eighth place respectively. In semiconductors, Japanese companies perform particularly well (Fig. 2.4). Although Intel moved into the lead, replacing NEC in 1993 as a result of sales of its microprocessors, six out of the top ten companies are Japanese. NEC, Toshiba, and Hitachi were in second, third and fifth places, while Fujitsu, Mitsubishi Electric, and Matsushita were in seventh, eighth, and tenth places respectively. NEC was the only company in the world to be in the top five in all three of these markets.

However, the enviable ranking of Japanese companies in these three markets does not imply that they enjoy dominant global competitive positions in these markets. Indeed, there is evidence that Japanese IC companies are weak in terms of global competitiveness relative both to Japanese consumer electronics and automobile companies and the leading Western companies in these markets (with the important exception of memory semiconductors).

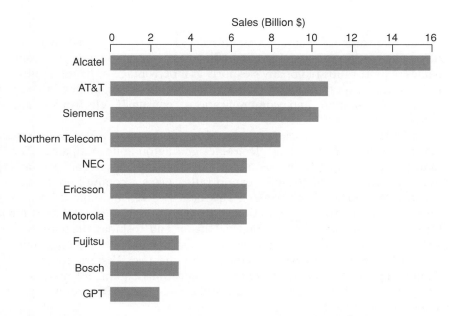

Fig. 2.3 Largest telecommunications equipment companies (1991)
Source: Dataquest.

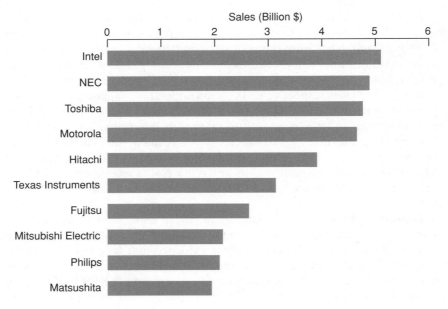

Fig. 2.4 Largest semiconductor manufacturers
Source: Dataquest.

One indicator of global competitiveness—indicating what may be referred to as 'revealed global competitiveness'—is provided by the companies' export ratios (company's exports as a percentage of its total sales). In Table 2.1, export ratios are shown for the major companies in three sectors: information and communications, consumer electronics, and automobiles.

As Table 2.1 shows, the export ratios of the IC companies are significantly lower than for the consumer electronics and automobile companies. The same picture emerges from a breakdown of company sales by Japanese and overseas markets (which, unlike export ratios, takes account of production overseas by Japanese companies). This data is given in Table 2.2 which shows that while overseas sales ranged from 23% to 33% of total sales for the main IC companies (NEC, Fujitsu, Hitachi, and Toshiba), the figure was 49% and 74% for the two major specialist consumer electronics companies (Matsushita and Sony). The percentage for the two Western companies dominating the computer and telecommunications equipment markets— IBM and Alcatel as shown in Figs. 2.2 and 2.3—in the early 1990s was 61% and 67% respectively.

This data raises three questions that are answered in the remainder of this paper. First, how is the prominence of the Japanese IC companies in

Table 2.1 Export ratio of selected Japanese companies, 1992

	Export ratio
Information and communication companies:	
NEC	18
Fujitsu	14
Hitachi	16
Toshiba	25
Mitsubishi Electric	18
Oki	25
Consumer electronics companies:	
Matsushita Electrical Industrial	35
Sony	64
Sharp	45
Canon	78
Automobile companies:	
Toyota	36
Nissan	41
Mitsubishi Motors	48

Note: Export ratio is a company's exports as a percentage of total sales, and includes direct exports by the company and all exports through trading firms. See *Japan Company Handbook* 1992, 29.

Table 2.2 Breakdown of 1993 sales, Japan and overseas (percentages)

Company	Japan	Overseas
NEC	77	23
Fujitsu	67	33
Hitachi	76	24
Toshiba	70	30
Matsushita	51	49
Sony	26	74

Source: Company Reports, 1993.

Figs. 2.2, 2.3, and 2.4 to be explained, that is, how were they able to achieve their relatively large size in terms of sales? Second, how is the relative ranking of the Japanese IC companies to be explained? Third, why have the Japanese IC companies been relatively weak in terms of global competitiveness.

Closer scrutiny of Figs. 2.2, 2.3, and 2.4 shows that of the Japanese companies in the top ten in these markets, three have dominated: NEC, Fujitsu, and Hitachi. NEC is third in computers, fifth in telecommunications equipment, and second in semiconductors; Fujitsu is second in computers, eighth in telecommunications equipment, and seventh in semiconductors; while Hitachi is sixth in computers, and fifth in semiconductors. The only other Japanese company to hold a place in the top five in one of these three markets is Toshiba, which was third in semiconductors.

The major circumstance that NEC, Fujitsu, and Hitachi have in common is the origin of their information and communication activities in the telecommunications sector in the prewar period. In the following section it will be shown that it was in the telecommunications sector that these three companies first accumulated the competences that in the 1950s they would use to enter the new but competence-related areas of semiconductors and computers.

2.4.2 Evolution of the Competences of the Japanese IC Companies

Company competences are central in the discussion of the three issues identified in the previous section posed above. In this section the evolution of the competences of NEC, Fujitsu, and Hitachi is examined. Later, the selection environment which influenced the competences that were accumulated is analysed.

Until 1950: development of telecommunications competences

During this period the three companies, (together with Oki, the fourth major supplier of telecommunications equipment) accumulated competences in four main areas: switching (at this time primarily electromechanical switching), transmissions (including land-based carrier transmissions systems and, from the 1920s, radio-based systems for telephone and TV), components (such as vacuum tubes), and customer premise equipment (like telephones). In view of the Japanese terrain and the proneness of the country to earthquakes, radio communications became particularly important and this later enabled Japanese companies, notably NEC, to establish an international competitiveness in microwave communications from the 1960s, subsequently used in satellite and mobile communications.

As will also be shown in the next section, the late 1920s and 1930s were very important for the accumulation of Japanese competences as the selection environment changed dramatically under the twin influences of financial crisis and growing nationalism. There were two crucial results. The first was increased competition between the suppliers of telecommunications equipment, a process that decreased NEC's dominance and gave greater access to the government telecommunications equipment market to Hitachi, Fujitsu and Oki. The second result was a significant reduction in the dependence of these companies on their foreign sources of technology. Both these factors resulted in the enhancement of Japanese technological competences.

1950–1960: entry into the new electronics paradigm

During this period these companies used the competences they had already accumulated in the telecommunications area as a springboard to enter the emerging product markets of the new electronics paradigm: transistors, computers, and electronic switches. While these were new products for the companies, and while they were based on new electronics technology, there was an important degree of continuity between the competences that had been accumulated under the previous technological regime in telecommunications and the competences required for the new electronics paradigm.

For example, the competences that Toshiba and NEC had accumulated in vacuum tubes in the 1920s and 1930s facilitated their mastery of transistor technology licensed from General Electric in the 1950s. Similarly, it was some of NEC's engineers, who first cut their technological teeth in telecommunications transmissions technologies, who went on to use the competences they had already acquired to build their company's first computers with the assistance of prototypes developed in government laboratories.

This competence-continuity has important implications for the assessment of the Japanese government's industrial policy. The success of many of the programmes established by the Ministry of International Trade and Industry (MITI), aimed at facilitating the entry of Japanese companies into the new product markets created by the electronics paradigm, was partly the result of competences that these companies had already accumulated before the war. Seen in this light, although MITI's programmes certainly aided the entry of the participating Japanese companies (Fransman, 1993), the necessary condition for their success, namely their prior acquisition of competences, had already been established in the prewar period.

1960–1980: catching up

From 1960 to 1980 the Japanese IC companies caught up with the Western leaders. In the area of electronic devices they moved from transistors to integrated circuits to global dominance of the memory semiconductor market. Their failure to achieve a similar position in microprocessors (for reasons that will be discussed shortly) was not the result of a lack of technological competence. Indeed, in April 1972 NEC produced Japan's first microprocessor, only six months after Intel produced the world's first microprocessor, the i4004, in response to a request from a Japanese calculator company.

In some other devices Japanese companies were able to develop internationally strong technological competences in response to the demand conditions in the Japanese market. One notable example is in optoelectronic integrated circuits, largely III–V compound devices such as LEDs (light-emitting diodes) and semiconductor lasers. In addition to the Japanese information and communication industry, strong demand for these devices comes from the country's internationally competitive consumer electronics industry. These optoelectronic devices have also readily proved their international competitiveness in global markets.

In computers the main Japanese computer companies—Fujitsu, NEC, and Hitachi—developed the full range of computers, from supercomputers to personal computers. By as early as 1976 Fujitsu had caught up with IBM in terms of the technological performance of its computers. However, it was IBM's continuing dominance of computer standards, particularly in mainframes, the installed software that its customers had already invested in, and the company's sophisticated global distribution network which prevented the Japanese companies from making significant headway against IBM outside Japan. In Japan their own networks and customer loyalties gave them a far stronger position.

In personal computers and workstations—the area that would increasingly come to dominate both computer sales and standards—the Japanese companies were seriously impeded by the slow development and diffusion of personal computers in Japan. The main reason was the difficulty of processing the Japanese *kanji* characters. As a result of this difficulty, Japan still has a far lower rate of diffusion of personal computers than Western countries. In turn this has inhibited the development of data networks and therefore so-called information superhighways. The specificity of the Japanese personal computer market also meant that different standards evolved in Japan compared to Western countries. Largely as a result of these shortcomings in the Japanese market for personal computers—a market on which the Japanese companies mainly depend—these companies were unable to compete to 'stamp their authority' in the area of computing. They were therefore unable to compete with companies like Intel and Microsoft whose success in microprocessors and operating systems respectively was based primarily on the rapid growth of the personal computer market.

Japanese technical competence in the broad area of microprocessors, however, is evident in their performance in microcontrollers which are technically similar although less complex than microprocessors. In microcontrollers the Japanese market played a more positive role. More specifically, Japan's large domestic market in consumer electrical and electronic products and its strong international competitiveness in consumer electronics created a substantial market for microcontrollers. (Microcontrollers are used in consumer products such as washing machines, microwave ovens, and video casette recorders.) Furthermore, the microcontrollers developed for this market were also suitable for use in products manufactured in other Western markets. Indeed, NEC is currently the world's largest producer of microcontrollers.

Japanese competences in software have also been shaped by the characteristics of the domestic environment. Japan is alone amongst the industrialised countries in terms of the importance of its market for customised relative to packaged software (packaged software is bought 'off the shelf' not customised to the needs of particular users). To some extent this characteristic of the Japanese software market is a reflection of the relatively low rate of diffusion of personal computers already referred to, since a substantial amount of packaged software is produced for personal computer applications. However, it is also a result of the greater tendency of large computer users in Japan compared to Western countries to rely on their close long term links with the Japanese computer companies to cater for their specific software needs.

Largely as a result of these characteristics of the Japanese software market, Japanese companies have not featured strongly in the global market for packaged software. (In a television interview, Bill Gates of Microsoft said he saw no sign of a challenge from Japanese companies in this market.) The weakness of Japanese companies here, however, contrasts strikingly with assessments of their strong software competences made by experts from leading Western computer companies and software houses.

In the field of telecommunications switches the Japanese companies during this period made significant progress in developing first electronic switching systems, notably the D10 used by NTT in the Japanese network, and then digital systems, primarily the D70 and D60 switches. Unfortunately for NEC and Fujitsu, however, they missed the window of opportunity that opened for digital switches in the USA in the late 1970s. The reason had partly to do with NTT's decision to delay development of digital switching in cooperation with these two companies and Hitachi and Oki. As a result, in contrast to practically all other cases where Japanese companies successfully entered Western markets, NEC and Fujitsu were forced by the emerging demand in the USA for digital switches to develop a product for the export market *before* testing and improving it on the Japanese market.

A further source of weakness in this field was the inability of NEC and Fujitsu to provide adequate software support for the users of their switches in the USA. (Switches are complex products which are highly software-intensive. The different characteristics of the American and Japanese telecommunications network means that a significant amount of the software must be re-engineered in order to adapt a Japanese switch to the American network.) In the event it was the Canadian company, Northern Telecom, an early entrant into digital switching, which benefited most from the window of opportunity. Its DMS digital switch was developed before

AT&T's comparable medium-sized 4ESS, giving Northern Telecom access to the US switch market and ultimately a market share roughly equal to AT&T's. In the 1980s, however, Fujitsu and NEC regrouped and concentrated their switching efforts on developing the next-generation broadband ATM (asynchronous transfer mode) switch used for multimedia switching. Fujitsu became the first company to offer commercially ATM switches and the company is currently hoping to become a leader in this area in the US, taking advantage of the new window of opportunity that will emerge with the adoption of this new generation of switches. This time, however, Fujitsu and NEC have been able to benefit from the joint ATM research and development project which NTT established, a project that also includes Northern Telecom as well as Hitachi and Oki.

Facsimile, however, provides a case where conditions in Japan resulted in the development of competences by Japanese companies which soon resulted in a dominant competitive position in global markets. The basic idea of electrically transmitting an image over a distance is by no means new. The first fax patent was taken out in 1843 and its first commercial use was in 1865. Thomas Edison's improvements to fax technology were motivated by his farsighted belief that this mode of communication would result in an important market in countries like China and Japan whose script used large numbers of complex characters. The first Japanese fax was developed by Yasujiro Niwa, a senior engineer in NEC who previously was involved in research and development in the Ministry of Communications, in 1928. Due to a perceived lack of profitability in faxes, however, Western companies failed to put much resource into this area. But in Japan, in line with Edison's earlier reasoning, Japanese companies became interested as the enabling technologies made faxes increasingly technologically and economically viable. A major facilitating role was played by NTT which by the 1970s had the world's largest fax research capability. When NTT harmonised the fax standards of the competing Japanese companies and cooperated with them in providing fax services through its telecommunications network, fax began to diffuse rapidly in Japan. With Japan as a springboard, Japanese companies moved quickly and successfully into global markets. By the late 1980s, Matsushita Graphic Communications Systems, with 60% of the market in Japan, had won about 40% of the world market. IC companies such as NEC, Hitachi, Fujitsu, and Oki also successfully entered the Japanese and global markets (Coopersmith 1993).

For the purposes of this chapter, this brief survey of the development of competences in Japanese IC companies in some of their main markets, and the extent of their international competitiveness in these markets, has served to illustrate the extent to which their performance has been influenced by the conditions prevailing in the Japanese market. As this survey shows, the Japanese market acted as a powerful conditioning environment which shaped the competences of the Japanese IC companies. In turn it was these competences which determined the international strengths and weaknesses of these companies.

1980 to the present: sharing global technological leadership

Since the late 1970s, Japanese IC companies, having reached the international technological frontiers in most of their areas, began to pay increasing attention to 'oriented basic research'. More recently, the various organs of the Japanese government have committed themselves to supporting this trend in the companies by giving greatly increased priority to basic research.

How and why were these Japanese IC companies able to accumulate the competences documented in this section, responding as they did to the conditions in the Japanese market? To answer this question a more detailed analysis is needed of the selection environment of these companies.

2.4.3 Selection Environment and the Evolution of Competences

Apart from the demand characteristics of the Japanese market discussed in the last section, there were five further features of the selection environment in Japan which shaped the evolution of competences in the Japanese IC companies. These were: government-facilitated entry into new products and their technologies; government-created markets; the uniquely Japanese form of organisation in telecommunications, 'controlled competition'; the acquisition of foreign technology through collaboration with Western companies; and strong competitive pressure in Japanese markets. As will be seen, the significance of these features changed over time.

Government-facilitated entry

Government users of information and communication products and government laboratories played an important role in facilitating the initial entry of Japanese IC companies into new products and their related technologies. The Japanese government continues to play a significant role, although since the 1970s, with the growth and globalisation of Japanese IC companies and their increasing R&D competences, the relative importance of government has decreased.

The facilitating role played by the Japanese government is apparent from the time when the country's information and communication industry was founded. This can be seen from the impact of the Ministry of Industry (Kobusho) in the late 19th century. For further discussion of this issue see Fransman (1995a), Fruin (1992) and, within a different interpretive framework, Odagiri (1993).

In 1868, the first year of the new post-Tokugawa Meiji regime, the

Japanese government, through the Ministry of Industry, established a government-owned telegraph factory which aimed at supplementing imported telegraph equipment with domestically produced products. A famous Japanese inventor already in his seventies, H. Tanaka, was invited to develop the equipment in this factory. In turn, Tanaka gathered a talented group of engineers. It was some of the members of this group who subsequently set up the private companies which constituted the core of the emerging information and communication industry.

In 1875 Tanaka himself left to establish Tanaka Seisakusha, a company which in 1904 became Shibaura Engineering. In 1939 Shibaura merged with the Tokyo Electric Company to form *Toshiba*. The origins of the Tokyo Electric Company go back to 1890 with the founding of a company, Hakunetsusha, by I. Fujioka, a professor at the College of Engineering in Tokyo (which later became the Engineering Department of the University of Tokyo). In establishing Hakunetsusha, Fujioka was assisted by S. Miyoshi who was one of the engineers in Tanaka's group in the Ministry of Industry's telegraph factory. In 1899 Hakunetsusha became the Tokyo Electric Company.

S. Miyoshi later went on to establish his own telecommunications equipment factory. By the late 1890s, however, Miyoshi faced bankruptcy and was forced to sell out to K. Iwadare who bought the factory in order to establish the Nippon Electric Company (*NEC*) in 1899. NEC was a joint venture with Western Electric which owned 54% of the company's shares. K. Iwadare studied engineering at the College of Engineering a year after Fujioka and worked for four years for the Ministry of Industry.

Another one of Tanaka's group was K. Oki who left the Ministry of Industry's factory to establish his own company, Meikosha, which later became *Oki*. In the early years of the 20th century, Oki was the largest supplier of telecommunications equipment and by the time of the Second World War it was second only to NEC.

Fujitsu and Hitachi also owe their origins in information and communications to government activities. In 1885 the Ministry of Communications (Teishinsho) took over responsibility for communications from the Ministry of Industry. The Ministry of Communications also controlled electric power generation, railroads, shipping, and postal services. In 1896 Furukawa Mining established Furukawa-denko (Furukawa Electric Industry) to supply electrical wire to the Ministry of Communications. With the expansion of the Ministry's expenditure on telecommunications, Furukawa Electric decided to begin making manual switchboards and telephones. Furukawa Electric's entry was facilitated by the transfer to the company of Dr M. Tonegawa, Director of the Ministry of Communications' laboratories, and some of the engineers who worked under him. In 1923 Furukawa Electric concluded an agreement with Siemens with the purpose of gaining access to the latter's switching technology. This resulted in a joint venture,

Fuji-denki (Fuji Electric). In the same year Fuji Electric became an official supplier to the Ministry. In 1935 Fuji Electric spun-off a subsidiary, Fuji Tsushinki (Fuji Telecommunications), to specialise in the production of Siemens' switches. In 1967 Fuji Tsushinki changed its name to *Fujitsu*.

Hitachi's entry into telecommunications, and through this the other information and communication activities which now constitute the largest part of its business, began with its acquisition of Kokusan Kogyo in 1937. Kokusan Kogyo's telecommunications business is traced back to its merger in 1934 with another company, Toa Denki Seisakusho (East-Asia Electric Machine Manufacturing). Toa Denki was founded in 1918 by K. Munesue, formerly Director of the Electricity Bureau of the Ministry of Communications. Hitachi itself began in 1908 when Kodaira Namihei, an entrepreneurial engineer, established the Kuhara Mining company. Hitachi began as the electrical-machinery repair shop of Kuhara Mining at its Hitachi mine. When Kuhara Mining moved its corporate headquarters to Tokyo in 1918, Hitachi Limited was established in 1920 as an electrical machinery company.

The Japanese government, largely through the Ministry of Communications, continued to exert an influence for growth on the Japanese IC companies until the end of the Second World War, when this Ministry was abolished. Particularly important were the laboratories of the Ministry which incubated many of the telecommunications-related technologies that were subsequently transferred to the supplying companies. After the war, the role of the Ministry was continued by NTT, formed in 1952 as a government-owned company, which inherited the Ministry's telecommunications responsibilities under the regulation of the new Ministry of Posts and Telecommunications. NTT's laboratories, the Electrical Communications Laboratories, continued to play a central role in the research and development of new telecommunications equipment, often working jointly with its 'family' of suppliers the main members of which were NEC, Fujitsu, Hitachi, and Oki. The other two major industrial electronics companies, Toshiba and Mitsubishi Electric, were not members of NTT's privileged family of suppliers. It was only after NTT was partly privatised in 1985 that the 'family' was broadened to include other Japanese and Western telecommunications companies.

NTT's Electrical Communications Laboratories (ECL) supported the accumulation of competences by the leading Japanese IC companies. ECL played a major role in the development of switching and transmission systems competences in NEC, Fujitsu, Hitachi, and Oki. ECL also assisted their entry into important new product areas. One example is in computers. The Musashino series of computers developed in ECL's Musashino laboratories was adopted by NEC, Fujitsu, and Hitachi, becoming one of their first computers. A similar role was played by MITI's Electrotechnical Laboratories (ETL). Its ETL series were similarly adopted by the main

Japanese computer companies. In the field of optical fiber in the 1970s, ECL's Ibaraki laboratories played a major role in developing a Japanese version of the technology developed originally by Corning and AT&T's Bell Laboratories. This technology was transferred to NTT's 'family' cable suppliers, notably Sumitomo Electric, Furukawa, and Fujikura.

ECL has continued to play its supportive role in research and development, leaving manufacture to the suppliers, although, as mentioned, NTT has since broadened its group of suppliers. The growing size, strength and global operations of the Japanese suppliers, however, particularly NEC and Fujitsu, has meant that they have come to depend less on ECL's R&D competences. The reduction in dependence is even greater in the case of MITI's ETL which in consequence now concentrates more of its activities on longer term and more basic research.

Government-created markets

Complementing its role in facilitating the development of new products and related technologies by the IC companies, the Japanese government gave further crucial assistance by providing the markets on which these companies largely depended in the information and communication area until the 1960s and 1970s. By this time the competences which they had accumulated allowed these companies to extend their activities into the private sector in Japan, which was expanding rapidly as a result of the high growth of national income, and into the export market.

Particularly important were the government's telecommunications expansion programmes which provided a regular and growing source of sales for the IC companies, particularly those that were members of the 'family of suppliers' of the Ministry of Communications and later NTT. Since these programmes were to some extent immune to the fluctuations of the business cycle, they provided an important source of stability for these companies, facilitating their steady accumulation of competences.

NEC, the main telecommunications equipment supplier, illustrates the importance of government-created markets. In the mid-1930s about 75% of NEC's sales were to the Japanese government. By as late as 1967 the figure was still around 50%. In 1975, 32% of NEC's sales were to government, primarily NTT, and in 1985—the year when NTT was partly-privatised—the figure was still 13%. Sales to government and NTT were also important for the other IC companies. This was true for Fujitsu and even more so for Oki, which remained more dependent on sales to NTT than NEC or Fujitsu. The same was the case with Hitachi, although as the largest of the IC companies with diversified activities which included heavy electrical equipment and consumer electronics, Hitachi depended less on government and NTT for its overall sales. However, in areas such as switching and transmissions, where Hitachi is far weaker than NEC or Fujitsu, sales to government are crucial. In the early post-war period Hitachi also benefitted significantly from government reconstruction programmes involving expenditure on heavy electrical equipment.

NTT and other organs of the Japanese government, such as the Ministry of Education, also provided crucial markets for the first computers that were produced in the 1950s and 1960s by Fujitsu, NEC, and Hitachi. Since they were not members of NTT's privileged 'family' of suppliers, Toshiba and Mitsubishi Electric benefited less from sales to NTT until 1985. NTT's support for its family suppliers was particularly critical in the early 1970s in the aftermath of IBM's great leap forward with the introduction of its System 370. It was this computer system that sent shock waves through the world of computer producers, leading to the exit of such substantial players as GEC and RCA. Sheltered, however, by NTT's significant purchases of computers, and with their competences buoyed both by NTT's joint development with them of its DIPS computer and MITI's cooperative research and development programmes, NEC, Fujitsu, and Hitachi remained as Japanese producers of mainframes. On the other hand, Toshiba, Mitsubishi Electric, and Oki, lacking NTT's support, abandoned the mainframe business. Nevertheless, the latter three companies participated in MITI's co-operative programmes in the information and communications areas and also benefited from the government's other measures aimed at promoting the IC companies. These included tariff protection and other mechanisms to ensure that Japanese companies had privileged access to the Japanese market for IC products.

The role of the Japanese government

In terms of selection environment, the main role of the Japanese government was to nurture the Japanese IC companies which, in the absence of government intervention, would not have been able to survive in a world dominated by Western companies which were significantly more powerful technologically and financially. The power of these Western companies is evident in the role that they continued to play as suppliers of technology to the Japanese IC companies as shown later. There can be little doubt, therefore, that the nurturing selection environment created by the Japanese government was a necessary condition for the entry of the Japanese companies into the markets of the information and communications industry.

Nevertheless, having accumulated competences that became increasingly internationally competitive, the Japanese IC companies have come to depend less and less on the Japanese government. This is reflected in MITI's transformed role which increasingly confines the role of the ministry to areas such as international trade conflict resolution, environmental and energy issues, and longer term and more basic research.

'Controlled competition' in telecommunications

A further important feature of the selection environment of the Japanese
IC companies was the evolution of a uniquely Japanese form of organisation in the area of telecommunications, referred to here as 'controlled competition' (Fransman, 1995a). This is a cooperative form of organisation that
was perfected in the 1920s and 1930s in Japan. It involves a cooperative
division of labour between the organisation running and further developing the Japanese telecommunications network—first the Ministry of
Communications and then NTT—and a closed group of companies with
which it jointly develops advanced telecommunications equipment. While
this joint activity results in the development of prototypes, manufacture is
left to the individual companies in the group.

There is controlled *competition* in that the supplying companies in the
group constitute alternative sources of supply and improvements made by
one company pressurising the others into making at least matching
improvements. Each of the suppliers is therefore subjected to a degree of
competitive pressure to make improvements. However, the competition is
controlled in that the purchases of the Ministry/NTT are shared amongst
the group of suppliers and entry into the group is restricted. (Until 1985
entry was strictly limited with the result that it was virtually impossible for
new companies to enter the group. After 1985, with the new procurement
regulations—the Track Three procedures—NTT invites bids for the joint
development of new telecommunications equipment not yet adequately
available on the market. In this way a group of suppliers is selected, usually
including both Japanese and Western companies. After selection, however,
entry to the joint development programme is closed, although in principle
any company can bid subsequently when NTT announces its procurement
demands for the equipment in point.)

How did controlled competition come about? What were the advantages
and disadvantages of controlled competition? And what were the consequences of controlled competition for the evolution of Japanese IC
companies?

We turn now to a discussion of controlled competition, and its consequences for Japanese IC companies. From the beginning, the Ministry of
Industry and then the Ministry of Communications left the manufacture of
telecommunications equipment to private Japanese supplying companies.
However, the Ministry, as a sophisticated user of this equipment with its
own substantial R&D competences, worked closely with its suppliers
strengthening their competences. Until the mid-1920s this pattern resulted
in the strong dominance of one supplier, Oki at the turn of the century, and
NEC thereafter. In 1926, NEC received 68% of the Ministry of
Communications' procurement of telecommunications equipment. The
figures for Oki, Fujitsu, and Hitachi were 17%, 11%, and 1% respectively.

By the late 1920s two important events occurred. The first was several financial crises while the second was the growing nationalism that swept Japan. In an attempt to deal with the former, the Ministry of Communications decided to strengthen the competition facing NEC by increasing procurement from the other suppliers. At the same time the Ministry, a hotbed of nationalism, attempted to decrease the dependence of the Japanese companies on Western technology. (The main Western suppliers of technology are discussed below.) The main beneficiaries of these attempts were Hitachi and Oki. Hitachi received privileged treatment from the Ministry because it did not have any major technology agreements with Western companies.

By 1931 controlled competition had significantly reduced NEC's dominance by increasing the degree of competition in the telecommunications equipment market. Between 1926 and 1931 NEC's share of the Ministry's procurement fell from 68% to 54%; Hitachi's rose from 1% to 6%; while Oki's rose from 17% to 21%. Fujitsu's share remained constant at 11%. However, these figures reflected standing orders relating to equipment that the Ministry had already installed. NEC's reduced dominance is better indicated by its falling share of the Ministry's new purchases. From 1925 to 1931 NEC's share fell from 38% of these purchases to 11%.

Controlled competition was a crucial part of the selection environment of the Japanese IC companies and had important consequences for their evolution. First and foremost, the absence of a 'pure market' mechanism in the market for telecommunications equipment had several significant effects: it reduced concentration amongst the suppliers in this market (under 'pure market' conditions it is likely that only NEC and perhaps another supplier would have survived); it increased the diffusion of advanced technology to the other supplying companies in the group thereby strengthening their competences; yet through the competitive pressure that it provided (albeit controlled) controlled competition ensured that all the companies would continue to innovate rather than stagnate; finally, by providing a reasonably certain market through the long term and a stable relationship that the suppliers enjoyed with the Ministry/NTT, controlled competition created conditions conducive to the accumulation of competences and transaction specific assets such as equipment and trained personpower. In this way, controlled conditions competition provided Japan with a mechanism for using telecommunications in order to facilitate the accumulation of competences in several large, competing companies. The companies went on in the postwar period to use the competences they had accumulated in telecommunications before the war to enter the new, competence-related fields of transistors and computers.

The contrast with the situation in the USA is striking. There, from the time that Alexander Graham Bell cooperated with instrument-maker Thomas Watson in producing the first telephone sets, it was the same organisation that both developed the telecommunications network as well as developed and manufactured the equipment that it required. This pattern was firmly established in 1880 when the American Bell Telephone Company purchased Western Union's telephone supplying subsidiary, the Western Electric Company of Chicago. According to a 1882 agreement, American Bell restricted itself to purchasing all its telephone equipment from Western Electric while the latter agreed to limit its activities to supplying American Bell and its licensees.

In the USA this situation resulted in the emergence of only one major supplier of telecommunications equipment, Western Electric, which is now part of the divested AT&T. (The second major US company involved in telecommunications equipment, Motorola, achieved its present position not through the development of equipment for the national telecommunications network, but through the competences that it accumulated from the 1920s and 1930s developing radio-based equipment for the non-telecommunications private sector. Motorola's weakness in the core telecommunications area of switching continues to impede its competitiveness in areas such as mobile communications systems.)

In the USA, furthermore, the regulations governing AT&T until divestiture produced a major split between the telecommunications and computer industries. As a result, none of the major American computer companies had a background of competences in telecommunications. (IBM failed in its bid to acquire telecommunications competences in the early 1980s with its acquisition of Rolm—spurred by its belief in the importance of the convergence of computing and communications. Furthermore, the jury is still out regarding AT&T's success in realising competence synergies through its takeover of NCR.)

In stark contrast, the three Japanese companies which rank highest in the major IC markets (as shown in Figs. 2.2, 2.3, and 2.4)—namely NEC, Fujitsu, and Hitachi—have competences in all of the key IC areas, namely computers, communications, and semiconductors. However, it is not yet clear whether synergies between these three areas can be realised in order to give these Japanese companies an international competitive advantage. Furthermore, beliefs in the major Western companies remain divided over the question of whether in-house competences in all three of these areas are necessary for competitive advantage.

Acquisition of foreign technology

A further crucial feature of the selection environment was the access that Japanese IC companies had to Western technology. This was particularly important for the two Japanese companies that are now the leaders in the IC industry, NEC and Fujitsu. In 1899 NEC was formed as a joint venture with Western Electric. (These interests of Western Electric were later taken over by ITT.) The technology that NEC obtained from this source was crucial until the 1960s by which time NEC's indigenous competences had advanced sufficiently for it to begin to sell its own technology, notably in microwave communications, to ITT. In 1923 the joint venture was set up with Siemens which led eventually to the establishment of Fujitsu. Siemens' technology was similarly crucial in the prewar period for the accumulation of Fujitsu's competences.

The other Japanese IC companies benefited likewise from technology supplied, directly or indirectly, by the major Western IC companies. For example, Toshiba's link with GE in the 1920s gave it access to vacuum tube technology, making it the most important producer of these devices in Japan. GE also helped Toshiba to accumulate its competences in radio-related areas. Mitsubishi Electric benefited in similar ways from its link with Westinghouse. Although before the war Hitachi did not have a major technology alliance with a Western company (it was the weakest of the major Japanese IC companies, a weakness that continues today in the area of telecommunications equipment), it also benefited, through activities such as reverse engineering, from the Western technology imported into Japan.

In the immediate post-war period, Western companies played a crucial role in facilitating the rapid move of the Japanese companies into the new electronics paradigm. In the case of transistors, for example, companies like RCA, GE, Philips, and Western Electric transferred this crucial generic technology to Japan.

In 1952, Hitachi, on the basis of a transistor license from RCA, opened a factory which produced transistors. RCA and GE sold transistor licenses to the specialist consumer electrical and electronics company, Matsushita. In 1952 Matsushita benefited enormously from a joint venture which it established with Philips—Matsushita Electronics Industry, 70% owned by Matushita—which helped it to move from electrical products such as light fittings, batteries, lamps, and vacuum tube radios into the new electronics paradigm. In 1953 Sony, then a small start-up, concluded an agreement for transistor technology with Western Electric (in the face of opposition from MITI which felt it was too small to benefit). Despite being told by Western Electric's engineers that the only consumer product for which the transistor was suitable was hearing aids, Sony's university-trained engineers were able to reverse the polarity of the transistor and develop a new transistor which it used in Japan's first transistorised radio. In 1958, NEC, after debating whether it should attempt to be self-reliant in transistor technology, entered into a licensing agreement with GE.

Western companies played a similarly important technology-supplying role in the development of the second generation of computers in the Japanese IC companies. Significantly, however, the first generation of computers were developed primarily in government laboratories, notably MITI's ETL and NTT's ECL, with Western companies playing a negligible direct role. (Interestingly, ECL's early Musashino computers used an alternative device to the transistor, the parametron, developed by Eichi Goto, then a student at Tokyo University who has since become a well-known semiconductor researcher. However, the parametron was not able to keep up with the great rate of incremental improvement made to the transistor which was widely adopted by most companies and researchers.)

In order to strengthen their early competences in computers, Hitachi signed an agreement with RCA, Toshiba with GE, and NEC with Honeywell. While Fujitsu, which was to become Japan's largest computer producer, had discussions with IBM, the latter's terms were too exacting and Fujitsu eventually decided to go it alone. However, Fujitsu was soon fortunate to be able to link up with Gene Amdahl, a leading IBM computer designer who had left IBM to set up his own company. Fujitsu's opportunity came when Amdahl ran into financial difficulties and by injecting capital into Amdahl Fujitsu was able to gain significant access to IBM-type technology.

The point, however, is not so much that the Japanese IC companies had access to Western technology, but that they used it, not as a substitute for their own efforts, but as a way of boosting their own accumulation of competences. Unlike many firms in developing countries and the former Soviet Union, which continued to depend to the same degree on external technology, the Japanese IC companies made rapid strides in first mastering the acquired technology and then improving it. This difference in behaviour was not due to the need to remain competitive in export markets (as has largely been the case for Korean electronics companies) since until the 1970s the Japanese IC companies had relatively little involvement in export markets in these areas. The reason rather was another crucial feature of the selection environment which these companies faced, namely strong competition in the Japanese markets.

Strong competitive pressure in the Japanese markets

The competitive process in Japan tends to differ in a number of important respects from that in Western countries. To begin with, the long-term obligational relationships that characterise many Japanese interfirm transactions tend to constrain the domain in which particular firms compete to sell their products. For example, it is rare to find any other car being purchased by firms associated with the Mitsubishi group of companies than one of the models made by Mitsubishi Motors. As this example shows, the long-term loyalty that often links sellers with their customers implies a degree of fragmentation in product markets that does not exist in Western countries. But it is important not to exaggerate the extent of this fragmentation. The walls that separate these fragmented markets are 'knee high' rather than 'unscalable'. If the price/quality differential between a traditional supplier and a would-be new entrant is sufficiently high for long enough, even a firm bound by long-term obligational relationship to its traditional suppliers will switch. Nevertheless these obligational relationships do imply a greater degree of market fragmentation than is found in Western product markets.

This market fragmentation has important implications for the competitive process in Japan. The main implication is that market fragmentation has meant that in many cases (but by no means all) there are a larger number of firms contesting particular product markets than in corresponding Western markets. To put the same point slightly differently, in an economy characterised by spot-markets (where buyers respond instantaneously to favourable price/quality differentials), rather than long-term obligational markets, all other things equal, the degree of market concentration will be higher. The degree of competitive pressure put on all of the sellers will therefore be lower.

The larger number of Japanese market contestants (relative to national market size) is evident, for example, in motor cars where competitors include Toyota, Nissan, Honda, Mitsubishi Motors, Mazda, and Suzuki. In mainframe computers there are three equally strong competitors, Fujitsu, Hitachi, and NEC in addition to IBM Japan. In central office telecommunications switches there are four, NEC, Fujitsu, Hitachi, and Oki. In optical fiber cables there are five, Sumitomo Electric, Fujikura, Furukawa, Hitachi Cable, and Showa Electric. Controlled competition in the telecommunications industry (a particular form of long-term obligational relationship mediated by NTT) has played its part in fragmenting markets and increasing the degree of competition and competitive pressure. Without controlled competition, for instance, it is likely that Oki would have exited from the telecommunications market a long time ago, and it is unlikely that Hitachi would have survived in central office switches. Similarly, it is unlikely that Hitachi Cable and Showa Electric would have been able to enter the optical fiber cable market. See also Porter (1980) for data on the number of Japanese companies contesting several markets in Japan, although he does not provide an adequate explanation of this phenomenon and in some cases his data is questionable.

The result has been that the Japanese selection environment is characterised by intense competition. In turn, this competitive pressure has encouraged Schumpeterian competition-through-innovation.

However, another form of competitive pressure, pressure operating through equity markets, has been more muted in Japan, especially compared to the USA and UK where stock markets and arm's-length investors play a particularly important role. In Japan not only do banks often play a larger role in corporate financing through the provision of loans, large companies also benefit to a greater extent than their US and UK counterparts from their 'committed shareholders'. The different role played by capital markets in Japan compared with Western countries constitutes a significant characteristic of the Japanese selection environment, often allowing Japanese managers to take a longer term view in their decision-making. (A committed shareholder may be defined as one which will retain shares in a company even when a greater expected profit may be made by selling the shares and buying others. Committed shareholders forgo the opportunity for expected gain since they have a long term stake in the company, for example as one of its major bankers, providers of insurance services, customers, or suppliers.)

2.4.4 Vision, Competences, and Selection Environment

Up to this point, competences and their interaction with the selection environment have been discussed entirely in an *ex post* way. This has meant abstracting from the processes involved in the making of decisions to accumulate competences, and the impression has incorrectly been conveyed that selection environments automatically, though over time, produce competences of various kinds. When these decision-making processes are examined, however, that is when competences are analysed from an *ex ante* point of view, it is clear that the beliefs embodied in vision play a central role and that the outcome of these processes are usually unpredictable.

These points may be illustrated by taking a particularly important 'competence creating moment' in the evolution of Fujitsu, namely the point at which this company, which was to become Japan's largest computer producer and the second in the world, decided to enter the new product area of computers.

The 'moment' was the later 1950s. Fujitsu had already produced its first computers, significantly not with its own resources but with funding obtained from MITI designed to facilitate the development of new industrial products. However, there was still incomplete information, and therefore considerable interpretive ambiguity, regarding the future for Fujitsu in the field of computers. Important uncertainties related to the company's ability to acquire the necessary new technologies, to the future size and growth of the computer market in Japan, and to the competition that Fujitsu would face in this market. Furthermore, controlled competition meant that Fujitsu already had a relatively certain and stable market in its sales of telecommunications equipment to NTT. Under these conditions, it was hardly surprising that different Fujitsu leaders derived different beliefs from the incomplete information regarding the direction that the company should prioritise for the future. As Taiyu Kobayashi, who became Chairman of the Board of Fujitsu in 1981, recalled: [M]ore than half of the directors preferred a more cautious course of action which dealt with known quantities. Rather than attempting some unknown [i.e. developing computers] ... if we stuck to contract work for Nippon Telegraph and Telephone

[NTT], it had the advantages a long and steady relationship offers, as well as the prospect of assured profitability (Fransman, 1995a).

There was, however, a group of engineers already in Fujitsu, including Kobayashi, who had been involved in the development of the company's first computers and who wanted to see computers becoming a priority for Fujitsu. However, as a result of the vision of the majority of directors, Kobayashi remembers, 'Regardless of the merits of our plan [to develop computers in Fujitsu], because we were still viewed with the bias accorded a stepchild, we could expect a predictably sour response' (ibid., 44).

A major change was required within Fujitsu before the company's prevailing vision—even though it was a vision contested by a minority of directors—could change in favour of computers. As it happened, this change came about at the right time, although fortuitously. In 1959 Wada, overburdened by his responsibilities as President of both Fuji Electric and Fujitsu, asked Kanjiro Okada to become President of Fujitsu. Before the war, Okada had been President of the Furukawa company but had been ousted in a realignment. By as early as 1955 Okada, who had been moved to a cement company in the Furukawa group, Ube Industries, had come to the belief that computers had an important future for Japanese companies. Kobayashi recollected his visit in this year to discuss computers with Okada: 'What excited me was that Okada had listened to our presentation, nodding from time to time as if in agreement, and had shown a great enthusiasm for computers' (43).

It was Okada who was responsible for the emergence of a new vision in Fujitsu, a vision which put computers at the center of the company's future. When he became President of Fujitsu in 1959, 'Okada disregarded the advice of the directors set in their old ways. He quickly picked a number of young men like our computer group and assigned them to important positions in the company. Although it was a radical recasting of the company, I do not think our [computer] business could have been transformed so quickly had he not done so. . . . From the point of view of the people directly involved it was strong medicine and only possible because of Okada' (45).

However, being armed with this new vision did not bring the end of Fujitsu's problems. The company still had to cope with a selection environment that severely restricted its access to the emerging markets for computers. At this time government markets, and especially NTT, were particularly important since a large private market for computers had not yet emerged. Kobayashi explained the difficulty that Fujitsu confronted (at the same time pointing indirectly to market fragmentation as discussed earlier in this chapter): 'NTT is one of Fujitsu's main customers—primarily for telephone switching equipment. We also . . . tried to sell them computers . . . however, they had an unwritten policy [part of NTT's controlled competition] that worked against us: regardless of how hard we strove, as a manufacturer late to the market [for computers] we were not able to displace NEC which was there first. A friend of mine at NTT told me, "If you want to obtain a lion's share of the orders from us, you have to become the undisputed leader so well known in markets outside NTT's sphere of influence, that everyone will be asking why we are not buying Fujitsu's equipment" ' (46).

Facing difficulties such as this in access to new computer markets and being relatively weak in telecommunications equipment compared to NEC, Okada and his supporters in Fujitsu believed that it was important for the future well-being of the company to rapidly build strong competences in computing. It was this competence-creating decision and related subsequent decisions which led to Fujitsu in 1968 overtaking NEC and Hitachi as the leading Japanese computer producer, second only to IBM Japan. Later they resulted in Fujitsu becoming the second largest computer company in the world (in terms of total sales) after IBM (see Fig. 2.2).

2.4.5 Competences and Competitiveness: The Present as History

As detailed earlier in this chapter, competences take a long time to accumulate—decades rather than years—and it is in their competences that companies carry their history. This is evident in the case of the Japanese IC companies.

NEC, for example, remains, as it was since the early decades of the twentieth century, the leading Japanese telecommunications equipment company. Its strong position in complex telecommunications equipment such as central office switches in Japan and many developing countries, and its international competitiveness in areas such as microwave communications equipment and simpler telecommunications products such as faxes and mobile digital phones, have given it fifth place in the rankings of the world's largest telecommunications equipment companies. That NEC does not have as high a ranking as Alcatel, AT&T, Siemens, and Northern Telecom (see Fig. 2.3) is largely a reflection of the fact that the competences which it accumulated in complex telecommunications equipment such as central office switches were not directly exploitable in the major Western markets. Its ranking is also partly the result of the relatively closed nature until recently of the markets of most large Western countries for such equipment (a constraint, however, that also applied to the other international telecommunications equipment companies).

Although, like Fujitsu and Hitachi, NEC developed competences in the whole range of computers, from supercomputers through mainfranes to personal computers, NEC's ranking in third place in computers is partly the result of its relative strength in smaller computers and particularly in personal computers where it controls about 50% of the Japanese market (see Fig. 2.2). Its strength in smaller computers is due largely to the beliefs of

Koji Kobayashi whose vision from the late 1950s of the convergence of computers and communications led him on to a strategy of developing distributed systems of smaller computers rather than centralised mainframe-based systems. Unlike Fujitsu and Hitachi which followed closely in IBM's footsteps and in the early 1990s, like IBM, owned about half of their revenues to mainframes, in NEC's case mainframes account for only about a third of computer revenues. NEC's strength in personal computers, which provide about 10% of its total revenues, originates from the competences that it developed in microprocessors. Indeed, its first personal computer was produced as a way of selling microprocessors.

In semiconductors, however, NEC's main competences have been in memories and microcontrollers, making it the second largest semiconductor company in the world (see Fig. 2.4). The company's competences in these products were accumulated largely in response to the large market in Japan. With the far lower and slower rate of diffusion of personal computers in Japan compared to other Western countries, and with the different standards for both personal computers and their microprocessors that originally evolved in Japan to deal with Japanese-language processing, NEC (like the other main Japanese semiconductor companies Toshiba and Hitachi) were unable to establish themselves in a dominant international position in microprocessors. In stark contrast, Intel—benefiting from IBM's (with hindsight mistaken) decision to subcontract the microprocessor for its personal computer to Intel—was able not only to accumulate further competences in microprocessors (which NEC also did) but also to come to dominate the *de facto* standard for microprocessors which became increasingly personal computer-driven. In 1992 Intel controlled 73% of the market for 32-bit microprocessors, followed by Motorola and AMD with 8.5% and 8.0% respectively. NEC, the largest Japanese producer, had 1.1%.

Despite many attempts, however, NEC never managed to establish a significant foothold in the consumer electronics market. The problem was not a technical or manufacturing one but rather had to do with the company's weak distribution network for consumer electronics goods, underlining the fact that the concept of competences refers to the whole value chain and not only to technological capabilities. In 1993 consumer electronics accounted for only 5% of NEC's total sales.

Fujitsu's second place in the global computer industry (see Fig. 2.2) can be traced back to the competences which it began to build from the 1950s, as outlined in the last section. Despite this high ranking, despite the inroads it has made into the U.S. and European markets through its part-ownership of Amdahl and ICL, and despite its OEM sales of computers and computer subsystems, Fujitsu has not made very significant headway in computers outside Japan. In telecommunications equipment, Fujitsu is the only other Japanese company (second to NEC) to have a chance of remaining a substantial global player into the next century. Since the late 1920s, when

Fujitsu was in third place in this market in Japan, the company has managed to eclipse Oki which was in second place.

Fujitsu, however, has never managed to establish strong competences (including external sales) in semiconductors or consumer electronics. Competence-weakness in these areas has been a constant feature of the company's history since its founding.

Hitachi has been fairly strong in semiconductors and computers where it is in fifth and sixth positions globally (see Figs. 2.4 and 2.2). However, its relatively weak competences in telecommunications equipment can be traced back to the 1930s when it ran fourth to NEC, Oki, and Fujitsu. As a more diversified company than NEC or Fujitsu, Hitachi also has strong competences in heavy electrical equipment and in consumer electronics. Although its competences in consumer electronics are considerably greater than those of NEC or Fujitsu, Hitachi's presence in this area is small compared to the main specialist consumer electronics companies such as Matsushita and Sony. In 1993 Hitachi's sales of consumer products was $8.1 billion compared to total sales of $60.8 billion for Matsushita and $34.4 for Sony.

Toshiba is the only one of the Japanese IC companies featuring in the top five rankings in at least one of the three major IC markets—computers, telecommunications equipment, and semiconductors—which was not one of NTT's 'family' of suppliers. Again the weight of history is evident in Toshiba current competences and competitiveness. Toshiba's strength in semiconductors—it is ranked third in this market (see Fig. 2.4)—can be traced back to the 1920s to its involvement in vacuum tubes through its alliance with GE. It continued to emphasise the importance of electronic devices which it used in its information, communication, and consumer products. Largely as a result of its strength in electronic devices it was able to establish an early dominant position in the market for laptop computers. In larger computers, however, Toshiba's exclusion from membership of the NTT 'family' was a major reason for its exiting from the mainframe market in the early 1970s after IBM introduced its System 370. As Fig. 2.2 shows, Toshiba was ranked tenth in the global computer industry, largely as a result of its sales of lap-top computers. Like Hitachi, Toshiba's competences in consumer electronics can be traced back to the origins of the company.

Of all the Japanese IC companies, Oki is one of the most interesting as a result of its failure to use the relatively strong competences that it accumulated in telecommunications in the first few decades of the twentieth century to move successfully into the competence-related areas of semiconductors, computers, or consumer electronics. Like the other IC companies, Oki was a 'Japanese' company with the typical Japanese management and organisational characteristics. But unlike the others mentioned here, it has been a relatively unsuccessful Japanese company. This suggests that its failure is to be attributed, not to these management and organisational characteristics, but to other shortcomings. Most important of these has been vision-failure on the part of Oki's leaders which led to the company remaining too closely tied to NTT. As a result, Oki failed to broaden its competences sufficiently into the main growth areas of the new electronics paradigm. And due to the specificities of the Japanese market in its main area of competence, namely telecommunications equipment, and the closed nature of markets in Western countries in this area, Oki was unable to 'leverage' its competences in this area to grow as rapidly as the average for the main Japanese IC companies.

As the above makes clear, therefore, the burden of history has made itself strongly felt for all the large Japanese IC companies.

2.4.6 The Organisation of Competences

As argued in the first part of this chapter, a competence-based theory of the firm requires an analysis of the organisational architecture of the firm, an analysis that spells out the principles according to which competences may be organised. In this section, attention is confined to one of the distinguishing features of the organisational architecture of many large Japanese companies, namely the degree of decentralisation or segmentation of their activities.

As Fruin (1992) has noted, several of the large Japanese firms involved in the information, communication, and consumer electronics industries have decentralised corporate functions—such as strategy formulation and marketing in addition to the more typical production, engineering, and development functions—to the level of the division and even factory. In addition they have made more use than comparable Western companies of spinning off activities to wholly or partially-owned subsidiaries and sub-contractors. On the basis of a comparison of AT&T, IBM, and NEC, I have argued that large Japanese companies in the IC industry have moved more rapidly than their Western counterparts to a segmented form of organisation, or S-Form (Fransman, 1994*a*). However, in the 1990s large Western companies such as AT&T and IBM have also adopted the S-Form.

If it is true that Japanese firms have from the beginning been more decentralised or segmented than their Western counterparts, then this important characteristic of their organisational architecture must be explained. The following factors are likely to form an important part of the explanation.

First, in the case of some of the Japanese companies, such as Toshiba, Hitachi, and Matsushita, opportunities in the early stages of Japan's industrialisation allowed the company to move through acquisition into activities that were largely competence-unrelated. For example, Toshiba became involved both in heavy electrical equipment through Shibaura Engineering and 'light' electrical equipment through Tokyo Electric. Hitachi entered a large number of competence-unrelated activities such as heavy electrical equipment, cables, chemicals, telecommunications equipment, and consumer goods. Two of the first products developed by Konosuke Matsushita, the founder of Matsushita—electrical light fittings and bicycle and household lamps—were largely competence-unrelated and from the outset were organised as distinct factories. Where activities are competence-unrelated, a segmented form of organisation is indicated.

But this was not the whole story. As late-comers to the industrialisation process, and with new opportunities rapidly emerging as a result of Japan's fast growth rate, the managerial competences of the new Japanese companies constituted a severe bottleneck. It was this *weakness* of Japanese management that encouraged an economising of managerial competences through the decentralisation and segmentation of activities. This is the second factor in the explanation.

The third is the long-term obligational relationships that were important in mediating the relationships between many Japanese firms. (The reader of the history of Japanese companies, such as those written by Konosuke Matsushita, is struck by the importance of these interfirm obligational relationships going back to the early decades of the twentieth century.) These obligational relationships made more feasible a division of labour which involved the delegation of activities to legally independent but cooperating suppliers. (In the language of transactions cost economics, obligational relationships, by reducing the possibility of opportunism and increasing beneficial flows of information, reduced the costs of transacting with complementary cooperating companies.) Although a specific kind of obligational relationship, life-time employment, only became widespread after the Second World War, it was already important in many companies in the early twentieth century (partly as a way of retaining skilled labour). Long-term employment within the company also facilitated the decentralisation and segmentation of activities by reducing both the need and the cost of monitoring and control at the head of the company.

These three factors, it is suggested, constitute an important part of the explanation for the degree of decentralisation and segmentation evident in the organisational architecture of many large Japanese companies.

2.5 The Global Weakness of Japanese IC Companies Relative to Japanese Specialist Consumer Electronics Companies

The success of the Japanese consumer electronics companies

The paradox of the Japanese IC companies mentioned earlier refers to their high global rankings in the three key IC markets—computers, telecommunications equipment, and semiconductors—coexisting with relatively low international competitiveness in most subsegments of these markets. The contrast in this regard with the Japanese consumer electronics companies is striking.

The global success of the Japanese consumer electronics companies (a degree of success enjoyed by Japanese companies in very few other markets) is truly remarkable. As the MIT study, *Made in America*, noted: 'In just four decades the Japanese consumer-electronics industry has progressed from making a few cheap, low-quality parts and radios to leading the world in market share and technology' (Dertouzos 1989, 228). For example, by the mid-1970s Japan accounted for over half of world production of colour TVs and three quarters of world exports. The study observes that 'Japan's ascendancy has come primarily at the expense of the US [consumer electronics] industry' (ibid. 228) and notes that as a result largely of the competition from Japan, this industry has been 'virtually eliminated' (217).

The outstanding success of the Japanese consumer electronics companies is evident from two inter-firm comparisons. In 1982 Matushita had sales of about $14 billion compared with $16 billion for Philips, the largest Western consumer electronics company. By 1992 Matsushita had sales of $61 billion against Philips's $32 billion. NEC, the largest Japanese IC company, was formed in 1899 (albeit as a joint venture majority-owned by Western Electric which may have limited its growth to some extent). Sony was formed as a tiny start-up in 1946. In 1993, NEC sales were $30.6 billion while Sony's were $34.4 billion.

How is the remarkable success of the Japanese consumer electronics companies to be explained? The answer to this question requires an understanding of the evolution of the Japanese consumer electronics companies.

The evolution of the Japanese consumer electronics companies

There are two main groups amongst the large Japanese consumer electronics companies. This first is the specialist consumer electronics companies led by Matsushita, Sony, Sharp, and Sanyo. The second is the general electrical and electronics companies which used their competences in electrical machinery and components to enter the consumer market. The major members of this group are Hitachi, Toshiba, Mitsubishi Electric, and NEC (although the latter two are much smaller in consumer electronics).

There were a number of factors which facilitated the rapid growth of these companies in the postwar period and their quick achievement of international competitiveness. The first was a conducive national selection environment. As Akio Morita of Sony put it, 'in 1958, the year after we produced our "pocketable" transistorized radio, only 1% of Japanese homes had a TV set, only 5% had a washing machine, and only two-tenths of 1%

had an electric refrigerator. Fortunately, the Japanese economy began to grow vigorously from the mid-fifties onwards. Double-digit increases in the gross national product and low inflation gave a great boost to consumer spending. . . . Japanese households needed everything, and because of the high savings rate, which . . . was over 20%, the people could afford to buy' (Morita 1986, 75).

Secondly, in the case of consumer electronics products—such as radios, tape recorders, TVs, video recorders, and audio products—the products developed for the Japanese market were with little modification also suitable for the major Western markets. This contrasts strongly with the information and communications products such as telecommunications switches, personal computers, and software which in many cases had to be tailored to the specific circumstances of the Japanese market and required substantial and costly modification before being marketable abroad. (The case of consumer electrical products such as refrigerators, washing machines, and vacuum cleaners was rather different, partly because of the conditions in Japanese households such as space constraints. As a result these products tended to have Japanese characteristics and were not sold in the same form in Western markets.)

The result was that Japanese consumer electronics companies, having designed and developed their products for the Japanese market, had immediate access to Western markets (although in some cases, such as TVs in Europe they were constrained by protective government measures). As Morita recollects, 'The idea of an international market for Tokyo Tsushin Kogyo [the predecessor of Sony] had been on our minds from early on, and it was inevitable that Ibuka and I would have to travel' (ibid. 63). Sony's first commercially successful product, a magnetic tape recorder, was first marketed in Japan in 1950. In 1952 Ibuka (with Morita, the co-founder of Sony) went to investigate the US market and Morita went the following year. In 1951 Konosuke Matsushita, the founder of Matsushita, made his first trip to the USA. In 1960, with substantial sales to the US, the Sony Corporation of America was established. By 1960, 12% of Matsushita's output was exported.

Thirdly, the companies quickly acquired the technical competences relating to the new electronics paradigm. But they acquired these competences from different starting points and in different ways. The first products produced by the tiny company that Konosuke Matsushita founded in 1918 were simple products such as light fittings and battery-powered lamps. These products emerged from the 'electricity paradigm' that at this time was transforming Japanese firms and households. Indeed, Matsushita's knowledge of electricity and electricity-related products was first acquired during his earlier stint working for the Osaka Electric Light Company. By the early 1930s the competences that Matsushita had acquired in these electrical products facilitated the company's move into radios. This required knowledge of areas such as electrical circuitry, electronic devices such as vacuum tubes, and techniques for the manufacture of electrical products. This knowledge, in turn, facilitated Matsushita's move into transistors and transistor-based consumer products from the early 1950s, although its competences in the electronics area were aided significantly by its joint venture company with Philips set up in 1952 (and 70% owned by Matsushita). The general electronics companies like Hitachi and Toshiba also made use of their prewar competences in electrical products in entering the new consumer electronics markets. However, they too depended on agreements with Western companies like GE and RCA for initial access to the new transistor technology.

Beginning in 1946, although with important war-time knowledge acquired in military-related electronic products, Sony was able to move directly into the electronics paradigm. In doing so it was greatly assisted by the high quality of its employees. Morita notes that around 1950 'we had forty-five people working for us, and over a third of them were college graduates [mostly engineers]. We were top-heavy with brains' (ibid. 57). Sony's brainpower was evident in the important incremental innovations that it made to the transistor. Although Morita may be exaggerating when he states that Sony's project team 'had to rebuild and virtually reinvent the transistor' (ibid. 67), it is clear that the company's engineers did make important innovations to the transistor in order to adapt it for use in radio.

Indeed, even the idea of using transistors in radios was innovative. When Morita concluded the license for the transistor from Western Electric in 1953, he was told that the only consumer product in which the transistor could be used was in hearing aids. In order to produce a transistorised radio it was necessary to develop a transistor with a higher frequency than the transistor originally invented in Bell Laboratories. In the attempt to achieve a higher frequency, Sony's engineers reversed the polarity of their transistor and experimented with different materials. The original Bell Labs transistor used a germanium slab (which provided the negative pole) which was 'sandwiched' between two pieces of indium alloyed to the germanium (which provided the positive pole). It was therefore a 'positive-negative-positive' device. Reasoning that negative electrons move faster than positive ones, the project team attempted to increase the frequency of the transistor by reversing its polarity, that is by producing a 'negative-positive-negative' device. The problem was to find appropriate materials. Eventually, through a process of trial-and-error, a Sony engineer developed a phosphorus doping method which achieved the desired result, a method that researchers had already tried at Bell Laboratories but without success. (It was also through the transistor research, particularly that using phosphorus, that a Sony physicist, Leo Esaki, 'discovered and described the diode tunneling effect, how subatomic particles can move in waves through a seemingly impenetrable barrier' (ibid. 68). As a result of this research Esaki won a Nobel Prize in 1973.

Fourthly, the consumer electronics companies not only mastered the technologies of the new electronics paradigm but also developed the competence to innovate. Some of these competences were product-related. For example, apart from its transistorised radio (produced a few months after the world's first was introduced by an American company, Regency, which used transistor technology provided by Texas Instruments) Sony produced the world's first fully transistorised television set in 1960. Other product-related competences that were to have important competitive consequences were miniaturisation and design capabilities that facilitated the use of fewer components and more efficient manufacturing methods. In addition, process-related competences were developed which allowed costs to be reduced while quality was improved. The competence to innovate was greatly aided by the intensely competitive selection environment that existed in Japan.

In addition, fifthly, the consumer electronics companies were assisted by the relatively low cost of labour in Japan in the 1950s and 1960s which helped to give them a comparative advantage in the reasonably labour-intensive consumer products.

Finally, the Japanese consumer electronics companies were also assisted by the failure of competing Western companies, particularly US companies, to seriously contest their growing strength. The MIT study explains this remarkable failure, a failure that later proved to be not only extremely costly for the firms themselves but also for the US economy as a whole, by arguing that 'A major reason was that the risks were higher and the potential profits were lower for US manufacturers in these contested areas, and the marginal return on investment was greater elsewhere' (Dertouzos 1989, 229). Indeed, the study goes so far as to conclude that 'The American retreat from the consumer-electronics market should not be attributed to mere incompetence or to poor judgment. The managers of the US firms acted rationally, guarding the interests of their shareholders' (ibid. 228)!

Precisely how this conclusion fits with observations made elsewhere in the study, such as the following, is not made clear: 'In 1987 RCA (including NBC) was bought by General Electric for $6.4 billion, and the consumer electronics units were sold later that year to the French firm Thomson. The Princeton laboratories responsible for thousands of RCA's innovations in consumer-electronics technology were given to Stanford Research Institute, a contract research firm' (227). The reader is left with the impression that the efficient operation of the American capital markets led to the efficient obliteration of the American consumer electronics industry. Yet at the same time the study notes that 'The US market [for consumer electronics products] has grown at a compound rate of 15.2% per year since 1976, reaching an estimated $30 billion in factory sales in 1986. Yet the share produced domestically by American-owned firms, which was close to 100% in the early 1950s, had shrunk to about 5% by the late 1980s. Consumer electronics contributed about $11 billion to the US trade deficit in 1986 . . . , with imports from Japan responsible for 74% of the total' (217). The implications regarding the outcome produced by the operation of market forces remain unexplored.

The insignificant role of the Japanese government in consumer electronics

It is also worth noting that the Japanese consumer electronics companies, unlike their counterparts in the IC industry, received practically no direct assistance from the Japanese government. It is true that they did benefit, like firms in all sectors of the Japanese economy, from the rapid postwar growth of the economy and from government-related advantages such as the relatively low cost of capital in Japan and R&D incentives. However, the Japanese government had few measures specifically aimed at the promotion of the consumer electronics industry. The view of MITI officials appears to have been that the consumer electronics companies could fend adequately for themselves. The contrast with the role of the Japanese government *vis-a-vis* the Japanese IC companies, discussed in the section above on the selection environment of these companies, is striking.

2.5.1 The Paradox of the Japanese IC Companies Revisited

In the light of a comparative understanding of the evolution of Japanese consumer electronics companies, it is now possible to explain the paradox of the Japanese IC companies. This paradox, it will be recalled, refers to the apparent anomaly whereby the Japanese IC companies rank highly in the global top ten places in the three key markets of computers, telecommunications equipment, and semiconductors in terms of total sales, while at the same time failing to hold dominant or even very strong competitive positions outside Japan in many of the major subsegments of these markets. For example, Japanese IC companies lack dominant or very strong market share outside Japan in subsegments such as: mainframes, minicomputers, workstations, personal computers, software, complex telecommunications equipment, optical fiber, and microprocessors. Japanese IC companies lack the international competitiveness of both their Japanese consumer electronics and automobile counterparts and their Western competitors which dominate these three markets.

The paradox begins to be explained once it is realised that the high ranking of the Japanese IC companies is the result of their dominant position in Japan, together with the rapid growth and large absolute size of the

Japanese economy. In other words, the high ranking of the Japanese IC companies has been achieved primarily on the back of the vibrant Japanese economy. However, a full understanding of the paradox also requires an explanation of why Japanese IC companies—unlike their counterparts in areas such as consumer electronics, automobiles, machine tools, cameras, semiconductor processing equipment, and amino acids—have been largely unable to use their strength in the Japanese economy, where they operate under highly competitive conditions, as the basis for achieving stronger competitiveness internationally.

In examining this issue, it is important to note immediately that in several areas the Japanese IC companies have managed to use their strength in the Japanese market in order to establish dominant or very strong competitive positions internationally. Notable areas where this has been the case include: memory semiconductors, microcontrollers, optoelectronic devices, liquid crystal displays, microwave telecommunications equipment, faxes, and digital mobile phones. But this raises a further question: why have Japanese IC companies managed to establish a strong international competitiveness in these areas but not in the other areas referred to above?

The answer to this question lies in an understanding of both the impact of the Japanese selection environment on the competences of the Japanese IC companies and the strength of the major Western competitors of these Japanese companies. The key point is that the Japanese IC companies have been driven primarily by the growth of the Japanese economy and by the demands of their customers in this economy. In view of the rapid growth of the Japanese economy and its consequent ability to sustain the rapid growth of their companies, the attention of the leaders of the Japanese IC companies has understandably enough focused largely on meeting the needs expressed in the Japanese economy. In turn, their competences have been shaped by this priority.

In some cases the competences that have resulted from meeting the needs of their Japanese customers have at the same time given the Japanese IC companies a strong international competitiveness. These include the cases of memory semiconductors etc. But in many other cases, the specificities of the Japanese needs have precluded the immediate establishment of an international competitiveness. Examples include complex telecommunications equipment such as switches, personal computers, software, etc. The international strength of the Japanese IC companies in the former areas is reflected in their export ratios, the proportion of their sales going to overseas markets, and some of their direct foreign investment activities. But, as shown earlier, their international strength as measured by these indicators is not as great as that of their counterparts in areas such as consumer electronics and automobiles.

In strong contrast, the Japanese consumer electronics companies, as shown in the last section, were able to turn their competences, honed under the rigorous conditions of highly competitive Japanese markets, immediately into an international competitiveness in areas such as radios, TVs, audio equipment, and video recorders. At the same time, as was also seen, the consumer electronics companies were aided by the weak competitive response of their Western, primarily US, competitors. Conversely, the Japanese IC companies faced strong competition from companies such as IBM, DEC, Apple, Sun, Microsoft, Compaq and Dell in computing; Alcatel, AT&T, Ericsson, and Northern Telecom in telecommunications equipment; and Intel, Motorola, AMD, and more recently Korean companies, in semiconductors. Many of these companies, furthermore, had won strong positions in *global* markets.

The future of the Japanese IC companies

What are the implications of this paradox for the future of the Japanese IC companies? The answer to this question is that the selection environment of these companies is in the process of significant change. In short, they are becoming gradually less dependent on the Japanese economy. Reasons for this include the rise of the Yen since the mid-1980s which has encouraged the transfer of productive activities outside Japan; trade conflict with Japan's major Western trading partners which is having the same effect; and, more recently, the severe recession in Japan. Over the last decade Japanese IC companies have strengthened their marketing and production activities in the USA and Europe, and more recently R&D operations have been added. The 'globalisation' of these companies is therefore steadily increasing, even though it still lags significantly behind comparable Western companies. This globalisation will with the passage of time allow the Japanese IC companies to integrate themselves more closely into the economic and business structures of the major markets outside Japan. In becoming more closely integrated in this way, they will have the opportunity to apply the potent competences which they have accumulated under the Japanese selection environment to the circumstances of these markets. Time will tell how successful they will be.

3

AT&T, BT, and NTT: A Comparison of Vision, Strategy, Competence, Path-Dependency, and R&D

3.1 Introduction

AT&T, BT, and NTT are the largest telecommunications service providers in the United States, Britain, and Japan respectively. Until the mid-1980s, the three companies were monopoly suppliers of telecommunications services in their own national markets. In the mid-1980s, the three companies confronted some similar changes in their environment. More specifically, due to changing beliefs on the part of their governments and regulatory authorities, all three companies faced competition from vigorous new entrants. At the same time, their legal status was changed, with AT&T being divested and separated from the regional Bell operating companies, and BT and NTT being partly privatised. Simultaneously, the three companies had to deal with the maturation of the market for telephone services, the growing importance of new telecommunications services, and the rapid globalisation of both service and equipment markets.

How have the three companies respond to these similar changes in their environment? Have they constructed similar visions in order to deal with the threats and opportunities resulting from these changes? More specifically, what are the differences in the strategies that the three companies have developed and in their beliefs regarding the competences they need in-house in order to take advantage of their changing circumstances? What

This chapter was written before AT&T's voluntary trivestiture into three separate companies in September, 1995: AT&T (telecoms services), Lucent (telecoms equipment), and NCR (computers). This chapter was originally published as 'AT&T, BT and NTT: A Comparison of Vision, Strategy and Competence', *Telecommunications Policy*, 1994, 18(2), 137–153 and 'AT&T, BT and NTT: The Role of Red', *Telecommunications Policy*, 1994, 18(4), 295–305.

I would like to acknowledge financial support on which much of this paper was based from the Institute for Japanese-European Technology Studies, University of Edinburgh, and from the PICT Programme of the United Kingdom's Economic and Social Research Council. I would also like to thank the many senior officials in NTT and BT for the time and information that they generously gave. In particular, appreciation is due to Dr Iwao Toda of NTT who has greatly improved my understanding of research and development in NTT, inadequate though this understanding undoubtedly still remains. It is from Dr Toda that the term 'network elements' comes and Fig. 3.1 in which this term is embodied. None of these people, of course, is in any way responsible for the information, analysis, and conclusions in the present paper.

role do they believe should be played by research and development in coping with these threats and opportunities? How do they think R&D should be organised within the company for it to play an appropriate role? These questions are analysed in this chapter.

3.2 Chapter Overview

This chapter is concerned with an apparent puzzle. While the major global telecommunications equipment companies, such as Northern Telecom, Siemens, Alcatel, Ericsson, and NEC, spend a similar amount on R&D (as a proportion of sales), there is a significant difference in the allocation of resources to R&D (by the same measure) by AT&T, BT, and NTT. Why is this the case, given that all three of the latter companies are increasingly having to compete in the same global selection environment? To what extent is this difference to be explained by the unique historical background of each company (its 'path-dependence'), to what extent by the strategic choices they have made? In so far as the difference is a reflection of strategic choice, can anything be said regarding the rationale for the company's choice and the factors that are likely to determine the longer run success of this choice? The present chapter will analyse these questions.

The chapter begins with a description of the differences between AT&T, BT, and NTT in terms of size, profitability, and R&D. The major changes that have occurred in the global selection environment which confronts these three companies are then examined. The question is then posed and answered regarding whether the strategic choices that have been made by the companies are a result of their past history, that is their path-dependence. An overview is then presented of the strategic choices that they have made regarding how they are to acquire the competences they need in order to offer competitive telecommunications services. It is shown that while BT has chosen to use the market to acquire 'network elements' (broadly, telecommunications equipment), NTT has selected cooperative development with a small number of suppliers, and AT&T has opted for vertical integration. In the following section a detailed analysis is provided of the differing visions of the three companies which underlie their varying strategic choices and the reasons for the differences are explained. A more general analysis is then undertaken of the advantages and disadvantages of the market, cooperation, and internal development as alternative modes of coordinating complementary competences. Finally, attention is turned to a major focus of the chapter, namely the role of research and development in the three companies. This role is examined in terms of the way in which these companies have dealt with four major questions related to research and development: What research does the firm need now? (an information problem): How to prevent 'irrelevant' research? (a control problem): What research is needed for the future? (an uncertainty problem): and Should the required research be undertaken in-house or ex-house? (an assignment problem). In examining these four questions particular attention is paid to the role of the internal market for research and development. It is shown, however, that while such a market can be crucial, it is also necessary to go beyond the internal market in providing longer term, radical innovation.

3.3 AT&T, BT, and NTT: Size, Profitability and R&D

Data on the size and profitability of AT&T, BT, and NTT are provided in Table 3.1.

As can be seen, AT&T and NTT are of a similar size in terms of sales. While in 1991 the sales of the former were $45.07 billion, for NTT they were $42.22 billion. BT was a little over half the size of the other two companies with sales of $24.31 billion in the same year. In terms of market value, however, the picture was significantly different. As a result of the different values that at the time ruled on the Tokyo Stock Exchange, NTT's market value was significantly different from the other two companies. Accordingly, NTT's market value of $103.00 billion compared with $40.43 billion for AT&T and $40.03 billion for BT. This difference in valuation is reflected in the price/earnings ratios for the three companies. While for NTT this ratio was 60, for AT&T it was 15, while for BT it was 11.

The valuation difference also shows up in one of the measures of profitability, namely the return on equity. While in 1991 this was 22.3 per cent for BT, and 19.7 per cent for AT&T, for NTT the figure was only 5.9 per cent. Another measure of profitability, namely profit as a percentage of sales, yielded similar figures. For BT this latter ratio was 22.4 per cent, while for NTT the figure was 8.8 per cent. Other measures of profitability also put BT significantly ahead of NTT. IN 1991 operating return on net property, plant and equipment was 22.6 per cent for BT and 7.3 per cent for NTT; operating margin (before interest and tax) was 26.5 per cent for BT and 11.4 per cent for NTT; net income per line $139 for BT and $36 for NTT; and cash surplus/(deficit) per line $33 for BT and $6 for NTT. In terms of one (debatable) measure of productivity, however, namely number of lines per employee, the figure for BT was 112 while for NTT it was 204. (It is, however, worth noting that these measures of BT's relative profitability and their appropriateness were hotly debated in the pages of the *Financial Times*.)

The R&D intensity of telecommunications equipment companies and operating companies is shown in Table 3.2.

The top part of Table 3.2 gives figures for a number of equipment companies for R&D as a percentage of sales for 1987. These show that R&D

Table 3.1 Size and profitability of AT&T, BT, and NTT

Indicator	AT&T	BT	NTT
Sales (1991)	$45.07 bn*	$24.31 bn	$42.22 bn
Market value (1991) (by week 15 July 1991)	$40.43 bn	$40.03 bn	$103.00 bn
Price/book value ratio (ratio of May 1991 closing price to net worth per share or common stockholder's equity investment)	2.9	2.5	3.6
Price/earnings ratio	15	11	60
Return on equity (earnings per share at May 1991 as percent of most recent book value per share)	19.7%	22.3%	5.9%
Profit as% sales		22.4%	8.8%
Operating return on net property, plant and equipment, 1991[a]		22.6%	7.3%
Operating margin (before interest and tax), 1991[a]		26.5%	11.4%
Net income per line, 1991[a]		$139	$36
Cash surplus/(deficit) per line, 1991[a]		$33	$6
Lines per employee, 1991[a]		112	204

* AT&T sales figure consolidates NCRP.

Sources: *Business Week*, 2 December 1991, 20 January 1992; [a] *Financial Times*, 1 November 1991, p. 21.

Table 3.2 R&D as percent of sales, 1987

Company	R&D as % sales
NEC[a]	13.7
Siemens[a]	12.8
Northern Telecom[a]	12.3
Alcatel[a]	9.8
Ericsson[a]	9.1
AT&T[b]	7.3
NTT[b]	3.8
BT[b]	2.1

[a] R&D as percentage of telecommunications sales (estimated). Calculated from Grupp and Schnoring (1992, p. 58, table 4).
[b] Total R&D as percentage of total sales. From Grupp and Schnoring (1992, p. 53, table 2).

Table 3.3 R&D in AT&T, BT, and NTT

Indicator	AT&T	BT	NTT
Sales, 1991[a]	$45.07 bn*	$24.31 bn	$42.22 bn
R&D, 1991[a]		$0.45 bn	$1.74 bn
R&D % sales, 1991[a]		1.9	4.1
R&D % sales, 1987[b]	7.3	2.1	3.8
R&D % sales, 1992/93[c]			4.7

* AT&T sales figure consolidates NCR.
[a] *Business Week*, 2 December 1991; [b] Grupp and Schnoring (1992); [c] *Nikkei Weekly*, 21 March 1992.

as a proportion of sales for NEC, with the highest R&D intensity, was 1.5 times that for Ericsson, which had the lowest intensity. On the other hand the bottom part of the table provides similar figures for the operating companies. These figures show that for AT&T, the company with the highest R&D intensity, the ratio of R&D to sales was 3.5 times that of BT, with the lowest intensity. Clearly, therefore, there was a greater difference in R&D behaviour between the operating companies as compared to the equipment companies. This difference is explained later in this chapter.

Further information on R&D in AT&T, BT, and NTT is provided in Table 3.3.

As Table 3.3 shows, while R&D as a proportion of sales increased in NTT from 3.8 per cent in 1987 to 4.1 per cent in 1991 the corresponding figure for BT *decreased* from 2.1 per cent to 1.9 per cent in these two years. Additional information has been obtained for NTT. This shows that in 1992/3 the R&D ratio increased to 4.7 per cent. As far as I am aware, there is no intention to increase the R&D ratio in BT.

Despite this significant difference in the R&D intensity of AT&T, BT, and NTT, these companies have confronted similar changes in their global selection environment. This is examined in greater detail in the following section.

3.4 Changes in the Global Selection Environment

Since the mid-1980s there have been a number of important changes in the global selection environment within which AT&T, BT, and NTT have had to operate. Amongst the changes have been the following:

1. Introduction of greater competition in telecommunications services on their domestic markets, leading, all other things equal, to a tendency for profits to be squeezed. (A *threat* to the companies.)

This tendency, however, has affected the companies in different ways. AT&T in 1991 managed to increase its net profit margin to 7.4 per cent, up from 7.1 per cent in 1990, after a period of severe cost-cutting. While BT has also successfully counteracted the squeeze on profits with its own cost-cutting measures, NTT has experienced a fall in profitability. For the fiscal year from 1 April 1992, for example, NTT's pre-tax profits are expected to decline by 6.4 per cent to Yen 351 billion. NTT's planned increase in R&D as a proportion of sales, therefore, is taking place against a background of falling profitability, which provides an indication of the company's strong degree of commitment to R&D.[1]

2. Gradual liberalisation of foreign service markets, leading to new possible sources of business. (An *opportunity* for the companies.)

In particular, it is now becoming possible for the operating companies to offer global telecommunications services to global multinational users. This had led to the emergence of several strategic corporate alliances as operating companies have attempted to stitch together alliances to offer 'end-to-end services' covering the world. At the same time this has created an 'outsourcing market' as the possibility has arisen for multinational users to contract out (vertically disintegrate) their telecommunications management activities. We shall return to this point later in an analysis of the corporate competences that AT&T, BT, and NTT believe they require in order to become and remain competitive in these emerging markets.

3. Gradual liberalisation of domestic and international telecommunications equipment markets, creating the possibility of multi-vendor purchasing environments for operating companies. (This is an *opportunity* for the operating companies, although it may simultaneously be perceived as a *threat* by those equipment producing parts of these operating companies which now face the possibility of greater competition from potential outside suppliers.)

As we shall see later, a crucial difference between AT&T, BT, and NTT has resulted from the strategic stance they have taken regarding the role of multi-vendor purchases.

4. Maturation of the 'plain old telephone' market, both domestically and internationally, leading to the necessity to introduce new telecommunications services. (This poses both a *threat* and an *opportunity* for the operating companies.)

For example, while spoken telephone calls constitute about 90 per cent of the world's telecommunications traffic, their growth rate is only about 7 per cent per annum. Other telecommunications services are growing far more rapidly, such as data communications which is increasing at about 25 to 30 per cent per annum.[2]

5. New technologies and standardisation which at one and the same time create the potential for innovative new services while increasing the likeli-

hood of increased competitive pressure through falling costs. (This is also both a *threat* and an *opportunity* for the operating companies.)

It is now widely accepted that in the future the new switching and transmissions technologies imply that the cost and price of telephone calls will be determined by the quantity of information sent (bit-rate tariff), rather than the distance over which it is sent. However, costs are likely to fall where demand is growing most rapidly, namely in long distance telephone and data calls. This will put increasing pressure on the operating companies.

In view of these changes in the global selection environment which affected all the major telephone operating companies, how is their significantly different allocation of resources to R&D, documented above, to be explained?

3.5 Strategic Choice of Corporate Competences and the Explanation of R&D Allocations

3.5.1 Path Dependence

There are important historical differences between AT&T, BT, and NTT, quite apart from their size and profitability. Perhaps most notable, from the point of view of the concerns of the present chapter with research and development, is AT&T's presence as both a major manufacturer of telecommunications equipment and a telecommunications operator. This reflects the incorporation of the former Western Electric into AT&T at the time of divestiture. Conversely, neither BT nor NTT were involved significantly in manufacturing activities prior to their privatisation and part-privatisation respectively. However, although both BT and NTT were at this prior stage closely involved with several domestic equipment manufacturers in the research, design and development of complex telecommunications equipment, there were important differences between these two companies in terms of their involvement. While for NTT the involvement with their 'family' of suppliers, primarily NEC, Fujitsu, Hitachi, and Oki, was on the whole satisfactory, it is probably fair to conclude that for BT the experience was far more ambiguous. This was particularly the case with the company's most ambitious project, namely the joint research and development of the System X digital switch. Furthermore, BT witnessed a significant change in the circumstances of its suppliers as GEC and Plessey first merged their telecommunications activities in the new firm GPT, which itself was subsequently taken over by Siemens and GEC, and STC, another major supplier, withdrew from switching. (NTT's relationship with its suppliers is analysed in Fransman (1992*a,b*), while BT's experience is recounted in Molina (1990).) AT&T, BT, and NTT, therefore, each had significantly different experiences regarding the research, design, development, and manufacture of telecommunications equipment.

Are these contrasting experiences sufficient to explain the different role in the three companies of research, design, development and manufacture (differences that will shortly be documented in detail)? The short answer is that such an explanation, couched in terms of path-dependence, is inadequate. The reason is that since their divestiture, privatisation, and part-privatisation, the three companies have had ample opportunity to *change* their activities in these fields. And, indeed, they have made significant changes. As we shall shortly see in greater detail, AT&T has *deepened* its involvement in the research, design, development and manufacture of telecommunications-related equipment with its acquisition of NCR, the computer manufacturing company. At the other extreme, BT has significantly *reduced* its involvement in these areas by pulling out almost entirely from the joint research, design, and development of telecommunications equipment. Of the three companies it is NTT which has exhibited the greatest degree of *continuity*, retaining its joint activities with its former suppliers, while adding new suppliers, both Western and Japanese, and simultaneously moving to a multi-vendor supply situation. Clearly, it was both in principle and in practice possible for each of the three companies to have made different choices. Thus AT&T could have opted to reduce its commitment to the manufacture of telecommunications and telecommunications-related equipment; BT could have followed NTT in developing closer relationships with international equipment suppliers involving joint research and development; and NTT could have distanced itself from its suppliers, deciding to specify and purchase equipment rather than jointly researching and developing them.

Accordingly, it must be concluded that it is strategic choice rather than path-dependence which explains the role of research, design, development, and manufacture in the three companies. The point, it should be noted, is not that 'history did not matter', but rather that in the light of their historical experience, and their understanding of their changing global environment, decision-makers in the three companies made very different choices regarding these activities, choices which are reflected in the resources that they have allocated to R&D as documented earlier. It is, therefore, to a deeper analysis of their strategic choices that we now turn.

3.5.2 *Strategic Choice of Corporate Competence: An Overview*

At a conference at the Royal Society, London, Dr J. S. Mayo, President of AT&T Bell Laboratories, suggested that there is a widespread consensus regarding the telecommunications services that will be provided over the next decade.[3] These are voice, data, and image based services, and a com-

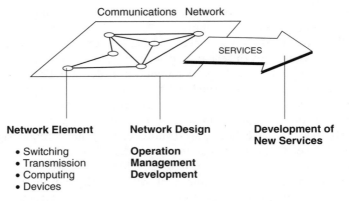

Fig. 3.1 A map of telecoms competences

bination of all three, available at any time. The provision of these services will require competence in three core areas: software, electronics, and photonics.

In Fig. 3.1 a more detailed 'map' is provided of the three main sets of competences that are required to provide these telecommunications services. These competences are in the area of 'network elements' (i.e. switching, transmission, computing, and devices); network design, operation, management, and development; and the development of new services. These competences may be divided into two complementary sets of activities, the first set involving running and improving network services (undertaken by the users of network elements), while the second set involves designing, developing, and manufacturing network elements (undertaken by the suppliers). These two sets of activities are shown in Fig. 3.2.

Clearly, the activities of the users and suppliers need to be coordinated in order to provide telecommunications services. However, as Richardson (1972) has pointed out in a criticism of the dualistic conception of industrial organisation in terms of firms as islands operating in a sea of markets, there are in fact three broad alternative modes of coordination: through the market, through interfirm cooperation, and through direction or development within the firm.

What strategic choices have been made by AT&T, BT, and NTT regarding the mode of coordinating these two sets of activities? Their choices are shown in Table 3.4 where it can be seen that while all three companies have chosen to develop in-house competences in the areas of network operation and development, and the provision of new services, they have made very different choices regarding the acquisition of network elements. More specifically, while each firm is a significant purchaser of telecommunications equipment on the market, BT has opted for greater use of the market as a mode of acquiring network elements, NTT has chosen interfirm

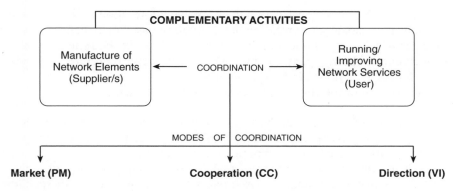

Fig. 3.2 Modes of coordinating user-supplier activities

Table 3.4 Strategic choice regarding acquisition of competence

Strategic options	Competences		Network elements			
	Network operation, development	New services	Switching	Transmission	Computing	Devices
Buy (market)			BT	BT	BT	BT
Joint development (cooperation)			NTT	NTT	NTT	NTT
Make/do (internal development)	BT NTT AT&T	BT NTT AT&T	AT&T	AT&T	AT&T	AT&T

cooperation to a more significant extent, while AT&T has selected internal development.

Why have these different strategic choices been made? This question is examined further in the following section.

3.6 BT—Using the Market

3.6.1 BT's Vision of the Future

Operating under conditions of complexity, imperfect information, and uncertainty, corporate decision-makers have no alternative but to construct 'images' of the future in deciding on the moves they should make. These images are not simply the result of processing the information which the company has obtained from its environment, as some would have us believe. While image construction does involve information processing, it is largely a process of interpretation of information based on belief. It is these images which are embodied in the company's vision of the future, a vision which allows the company to envisage the future and therefore to decide which present actions are best to undertake.[4]

BT's vision of the future embodies the following elements:

1. The key force driving the future competitiveness of telecommunications operating companies is the capability to cater to the needs of customers, particularly large multinational companies.

2. The essential element in this capability is the ability to tailor the characteristics of telecommunications services to the requirements of specific customers.

3. In turn, this ability is largely dependent on competences in the area of software and system engineering. These competences are so important that it is essential that they are developed largely by BT itself rather than relying on outside suppliers of software and system engineering. (Software and system engineering relating directly to the provision of competitive telecommunications services, therefore, are seen as core competences which are mainly to be developed within the company. Other software, such as packaged computer software, may be purchased from outside suppliers).

4. The ability to manufacture telecommunications-related equipment is seen as being largely irrelevant insofar as competitiveness in telecommunications services is concerned. Accordingly, BT will purchase the equipment that it requires on the market. Neither are there competitive advantages in engaging in the costly activity of jointly researching and developing telecommunications equipment.

5. Although many analysts have referred to the alleged 'convergence' of communication and computing technologies, BT does not believe that the realisation of synergies between these two areas will be an important determinant of competitiveness in the provision of telecommunications services. Accordingly the company has decided not to become a producer and supplier of computers and computer services.

6. Similarly, BT has decided that it does not for competitive reasons require substantial in-house competences in the design and manufacture of devices, including electronic and optical devices. While these devices are important components of telecommunications systems and the services which they provide, BT can rely on the market to satisfy its requirements. Besides, the escalating research and development costs of devices is constantly adding to the cost of competence in this area, without there being compensating benefits in terms of increased competitiveness.

7. The implications of all this for R&D are that BT can largely leave research and development in the areas of manufacturing telecommunica-

tions equipment, computing, and devices to the supplying companies. BT will rather concentrate its R&D in areas such as software and system engineering which directly and strongly affect its competitiveness. One of the roles of research, however, is to ensure that BT has sufficient knowledge of new technologies to be able to rapidly and efficiently assimilate them. Furthermore, research also has the aim of 'guarding against surprise' and this justifies a certain amount of long term research.

While the question of R&D is examined in more detail in a later section, we will now examine some of the evidence on which the above account of BT's vision rests.

According to Iain Vallance, Chairman of BT, 'what we know how to do well' is the 'running of telecommunications networks and the provision of services across them'. Vallance identified three levels of competence that he regarded as particularly important for BT: software competences in order to customise services and provide them rapidly and efficiently to customers; competences in operating telecommunications networks themselves; and, 'most importantly', competences in marketing, sales, and customer service. Technology *per se* he regarded as less important than customer services: 'We have to offer, not technological solutions, but services that our customers need'.[5]

In line with its emphasis on customer services rather than 'technological solutions', BT has decided that it does not need in-house manufacturing capabilities. Accordingly it has decided, in retrospect, that its investment in Mitel Corp., the Canadian telecommunications equipment manufacturer in which BT owned a 51 per cent share, was misjudged. As Richard Marriott, Director of BT's corporate strategy and formerly from IBM, put it: 'The one [overseas investment made by BT] that really hasn't worked out as well as we hoped is Mitel. . . . At the time, it seemed like a good idea to be in the hardware business. Our vision is now entirely based on being in network services. That, of course, in turn has meant a major shift in our research and development—moving from hardware into software and systems to give us an edge in meeting customers' increasingly complex needs. Mitel doesn't fit our new strategy' (Marriott 1992, 26).

If technological solutions are not a priority, neither is in-house competence in computer hardware and software. As Iain Vallance put it: 'What about "convergence"? Ten years ago that was the "in" word. AT&T and IBM were going to clash in the battle of the titans. On a lesser scale convergence was the rationale for STC's acquisition of ICL [the British computer company] five years ago. It never happened. ICL now belongs to Fujitsu, and STC will shortly be part of Northern Telecom [and now is]. And I was going to wonder aloud whether AT&T had lost as much money in computers as IBM had in telecommunications, but in the light of recent announcements by Bob Allen [Chairman and CEO of AT&T] that seems inappropriate'.[6]

A further reason for BT avoiding manufacturing equipment and getting involved with computers was to 'economise on bounded rationality', namely to reduce complexity by focusing on a narrower range of issues. As Richard Marriott put it: 'Our international strategy is perhaps the most focused of all of the major global players. We have no distractions, such as providing service to Third World organisations. Nor are we concentrating on manufacturing telecom equipment or computers—we're getting out of manufacturing. Our strategy is very, very focused' (Marriott 1992) Underscoring this point, Iain Vallance said, 'there is enough complexity to deal with. We do not want to take on these other activities'.[7]

3.7 AT&T—Reaping Synergies through Vertical Integration

3.7.1 AT&T's Vision of the Future

AT&T's vision of the future contains the following elements:

1. The key driving force behind the company's future competitiveness is the synergy that can be realised from its internal competences in software, switching and transmissions, computing, and devices. This synergy will allow AT&T to provide customers with better telecommunications services more rapidly than its competitors.

2. AT&T's distinctiveness lies in its in-house possession of competences in all of these areas. None of the other major telecommunications operating companies has such a wide range of competences. Neither do the equipment supplying companies, which have also begun to compete in some telecommunications service-related markets. While the latter may also have competences in the areas of hardware and related software, they do not have AT&T's competence in network management and services. They are therefore unable to provide the customer with the same package of services that AT&T can.

3. By implication, AT&T would not be able to realise the synergies on which its competitiveness rests by bringing together by agreement its own competences with those of other distinct companies. Hence, for example, rather than fostering close ties with one or more computer company, it was necessary to either develop the necessary computer competences internally or acquire a computer company, as eventually happened with NCR after the internal development strategy failed.

4. The implication of this vision for R&D is that AT&T must undertake research and development activities in all the areas in which it has chosen to develop internal competences. Furthermore, basic research has a role to play in providing the seeds for future improvements in services.

Nevertheless, as will be seen later, it is necessary to establish organisational mechanisms that will ensure that research and development activities contribute effectively and profitably to commercial competitiveness.

Let us now briefly examine some of the evidence on which this account of AT&T's vision is based.

In a recent interview with *Business Week*, Bob Allen, AT&T's Chairman and CEO, stated that 'There is no other company like AT&T. We are unique, and therefore we have a unique opportunity'.[8] *Business Week* elaborated on Allen's vision: 'Allen is convinced that, even after years of frustrated efforts, AT&T can be a global information powerhouse by putting together a set of resources that no other company can match: a sophisticated world-wide network to carry voice and data, plus the equipment to run it, plus the devices that hook up to it. . . . Put them under one roof, the Allen theory goes, and you can build complex, networked information systems that surpass anything available from a computer manufacturer, long-distance company, or phone-switch maker' (ibid. 35).

For AT&T the crucial point is that as a result of synergies, these competences *in combination* will be capable of yielding greater competitiveness and returns than they would deliver separately. Taken separately, the 'products and systems' part of AT&T has not been nearly as profitable as the 'communications services' part. (In 1991 products and systems—which includes computers, network switches and transmission equipment, office telephone systems, microelectronics, telephones, and answering machines—produced a net profit margin of only 3.0 per cent. This compared with 13.8 per cent for communications services, which includes long distance telephone and dedicated, high-speed data lines for business (ibid. 34–5)).

Although by and large the hoped-for synergies still remain to be realised, AT&T does have a number of examples to illustrate the potential gains. These examples include the intelligent networks that AT&T have developed for the Italian telephone operating company, SIP. According to Claudio Carrelli, head of SIP's research and development, AT&T's competitive advantage stemmed from its combined competences in switching and network operating: 'All switchmakers have the same technology but AT&T has the major operating experience. From that point of view, AT&T is far ahead of everyone else' (ibid. 38). Another example, combining communications networks and computing, is the computer network for after-hours trading at the New York Mercantile Exchange which will be installed by AT&T and NCR (ibid. 39). According to Gilbert P. Williamson, Chairman of NCR, synergies such as these could not have been achieved if the two companies had an arm's-length market-based relationship: 'If you really want to do something big, it gets very difficult to do it on an arm's-length basis' (ibid. 37).

3.8 NTT—Competing Through Cooperation

3.8.1 NTT's Vision of the Future

NTT's vision consists of the following elements:

1. In order to remain competitive domestically against the new common carriers and become increasingly competitive internationally, NTT must be a leader in the provision of new telecommunications services.

2. Leadership in new services requires that NTT plays a leading role in research and development. This means that NTT must be actively developing new services (and the technologies which underpin them) *before* they are developed by the telecommunications equipment manufacturers. This advanced positioning on the part of NTT is necessary since once new services are developed by the manufacturers, they will soon be made available to all the major telecommunications operating companies, depriving any one of them of a competitive lead. It is for this reason that NTT has decided to devote an *increasing* proportion of its sales to R&D.

3. For historical reasons NTT has not acquired manufacturing competences. In view of the costs of accumulating such competences, however, NTT has decided to leave manufacturing to the manufacturers rather than attempt to compete with them.

4. Nevertheless, NTT believes that it can benefit from cooperating closely with a number of equipment manufacturers and jointly developing telecommunications equipment and services that are not already available in satisfactory form and price on the market. In this way NTT will be able to 'marry' its competences with those of its suppliers in order to achieve its objective of service leadership through technological leadership.

5. NTT also believes, as the terms of its part-privatisation legally require it to believe, that it must continue to play an important national and global role (in addition to its private role) as a supporter and advancer of research and development in telecommunications-related technologies.

Since its part-privatisation in 1985, NTT has come under substantial pressure from the new common carriers on the Japanese market. By the financial year 1990 the new common carriers accounted for 12 per cent of the Japanese long-distance telephone services market and this increased to 16 per cent by 1991. The new common carriers controlled 40 per cent of the voluminous Tokyo–Nagoya–Osaka market in 1990, rising to 49 per cent in 1991.[9] In part the increasing market share of the new common carriers was facilitated by the lower prices that they charged relative to NTT, which in turn were made possible by the low access costs that they had to bear for access to NTT's network. Although by 1994 access charges are expected to reach an economic rate, the substantial share of the Japanese market controlled by the new common carriers, together with NTT's recent fall in profitability referred to earlier, put great pressure on NTT to ensure its longer term competitiveness.

How does NTT plan to increase its competitiveness? The answer according to Dr Iwao Toda, Executive Vice President of NTT, is that NTT intends to improve its services and offer new services through concentrating on research and development. By 1994 NTT expects that new services will account for a substantial 30 per cent of total annual revenue. According to Dr Toda, 'We think a substantial portion of [NTT's] earnings are attributable to research and development. For this reason, NTT's management believes R&D is the foundation of NTT's business activities'.[10] It is for this reason that, as is shown in Table 3.3, NTT's expenditures on R&D as a proportion of sales are expected to increase from 4.1 per cent in 1991, to 4.7 per cent in 1993.

Dr Toda has explained that NTT has three objectives for its R&D. The first is to develop new telecommunications services, the second is to improve the planning, administration and management of the telecommunications network, while the third is to innovate in the area of 'network elements' (which include switching, transmission systems, devices, and computers). Dr Toda elaborates on the rationale behind NTT's emphasis on network elements:

The technological progress in telecommunication fields is so rapid that the quicker we can introduce newer and more cost effective network elements, the more we can reduce network costs. This is why NTT develops key network elements by itself. Its aim is to produce the element much *earlier than outside manufacturers*. Usually we initiate our own R&D work for network elements which rely on rapidly advancing technologies and, furthermore, for which we can expect more than two years lead over outside organizations   (Toda, 5, emphasis added, see note 10).

This does not mean, however, that NTT does not cooperate closely with telecommunications equipment manufacturers. Again Dr Toda elaborates:

NTT has no manufacturing capability. Therefore, NTT has to collaborate with outside manufacturers to develop a network element. That is, we have to ask outside manufacturers to build a prototype of a network element *according to our design*. These collaborating manufacturers are called development partners   (ibid. 8, emphasis added).

But close collaboration with a selected group of manufacturers, however, does not mean that NTT forgoes the benefits of competition. Dr Toda explains the advantages of the NTT approach, which we outlined in Chapter 2, and refer to as '*controlled competition*':

The development partners for a particular network element are . . . selected by openly inviting tenders [from] the manufacturers world wide. This open and fair selection process encourages competition among manufacturers. We usually select more than two partners for development of a network element. The selected partners compete with each other during the development process   (Toda, see note 10).

Furthermore, NTT also benefits from the competitive pressure which non-partner manufacturers bring to bear through market competition with the partner companies that cooperate with NTT:

It should be noted that NTT's competition with non-partner manufacturers is most intensive. We believe such competition [between partner companies and between them and non-partner companies] contributes to better product development in a shorter period   (Toda, see note 10).

Dr Toda summarizes the advantages that accrue to NTT despite its lack of competences in the area of manufacturing: 'first NTT as a big user of network elements can innovate technologies, and second, NTT can always utilize the best manufacturing technology in the world'. However, he does acknowledge that 'a disadvantage is difficulty in accumulating the manufacturing know-how necessary for better design' (ibid. 9). This disadvantage NTT attempts to rectify through close cooperation with its partner manufacturing companies.

Examples given by Dr Toda, where network elements were developed more rapidly through cooperative development under conditions of controlled competition, include low-loss optical fiber cables and large capacity transmission systems. Examples include the ATM (asynchronous transfer mode) broadband digital switching system, where the partners in addition to Japanese companies include Northern Telecom, and the MIA (multivendor integration architecture) project to define interface specifications for NTT's future computer acquisitions which includes IBM (Japan) and DEC.[11]

3.9 Contradictions among the Visions

3.9.1 Vision, Bounded Vision, and Vision Failure

Returning to Table 3.4, it would appear that there is a significant contradiction between the visions of AT&T, BT, and NTT as reflected in their different strategic choices of the market, cooperation, and internal development in acquiring the network elements which provide the basis for the telecommunications services which they sell. As Table 3.4 shows, while BT has opted for the market as the means of acquiring network elements, NTT has chosen cooperation, while AT&T has selected internal development.

How is this different choice to be explained? Does it reflect inconsistent calculations regarding the costs and benefits of transactions involving the market, cooperation, and internal development?

The answer to these questions hinges on an understanding of the way in which corporate visions are formed. In short, it is proposed that the difference in the vision of the three companies is to be explained by the way in which the past experience of the company is interpreted by its decision-makers, and the beliefs of these decision-makers regarding the alternatives that exist and the consequences of these alternatives. Accordingly, it may be suggested that in the case of BT, the past history of joint research and development of telecommunications equipment was on the whole not interpreted very favourably. Seen in this light, the alternative of market procurement seemed to be relatively attractive. For NTT, on the other hand, the experience of joint research and development with a stable group of suppliers was interpreted far more positively. It is therefore perhaps not surprising that NTT has opted for a continuing close relationship with selected groups of suppliers in its attempt to take the lead in researching and developing advanced network elements while drawing on the manufacturing competence of these suppliers. Similarly, AT&T, with its internationally favourable track record in developing network elements internally (through close interaction between AT&T's operating units and its subsidiary Western Electric), emerged after divestiture with a positive interpretation of internal development as a suitable mode for obtaining such elements.[12]

According to this account, what a company 'sees' depends on its knowledge. But this 'knowledge', in turn, comprises the interpretations and beliefs of the company's decision makers. These interpretations and beliefs are influenced by (without being fully determined by) the past experience of the decision makers. This, however, raises the likelihood of 'bounded vision', namely where the company's vision is bounded by its interpretations, beliefs, and past experience. In some cases bounded vision may result in 'vision failure', where the company's vision results in a failure to correctly anticipate events with the result that inappropriate decisions are made. Thus the copper cable manufacturer may fail to anticipate the significance of optical fiber, the analog switch maker and buyer may fail to appreciate the speed with which digital switches will be introduced, the maker of large computers may underestimate the growth of demand for small computers, the producer of CISC microprocessors may not see the coming importance of RISC, etc. See Chapter 1 for a theoretical discussion of bounded vision. Similarly, it is also possible that telephone operating companies may overestimate, or perhaps underestimate, the advantages and disadvantages of markets, cooperation, and internal development.

3.9.2 *The Market* versus *Cooperation* versus *Internal Development*

We have seen that BT, NTT, and AT&T have made very different strategic choices with respect to the acquisition of 'network elements'. More

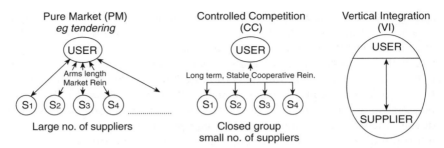

Fig. 3.3 Strategic options for procurement

specifically, BT has tended to rely to a greater extent on markets, while NTT, although also resorting to markets, has opted more than the other companies for interfirm cooperative development. Finally, AT&T, also using markets, has selected internal development (or vertical integration) as its preferred mode of coordination. Is it possible to make any analytical generalisations regarding the advantages and disadvantages of these alternative modes of coordination?

The first step in attempting to make such a generalisation is to construct stylised 'ideal types' of the strategic options each company has selected and then to proceed to analyse the advantages and disadvantages of the modes of organisation they have chosen. In so doing, however, it is necessary to stress that these are ideal types and may not accurately reflect all of the interactions between the telephone operating company and its suppliers of network elements.

The three alternative modes of organisation, or strategic options for the procurement of network elements, chosen by BT, NTT, and AT&T are illustrated in Fig. 3.3.

BT has tended to opt for the 'pure market' (PM) option typified by a potentially large number of suppliers (at least in the pre-contract stage) all of whom have an arm's length relationship with BT. NTT, by contrast, has chosen 'controlled competition' (CC) for developing those network elements which it believes will give it a competitive advantage and which are not available on the market. Controlled competition has involved a relatively long term and stable cooperative relationship with a selected group consisting of a small number of suppliers. Recently these suppliers have included non-Japanese companies such as Northern Telecom, DEC, IBM (Japan), and AT&T, and Japanese companies that before 1985 did not supply NTT, such as Toshiba, Matsushita and Mitsubishi Electric. Finally, AT&T has selected 'vertical integration' (VI) or internal development for those network elements which it does not wish to purchase on the market and which it would like to develop in a synergistic way.

What are the advantages and disadvantages of these three ideal type

Table 3.5 Advantages and disadvantages of PM, CC, and VI

PM	CC	VI
Advantage for carrier	*Advantage*	*Advantage*
1. Maximise static efficiency (choose best supplier)	1. Better coordination (compared to PM)/ better information flow	1. Coordination through direction may be more efficient (e.g. synergies)
2. Innovation responsibility of supplier/competition-induced innovation	2. Limited competition possible	2. Knowledge-leakage minimized
	3. Greater incentive to invest in transaction-specific assets	3. Greatest incentive to invest in transaction-specific assets
Disadvantages	*Disadvantages*	*Disadvantages*
1. Competition-induced uncertainty	1. Limited ability in short run to switch suppliers ($\rightarrow$ static inefficiency)	1. Innovation responsibility of user ($\rightarrow$ high R&D)
2. Limited incentive to invest in transaction-specific assets	2. Possibly high coordination costs (autonomous firms)	2. Absence of competition-induced innovation
	3. Some competition-induced uncertainty	3. No switching from internal to external supplier ($\rightarrow$ static inefficiency)
	4. Possible knowledge-leakage	

alternative modes of organisation? Some of the main advantages and disadvantages are shown in Table 3.5.

3.9.3 Advantages and Disadvantages of 'Pure Market' (PM)

One of the main advantages is that the carrier/buyer can choose the best supplier from amongst all those available in the market (and therefore maximise 'static private allocative efficiency'). Furthermore, under PM innovation is largely the responsibility of the supplier, and the carrier, therefore, does not have to commit as much resource to innovation and thus risk becoming 'locked in' to specific technological paths which it has chosen. In addition, insofar as there is competition between potential suppliers, there is also likely to be competition-induced innovation which may speed and improve the quality of new technologies offered by the suppliers.

PM, on the other hand, may also result in a higher degree of competition-induced uncertainty (relative to CC and VI) since suppliers, even those who have won orders, will be unsure from one round of tendering to the next whether they will win future orders. In addition, and following on from the point about increased uncertainty, there will under PM be limited incentive for potential suppliers to invest in 'transaction-specific assets', that is assets such as machinery and equipment and human skills which are specific to a supplier's transaction with a particular buyer and which are worth substantially less in alternative uses. The reason is that the supplier is uncertain regarding whether it will win orders and therefore be able to recoup reasonable returns on its investment in transaction-specific assets. Under these conditions suppliers are less likely to invest in such assets compared with where they are more sure of winning future orders.[13]

3.9.4 Advantages and Disadvantages of 'Controlled Competition' (CC)

One advantage that may follow from CC is more effective coordination between supplier and carrier compared with PM. While PM will provide for coordination through the market mechanism, specifically through the price mechanism and competitive process, it may be less effective in facilitating non-market-mediated flows of information between suppliers and carriers who have an arm's-length relationship to one another. Better flows of information between carriers and suppliers who enjoy a longer term, relatively stable relationship may lead not only to better coordination but also to more effective user-oriented innovation. Furthermore, although there is less competition than under PM since there is at any point in time a closed group of suppliers consisting of a small number of firms, there remains the opportunity to benefit from some competition between the members of this group. Less competition compared with PM also means that there is less competition-induced uncertainty and hence a greater incentive, again compared with PM, to invest in transaction-specific assets.

Against these advantages, however, must be set the limited ability in the short run to switch suppliers, which may lead to 'static private allocative inefficiency' relative to PM. It is also possible that there will be relatively high coordination costs under CC as the carrier attempts to share information and get agreement between several autonomous firms. Furthermore, although competition-induced uncertainty is likely to be lower than under PM (since there is controlled competition), to the extent that competition remains there will be some such uncertainty. In addition, there is, from the supplier's point of view, the danger that commercially sensitive knowledge will leak to the other competing suppliers who are also involved in the cooperative research and development.

3.9.5 Advantages and Disadvantages of 'Vertical Integration' (VI)

One possible advantage of VI may be more effective coordination between complementary activities (since the activities are under the same 'command structure' in the same firm) and therefore a greater realisation of synergies between these activities. In addition, under VI there will be the greatest incentive to invest in transaction-specific assets (relative to PM and CC) since the costs of diverting these assets to lower-earning alternative uses will have to be borne by the firm itself (a point that Coase made in his original 1937 article). Furthermore, the chance of knowledge-leakage to competing firms is minimis.ed and there is also a minimisation of competition-induced uncertainty, since the transactions occur within the same firm.

A major disadvantage of VI, however, is that innovation is the responsibility of the carrier and this is likely to lead to relatively high R&D expenses. Furthermore, there is the danger that, having invested in particular forms of innovation, the firm may become 'locked in' and therefore unable to as easily take advantage of alternative innovations that have been generated outside the firm. In addition, since by definition there is only one internal supplier, there is the absence under 'pure' VI of competition-induced innovation. Similarly, again under 'pure' VI, since there is by definition no opportunity to switch from an internal to an external supplier, there may well be greater 'static private allocative inefficiency' than under either PM or CC. (It is, of course, to avoid these consequences that vertically integrated firms usually leave some option for users in the firm to purchase from outside firms.)

3.9.6 Conclusion

In view of the complexity of the possible effects of PM, CC, and VI it is not possible to reach a definitive conclusion regarding the relative efficiency of these strategic options. It is no doubt for this reason that BT, NTT, and AT&T have been able to make different choices regarding these options and remain convinced that they have made the optimal choice. To a larger extent the efficiency of the choice depends on the company's competences including the extent to which it is able, organisationally and managerially, to exploit the advantages which have been analysed, while dealing effectively with the disadvantages. Furthermore, as mentioned at the outset, the three strategic options analysed in this section are ideal types and although the three companies have made broadly different choices with regard to these options, they have also modified the ideal typical modes of coordination in order to increase the net advantages, as is indicated in note 13 with reference to BT's concept of 'quality suppliers'.

However, the strategic choices that have been made regarding the acquisition of network elements must be sharply distinguished from the strategic choices that the companies have made in the area of research and development. It is accordingly to an analysis of research and development that we now turn.

3.10 The Role of Research and Development

3.10.1 Introduction

The first corporate research laboratories were established in the German chemical industry in the late nineteenth century and not long after in American companies such as AT&T, General Electric, and Du Pont (Reich 1985, and Hounshell and Smith 1988). While these laboratories allowed their companies to apply scientific principles and practices to industrial production and in some cases to increase the company's ability to appropriate returns from its investments by securing commanding patent rights, the laboratories also posed new and formidable organisational problems. These stemmed largely from the greater *fragmentation of knowledge* that accompanied the increased division of labour implied by the establishment of an industrial laboratory. Now a cadre of *researchers*, one step removed from the company's routine process of production and with a knowledge base significantly different from those involved in this production process, had to be integrated into the firm's activities in a value-enhancing way. It was not, and still is not, always clear to the management of the company concerned how this integration could be effectively achieved.

This organisational problem became increasingly pressing for the major telecommunications operating companies from the mid-1980s, faced as they were with increasing competition in their major markets. While hitherto their monopoly status in their domestic market afforded them a degree of protection from the necessity to generate immediate value from research, in the tougher world of short run competition the 'luxury' of research relatively uncoupled from direct value-creation could no longer be sustained. The result was organisational reform in these companies designed to integrate research more closely with the immediate value-creating process.

3.10.2 The Four Major Research Problems

Any company undertaking research has to resolve four major research-related problems (Fransman 1991):

1. What research does the firm need now? This is an *information* problem.
2. How to prevent 'irrelevant' research? This is a *control* problem.
3. What research is needed for the future? This is an *uncertainty* problem.
4. Should the required research be undertaken in-house or ex-house? This is an *assignment* problem.

How have the telecommunications operating companies dealt with these problems?

The information and control problems

To ensure that . . . [research] is well coupled to the needs of the business, the strategy demands that at least two-thirds of the work performed by the central laboratories should be sponsored and financed directly by the customers in the operating divisions [of BT]   (Rudge 1990, 124–5).

If researchers in the laboratories received payment from the operating divisions in NTT the benefit is that researchers would become more customer/business oriented. However, the cost is that they will become short-term oriented. The business people [in the operating divisions] cannot see the future. So right now we do not use a financial link [between the operating divisions and the central research laboratory]. Head Office funds most of the research in the laboratories   (Author's interview with senior NTT officer, 1991).

1. Using an internal market for research and development   In an important article, Alan Rudge, Director of Group Technology and Development at BT, has carefully explained how BT since privatisation has attempted to deal with the information and control problems relating to research. The central role in coping with these problems has been played by what Rudge calls 'the customer-supplier principle' (Rudge 1990, 127), or what is referred to here as the internal market for research and development.

In short, in order to provide information regarding the research and development priorities in BT and to ensure that the company's researchers allocate their time and other resources in accordance with these priorities, BT has established an internal research and development market. In this internal market, BT's Operating Divisions demand the research and development that is supplied by the company's 4,000 scientists, engineers, technicians, and support staff in the central research laboratories. This demand is expressed in the form of an explicit contract for the particular project, which is defined in terms of milestones and deliverables and stipulates a fixed time period and price. Every task undertaken in the central research laboratories is defined as a project in this way (ibid. 121). Overall, the central research laboratories are highly dependent on the internal market for the revenue which they need to employ their staff and cover their costs. Thus Rudge reports that in 1989 '75% of work of the central laboratories is funded, and therefore directed, by customers either in the

Operating Divisions [who provide the bulk of the revenue] or externally'. (ibid. 126)

Further organisational steps have been taken to 'couple' the central research laboratories, which Rudge sees as BT's 'engine of change' (ibid. 127), with their customers in the Operating Divisions. One of these steps has involved the appointment of Programme Office Directors whose main job is to coordinate all of the projects being undertaken in the laboratories for a particular customer in one of the Operating Divisions. While the Programme Office Director plays the entrepreneurial role of 'trying to anticipate the client's needs and his likely direction in the future', he is also a 'line manager', performing a significant part of his work for the same major customer (ibid. 123). In its attempt to make the boundary between the Operating Divisions and the central research laboratories a 'managed interface', BT has made use of what Rudge calls the 'flow management principle'. This provides a 'means of measuring the effectiveness of the company's R&D by monitoring the flow of technology, techniques, products and service ideas across the boundaries' (ibid. 128). Rudge argues that 'This kind of flow is measurable and can be quantified. It offers sensible advantages over measures based upon the numbers of publications, which are often totally inappropriate in commercial organizations' (ibid. 129).

AT&T has also attempted to make use of an internal market in order to coordinate the activities of its laboratories and operating divisions. In 1988 Robert E. Allen, AT&T's Chairman, reorganised the company into some twenty separate business units with profit-and-loss responsibility (See note 8). The following year, Arno A Penzias, Vice President of Research at Bell Laboratories, initiated a number of corresponding changes in the laboratories. One of the main objectives of these changes was to tighten the link between the laboratories and the business units. The changes included the consolidation of research projects into 15 laboratories divided among 4 divisions, requiring almost half of the 1,200 research staff to support projects in the business units, and assigning all of the 19 directors in the laboratories the task of working with one of the business units partly by establishing cooperative projects with them.[14]

Through changes such as these it was hoped that AT&T would be able to increase the value that it reaps from research and thus meet the criticism of critics, like A. Michael Noll, a former AT&T marketing executive and now Professor of Communications at the University of Southern California, Los Angeles, who have argued that AT&T's return on investment in research has been too low. According to Noll (1991), in '1984 [Bell] Labs employees were 5.3% of the total number of AT&T employees; in 1989 this doubled to 10.2%.' However, Noll argues, AT&T has not derived sufficient benefit from these employees. In support of his argument Noll has published the following rather remarkable claim:

One reason AT&T agreed to divestiture was to be free to develop the many new business opportunities that supposedly were available from the technological store-house of Bell Labs. This hypothesis was not investigated before divestiture. After divestiture AT&T Bell Labs did an internal study of all its ideas for new products, services and businesses. While at AT&T I had the opportunity to review the results of this study, a multi-volumed document. Of the hundreds of ideas submitted, fewer than half a dozen, as I recall, were realistic, and most of them were already under development in some fashion. The simple fact was that the Labs' cupboard was bare. The jewels of the Bell System, the operating telephone companies, had been given away in return for nothing!' (Noll 1991, 103).

NTT has also, after its part-privatisation in 1985, reorganised in order to strengthen the connection between research and development and the operating divisions. In 1987, under the influence of the new head of NTT, Dr Shinto, the four research locations of NTT's Electrical Communications Laboratories (ECL), based in Musashino, Yokosuka, Atsugi, and Ibaraki, were divided into 11 research laboratories.[15] In order to meet the develop-ment needs of the operating divisions, the remaining scientists, engineers, and technicians, who had been part of ECL but were not included in the laboratories, were moved to two new development centres, the Network Systems Development Center and the Software Engineering Center, which were closely tied to the activities of the divisions. In 1991 some 3,200 of NTT's approximately 8,200 scientists, engineers, and technicians were allo-cated to the eleven laboratories while the remaining 5,000 were based in the centers and in the development sections of the operating divisions. In the same year, while about 40 percent of NTT's total R&D budget went to the centers and development sections, 60 percent was allocated to the 11 laboratories.[16]

When Dr Shinto's reforms were first mooted, they caused a good deal of anxiety on the part of researchers and others high in the NTT hierarchy who feared that they may indicate a tendential swing against NTT's research-led approach to telecommunications. A top delegation of NTT's researchers accordingly went to discuss the matter with Dr Shinto who reas-sured them that as a former engineer he understood the importance of research. He had, he said, no intention of undermining the role of research in the company, although he felt that some reorganisation was necessary to increase the effectiveness of NTT's development activities. It was for this reason that he had formed the two new development-oriented centers and linked them more closely with the operating divisions.[17]

2. The internal market and beyond   Although, as documented, use is made of an internal market for research and development to deal with the infor-mation and control problems referred to, the internal market mechanism is of only limited value in taking care of a company's research needs. The limitations have been well expressed by Rudge (1990) who has observed that 'while research provides the in-depth knowledge, it is noteworthy that the majority of our customers [in BT] are not interested in buying research as such' (ibid. 117). However, 'If the central laboratories are to provide expertise on demand they must have in place a well-directed research programme to generate enabling technology and "know how" *in advance of the customer's need*' (124, emphasis added). This creates something of a dilemma: the central laboratories must generate knowledge *before* the customer has a need for this knowledge and therefore before the customer will be willing to pay for the creation of this knowledge. This raises the question of who will pay for the creation of this knowledge, that is if it is to be created at all. The answer in most cases given to this question is that it is the company's headquarters which will have to extend what is in effect a grant to the central research laboratories to finance the research that will result in output which the operating divisions will later be willing to pay for. This requires going beyond the internal market for research and development.

However, even if it is accepted that headquarters should play this role, further difficult questions are raised. For example, what proportion of the budget of the central research laboratories should be funded from headquarters? How should the company ensure that research funded in this way is relevant to the needs of the company? In dealing with questions such as these, significant differences have emerged among the companies being studied here. This takes us on to the third research problem referred to earlier, the uncertainty problem, namely: what research is needed for the future?

The uncertainty problem

There are significant differences between BT and NTT regarding the solutions that have been devised for dealing with the uncertainty problem. Reminiscent of the differences between these two companies with respect to the acquisition of network elements, which were analysed earlier, BT has tended to rely to a greater extent than NTT on market forces, albeit in this case internal market forces. This emerges clearly in Table 3.6.

From Table 3.6 it can be seen that in the two companies a similar proportion of total R&D is undertaken in the central research laboratories as opposed to elsewhere, namely 60 per cent in the case of NTT and 66 per cent in the case of BT. The big difference between BT and NTT, however, relates to the proportion of the central research laboratories' R&D which is funded from, headquarters rather than the operating divisions, about 18 per cent in the case of BT compared to about 95 per cent for NTT.

This substantial difference is indicative of a fundamentally different philosophy (or, more accurately, vision) in the two companies regarding both the role of research and the balance of market and non-market forces required to deal with the uncertainty problem. The differing philosophies

Table 3.6 R&D in BT and NTT

	BT	NTT
% R&D in central research labs (CRL)	66	60
% of CRL R&D funded by Headquarters rather than Operating Divisions	18	95
CRL staff BT, 1989	4,000*	
CRL staff NTT, 1991		3,200**
% of total R&D 0–6 year horizon	65	60
7–10 year horizon	25	30
11–20 year horizon	10	10
'Basic' research as % of total R&D	n/a	5

* Includes total research-related staff.
** Includes only scientists, researchers, and technicians.
Sources: Rudge (1990); NTT Annual Report, 1991; author's estimate for NTT.

emerge in the two quotations presented above (under the heading 'The information and control problems') which are sufficiently illuminating to justify repeating here:

> To ensure that . . . [research] is well coupled to the needs of the business, the strategy demands that at least two-thirds of the work performed by the central laboratories should be sponsored and financed directly by the customers in the operating divisions [of BT]   (Rudge 1990, 124–5).

If researchers in the laboratories received payment from the operating divisions in NTT the benefit is that researchers would become more customer/business oriented. However, the cost is that they will become short-term oriented. The business people [in the operating divisions] cannot see the future. So right now we do not use a financial link [between the operating divisions and the central research laboratory]. Head Office funds most of the research in the laboratories   (Author's interview with senior NTT officer, 1991).

The difference in philosophy between the two companies may be expressed in the following way: while both companies agree that a combination of 'internal market pull' and 'science-technology push' (funded from Headquarters) is required in order to deal with the uncertainty problem, they differ regarding the *balance* that is necessary between these two forces; BT ultimately gives greater weight to internal market pull, while NTT tends to favour science-technology push.

According to the NTT view, the vision of the staff in the operating divisions (including the development engineers working there) is bounded by the activities currently undertaken in the divisions. These activities in turn are determined by the existing markets and technologies of the operating divisions. This situation is appropriate as long as only incremental changes in markets and/or technologies are needed. If more radical changes are required, for example new services are introduced based on fundamentally different technologies, then the bounded vision of the operating divisions becomes a binding constraint. In the latter case the lead must come from the research laboratories where knowledge of the new technologies and their applications has been created.[18]

NTT's preference is also apparent in the choices that have been made regarding the appropriate location for the creation of knowledge required for the future and the way in which such knowledge, once created, is transferred to the operating divisions where it is to be used. Before Dr Shinto's reforms introduced in 1987 (referred to earlier), both radical changes in knowledge and applications of this knowledge were created in the central research laboratories and were then transferred to the operating divisions. Under the reforms, an attempt was made to move the site of such application creation to the development centers and operating divisions. However, it was soon discovered that the engineers in the development centers and operating divisions frequently were insufficiently familiar with the new technologies. Accordingly, it was decided to revert to some of the previous practices and locate the creation of applications based on radical improvements in technology in the central research laboratories. In order to transfer these applications to the operating divisions, engineers by and large, *from* the divisions *to* the laboratories where knowledge regarding the new applications is located, rather than the other way round. They then return to their divisions to complete the applications according to the division's requirements. In those cases where researchers from the central laboratories move to the operating divisions to assist the technology transfer process, they generally return to the laboratories rather than, as happens in many Japanese electronics companies, remaining permanently thereafter in the divisions.[19] In this way, the 'causal direction' of innovation is clearly from the central research laboratories to the operating divisions rather than the other way round.

With regard to the proportion of the budget of the central research laboratories funded from headquarters, practice in NTT differs significantly from that in the major Japanese industrial electronics companies such as NEC, Fujitsu, and Hitachi. The central laboratories in the latter companies generally receive about 50 per cent of their budgets from corporate headquarters (Fransman 1991). However, in a recent and important departure from previous practice, several of these companies have established advanced research laboratories which are intended to undertake long-term 'oriented basic research' and which receive all of their funding from corporate headquarters. These laboratories include Hitachi's Advanced Research Laboratory and NEC's Princeton Laboratory (ibid.) In funding terms these laboratories resemble NTT's central research Laboratories (the Electrical Communications Laboratories) more closely, although unlike ECL their mission is entirely longer term oriented with the result that they have significantly less interaction with the operating divisions in the company.

In BT, rather than an autonomous science/technology push from the central laboratories being given responsibility, as it were, for initiating the innovation process, as is the case in NTT, an attempt is made to have the research process itself pulled by the users of the research output. This is true even within the Central Research Laboratories, as Rudge (1990) makes clear: 'One way of enhancing [the flow of technology, techniques, products and service ideas across the boundaries between the laboratories and the operating divisions and between the research and development departments of the central laboratories] is to ensure that a significant number of projects on one side of the boundary are being funded, and hence directed, by a manager on the other side. In BT this process has been established not only between the central laboratories and their customers in the Operating Divisions, *but within the Central Research Organization.* While it is difficult for a manager of a corporately-funded research project to guarantee success of his work in the ultimate market place, he can often ensure that his output is sufficiently attractive to his customer *in the development laboratories*, that they will want to take it up, either by adopting his output or by funding extension work with him' (Rudge 1990, 128–9, emphasis added). As Rudge makes clear, for BT the 'causal direction' of innovation is largely, although not completely, from the users of knowledge to the creators of knowledge, rather than the other way round.

Comments on the difference between BT and NTT   Can the differences between BT and NTT just referred to be reconciled? One way of doing so is to suggest that in the case of intra-paradigmatic technological change (where the changes of technologies occur within a given technological regime) a causal direction from the users of knowledge to the creators of knowledge is indicated. Not only does this assist the knowledge creator by providing more information about the circumstances and needs of the user, it also helps the subsequent flow of knowledge from the creator to the user. However, in the case of inter-paradigmatic technological change (where there is a change in technological regime) a different causal direction is needed, namely from the creator to the user of knowledge. The reason, to give some examples, is that the users of electromechanical switches, or copper cable transmission systems, or records, are able to provide knowledge which is only of limited use to the creators of digital switches, or optical transmission systems, or optical disks. In these cases, therefore, it is necessary to go beyond the market, even the internal market, in order to ensure the creation and implementation of radical new technologies. However, how to ensure in this case that the knowledge created remains relevant for the users, and is therefore value-enhancing for the company, when the users themselves play only a limited role in the knowledge-creation process, is the organisational and managerial problem that remains.

Basic research and long-term research This raises the issues of basic research and long term research. Are there any differences regarding the role of these kinds of research in BT and NTT?

As shown in Table 3.3, both BT and NTT allocate about 10 per cent of their total R&D budget to projects with a commercial time horizon of 10 to 20 years. Nevertheless, as will become apparent, there are important differences between the companies regarding the roles of both long term and basic research.

Rudge elaborates on the role of long term research in BT:

The most difficult part of the R&D portfolio to direct effectively is the final 10% which is devoted to identifying the technological threats and opportunities which may effect (sic) the company's business activities in the longer term. Looking to the longer term there are an increasing number of scientific developments which could be of interest. The approach adopted [in BT] has been to provide a thin screen of relatively small projects which guard against surprises, combined with a lesser number of larger projects focused on the areas which are considered to be key to the Group's strategic development. To strengthen the longer term coverage, a managed programme of research with selected universities and other external research organizations has been put in place (Rudge 1990, 125–126).

However, even in the case of long term research, BT has applied its 'customer-supplier principle':

To provide a customer-supplier framework for the management of the Corporate Research Programme [i.e. corporate funded research with primarily a 7 to 20 year commercial time horizon], a 'Programme Office' structure has been established [analogous to the Programme Office Directors referred to earlier who coordinate the link between the central research laboratories and the operating divisions] led by the Chief Engineering Advisor supported by a small team of specialist staff. Their task is to establish a portfolio of research projects within the agreed corporate budget and to audit the projects on a regular basis. The corporate research portfolio is managed to comply with the broad strategic directives agreed by the Research and Technology Board and the portfolio is reviewed by the Board and an advisory committee of senior technical managers selected from business units across the group. Additional inputs to the Programme Office include commercial support from the Business Operations Division and advice from 30 specially identified technical specialists . . . chosen for their eminence in their field of expertise (Rudge 1990, 126–127).

As Rudge's account implies, there is little if any 'basic research' being undertaken in BT's laboratories, at least insofar as this refers to research undertaken without any practical or commercial objective in mind. According to this definition it may also be the case that there is little basic research undertaken in NTT. Nevertheless, there is a difference between the two companies. This becomes apparent in the role of NTT's Basic Research Laboratories which, together with so-called basic research in other parts of the Electrical Communications Laboratories, consumes about 6 per cent of NTT's total R&D budget and which has been protected as a priority area from budget cuts.[20] Although the Basic Research Laboratories is perhaps best characterised as undertaking longer term 'oriented basic research', it has differentiated its activities from the other laboratories in ECL also concerned with oriented basic research by concentrating largely on 'scientific' research, albeit research probably still undertaken with long term telecommunications needs in mind. According to a former director of this laboratory, the publications of this laboratory are now largely in scientific, as opposed to engineering, journals.[21]

Furthermore, in line with NTT's 'science/technology push' approach, neither the other ECL laboratories, nor the operating divisions, are given any formal role in influencing the agenda of the Basic Research Laboratories, although informally of course there is the possibility of influence.

In part this difference in emphasis is the result of the different obligation in BT and NTT to do research in the 'national interest'. Rudge is clear that this obligation, important pre-privatisation, is now non-existent: 'For research and technology [in BT], the first priority must be the BT Operating Divisions and the Corporate Headquarters. Recognizing BT's public sector background it has been emphasized that this first priority does not include "British Industry", the "UK Government" or even the "National Good" except where BT's interests coincide' (Rudge 1990, 117).

NTT's obligations are significantly different. Clause 2 of the NTT Company Law of 1984 (Nippon Denshin Denwa Kabushiki Kaisha Law), which provided for the part-privatisation of NTT, details NTT's responsibilities in connection with research:

NTT should make efforts to contribute to the improvement of telecommunications and increase the level of social welfare of the people by promoting basic-like and applied research in the area of telecommunications and also by diffusing the results of research, since telecommunications plays an important role for social and economic development of the future.

But although there clearly are important legal differences between BT and NTT regarding their obligations to do research in the public interest, it would be incorrect to reduce the differences between the two companies in the areas of basic and long term research to legal obligations. Enough has been said in this chapter about the differences in vision and managerial style between BT and NTT to support the conclusion that, even in the absence of legal obligations to do research in the national interest, a significant distinction between the two companies would still remain regarding the role of basic and long term research and the way in which this research is organised.

The assignment problem

Finally, we turn to the assignment problem, namely the question of whether R&D should be done in-house or ex-house.

Earlier we noted a significant difference between AT&T, BT, and NTT in terms of the strategic choices they have made regarding the acquisition of competences in network elements (broadly, telecommunications equipment). More specifically while AT&T opted for the internal development of these competences, BT chose to use the market, while NTT decided on the course of cooperative development with a small selected group of supplying companies.

It is necessary to emphasise, however, that these strategic choices do not simultaneously determine solutions to the assignment problem being discussed here. To take an example, even if a company decides to purchase switches or transmission systems on the market, it does not necessarily follow that it should do no research on switching or transmission. Similarly, if a company decides to internally or cooperatively develop switches or transmission systems it does not therefore follow that it should not buy-in some, even a significant part, of the research and development required. Accordingly, the strategic choice regarding the overall acquisition of competences does not determine whether R&D is required and, if so, whether it should be done in-house or ex-house.

To take this a little further, a company that buys its switches on the market may still require knowledge in the area of switching for at least two reasons. In the first place, the company will require switching knowledge in order to make an effective choice between the switching systems that are available on the market, and in order to install and efficiently implement the switches it purchases. Secondly, the company will also need knowledge to be able to anticipate future trends in the area of switching and to 'tap into' the networks that will provide information regarding trends. Such knowledge will help the company to make suitable decisions.

The question still remains, however, regarding whether the company should accumulate this knowledge in-house via research or whether it should rely on external sources for this knowledge. Choice of the latter alternative would have to confront the following conundrum: in order to acquire complex knowledge, an individual or company needs to already possess some of that knowledge. Furthermore, much of the knowledge that is needed is tacit with the result that it is difficult and costly to acquire, and perhaps in some cases even impossible. These kinds of difficulties may increase the incentive to accumulate the required knowledge in-house.

How have BT and NTT differed in terms of their decisions regarding the assignment problem? In the absence of available comparative information with which to answer this question we shall have to rely on circumstantial evidence. This evidence suggests that it is likely that, although both companies have accumulated knowledge through in-house research and have sourced knowledge externally, at the margin NTT is more likely than BT to have chosen the in-house option. This does seem to have been the outcome in the case of microelectronics. Thus Rudge (1990) has noted that as a result of BT's new forms of organisation analysed in this paper there has 'Over the past two years ... been a continuous change in the laboratories' activities. For example, in three technical areas of major importance to BT, we have seen a progressive decline in micro-electronics, a continued high level of activity in photonics and a major growth in software systems engineering.' Rudge continues, 'These relative changes have not been based upon scientific interest but the ability of the laboratories to provide specialist services to the operating divisions which are in keeping with their needs *and competitive with alternative sources which are available to them*' (129, emphasis added). Interestingly, a recent report on the re-organisation of Bell Laboratories stated that 'Over the past year [i.e. 1991] Penzias has ... begun sliding the balance of [research] funding away from high-cost and relatively low-payoff work, such as basic physics and materials science, toward the more lucrative software and information technologies'.[22]

In NTT research in areas such as microelectronics has continued, although the company's research leaders have acknowledged that they are coming under increasing pressure to demonstrate that research such as this pays.[23] Nevertheless, NTT is not without its critics regarding the wisdom of such research. In the case of microelectronics, for example, the prestigious Nikkei Communications has recently argued, not only that NTT's research in this area is now unnecessary as a result of the technological strength of the major Japanese manufacturing companies, but also that it may be counterproductive, interfering with the companies' research as NTT, a powerful customer, pulls research in directions that are not always productive (1990, Vol. 3, no. 4). The journal acknowledges that NTT made an important contribution to the early development of large scale integration in Japan, initiating the first major cooperative research programme in this area in 1975, a year before the much better known, but not necessarily more productive, cooperative programme initiated by MITI, the VLSI Research Project 1976–80.[24] It argues, nevertheless, that NTT's research in this area has now outrun its usefulness. While this is not the place to evaluate the arguments of Nikkei Communications regarding NTT's microelectronics research, it is simply noted that from the NTT point of view such research is seen as being important since it facilitates the design and development of more powerful devices which are crucial determinants of the effectiveness of network elements such as switches, computers, and customer premise equipment. With this in mind, NTT researchers believe that nanometer-scale fabrication technology and quantum-device technology will open the era of new visual, intelligent, and personal telecommunications services.[25] NTT's research leaders accordingly argue that microelectronics research, and device research more generally, should continue to play an important role in the company's overall strategy.

3.11 Conclusion

It is neither possible nor desirable to attempt to summarise the conclusions that may be drawn from the present complex comparison of AT&T, BT and NTT. Suffice it to say here that what we have analysed in this chapter are three very different 'beasts', which have reorganised themselves in the aftermath of divestiture, privatisation, and part-privatisation, and which are preparing themselves to do battle in increasingly integrated and liberalised global telecommunications markets. Although these beasts are operating in an increasingly similar global selection environment, their visions, strategies, and chosen competences are, as we have shown, significantly different. Whether these differences will be functional, in the sense that they will aid their growth in an increasingly difficult operating environment, or will be the source of significant shortcomings, is a crucial question, the answer to which will only emerge with time.

NOTES

1. See *Business Week*, 20 January 1992, p. 35 and Nikkei Weekly, 21 March 1992.
2. See *The Economist*, 10 March 1990, p. 12.
3. Conference on 'Communications after 2000 AD', the Royal Society, London, 18 and 19 March 1992.
4. For a more detailed discussion of the concept of vision, and the related concept of bounded vision, see Fransman (1990, 1991) and the introduction and first chapter to the present book.
5. Iain Vallance, quoted from Royal Society conference address. See note 3. See also Vallance (1990, pp. 84–7).
6. Remarks by Mr Iain Vallance, Chairman, British Telecom PLC to the Common Carrier Summit, Tokyo, 17 December 1990, p. 11.
7. Iain Vallance in answer to a question at the Royal Society conference.
8. See *Business Week*, 20 January 1992, p. 36.
9. Talk given by Mr Teruaki Ohara, Senior Vice President, Fair Competition Promotion Office, NTT, to the Anglo-Japanese High Technology Industry Forum, Tokyo, June, 1991, and talk given by Dr Iwao Toda, Executive Vice President, NTT, to the Royal Society conference; see note 3.
10. Interview with Dr Iwao Toda, NTT.
11. For a detailed account of the development of optical fiber technology in Japan and for the ATM and MIA projects, see Fransman (1992*b*).
12. For a comparative international analysis of the performance of NTT and AT&T in the area of switching, see Fransman (1992*a*).
13. The problems posed for market transactions by transaction-specific assets were first examined by Coase (1937). Williamson (1985) provides a more detailed elaboration on the importance of these assets. As we shall shortly see, these problems are reduced under CC and even more so, as Coase originally noted,

under VI. It is precisely because of problems such as transaction-specific assets and competition-induced uncertainty which arise under pure market conditions, and which can negatively affect the user-supplier relationship, which have led companies to attempt to modify these conditions while retaining the competitive option of switching suppliers. Thus, for example, BT in its publicity material intended for potential suppliers, has stressed that 'it is vital that we safeguard our position and that of our customers by buying only those goods and services which represent value for money'. This, however, requires that high standards of quality are attained by suppliers particularly of complex equipment that directly affects the services which BT sells to its customers. The attainment of these quality standards, however, requires that BT engage in quality-enhancing activities such as 'joint quality improvement projects', 'comprehensive monitoring of [post-purchase] performance', and the collection of 'information on whole life costs' (p. 4). But such activities are not always compatible with pure market practices where the user/purchaser may switch current suppliers in order to take advantage of more favourable price/performance offered by new suppliers. It is for this reason that Brian Rigby, BT's Director of Group Procurement Services, expresses the hope in the introduction to this document that 'if we choose to work together we can develop a long term, mutually beneficial relationship' (p. 1). Later it is reiterated that 'a close relationship with suppliers is essential. We need a partnership founded on trust, co-operation, support and, above all, continuous improvement' (p. 4). It is precisely these relational characteristics which the supporters of controlled competition claim necessitates the significant departure from a market relationship which controlled competition represents (BT 'Selling to BT. A Winning Partnership', undated).

14. See *Scientific American*, 'Rethinking Research', December 1991, pp. 92–3.
15. Of the eleven laboratories, three dealt with network and human interface issues (the Telecommunications Networks Laboratories, Communications and Information Processing Laboratories, and Human Interface Laboratories), three with systems (the Communication Switching Laboratories, Transmission Systems Laboratories, and Radio Communication Systems Laboratories), four with key technologies (the Software Laboratories, LSI Laboratories, Optoelectronics Laboratories, and Applied Electronics Laboratories), and one with basic research (the Basic Research Laboratories). In 1991 a new laboratory, the Communications Science Laboratory, was added, based in the Kansai area. At around the same time a new development center was announced, dealing with development of the optical subscriber loop.
16. Author's estimate and Table 3.6.
17. Interview with senior NTT research leader.
18. Interview with senior NTT research leader.
19. Interview with senior NTT research leader.
20. Author's estimate.
21. Interview with a former head of the NTT Basic Research Laboratories.
22. See *Scientific American*, Dec. 1991, p. 93.
23. Interviews with NTT research leaders.
24. For a detailed analysis of MITI's VLSI Research Project 1976–80 see Fransman (1990, ch. 3). For a brief discussion of the NTT VLSI project, see ibid. 87.
25. Communication from Dr Iwao Toda, NTT.

4

Visions of Corporate Organisation: From the Multidivisional to the Segmented Form of Organisation in AT&T, IBM, and NEC

4.1 Introduction

There has been a strong tendency for the modern large industrial corporation to become larger over time in terms of total sales as advantage has been taken of economies of scale and scope. Increasing size, however, raises new questions regarding organisation as the corporation grapples with the problem of how to coordinate, control, and formulate strategy for its activities. As this chapter shows, in answer to these questions of organisation the modern large industrial corporation has tended to become more decentralised at the same time as it has tended to increase in size. This tendency to become more decentralised is apparent in the adoption of the multidivisional form of organisation by some of the large US corporations from the 1920s.

However, while decentralisation provides a solution to some of the problems that arise with increasing size, decentralisation itself is the cause of further problems. Of particular concern in this chapter is the problem of interdependence of activities that have been decentralised. Such interdependence can be positively used by the corporation to produce important benefits flowing from synergies or economies of scope. However, synergies and economies of scope must be organised to be realised. This raises a key question: how should the modern large industrial corporation be organised in order to realise these benefits?

The difficulty may be expressed more concretely with reference to the three companies that are analysed here, namely AT&T, IBM, and NEC. All of these companies are fairly widely diversified, being multitechnology, multiproduct, and multidivisional companies in the information area. All face

This chapter was written before AT&T's voluntary trivestiture into three separate companies in September, 1995: AT&T (telecoms sevices), Lucent (telecoms equipment), and NCR (computers). This chapter was originally published as 'Different Folks, Different Strokes—How IBM, AT&T and NEC Segment to Compete', *Business Strategy Review*, 1994, 5(3), 1–20.

the problem of organising sufficient focus, flexibility, speed of response, and efficiency in order to compete. All confront vigorous competition from more highly specialised rivals such as Apple, Compaq, Intel, Microsoft, and Northern Telecom which operate in a more limited range of technologies and products. However, AT&T, IBM, and NEC also share a common vision regarding the potential competitive advantage that they can derive from their broader range of competences compared to their more specialised opponents. More specifically, they believe that their in-house possession of competences in areas such as semiconductors, software, and computers may allow them to deliver better information solutions to their customers than their specialised rivals.

The problem, however, is that synergies and economies of scope do not flow automatically. They have to be organised and there are costs of organising them. Furthermore, as already noted, there is a contradiction between the decentralisation of these companies and their need to coordinate activities across decentralised units if they are to realise the benefits of synergies and economies of scope.

What forms of organisation do these companies need to deal with these circumstances? There is a good deal of interpretive ambiguity surrounding this question. In the light of this interpretive ambiguity, what beliefs and visions of organisation have AT&T, IBM, and NEC constructed in order to cope with this question? It is the latter question that constitutes the crux of the present chapter.

4.2 Chapter Overview

The chapter begins by analysing the tendency for the modern large industrial corporation to decentralise by examining the transition from the unitary form of organisation (or U-Form) to the multidivisional form (or M-Form). The discussion then moves on to consider the difficulties arising in IBM and AT&T which led to major reorganisations of both these companies around 1990. It is shown that in order to deal with these difficulties IBM and AT&T have come to believe that their activities need to be further decentralised. It is this vision of organisation which led them to construct what is referred to in this chapter as a segmented form of organisation (or S-Form). The characteristics of the S-Form are then analysed by comparing it with the U-Form and the M-Form.

The case of NEC is then examined. It is shown that it was in 1965, when the company underwent its most significant organisational change since the war, that NEC adopted an S-Form of organisation. However, by the early 1990s NEC's leaders came to the conclusion that their existing form of organisation needed further changes in order to realise the company's vision of competing through synergies and economies of scope in the areas of semiconductors, computers, and communications. This resulted in a major reorganisation of the company in 1991–2, the biggest since 1965.

The final part of the chapter deals with the different ways in which AT&T, IBM and NEC, in the light of their different visions of organistion, have attempted to coordinate their activities in order to realise synergies and economies of scope within the context of their decentralised S-Forms of organisation. These modes of coordination are categorised and their strengths and weaknesses analysed.

4.3 Decentralisation in the Large Corporation

Decentralisation has been one of the main long run tendencies in the organisation of the modern large corporation. This tendency can be seen clearly in the transition from the so-called unitary form of organisation to the multidivisional form. The tendency is further accentuated with the emergence from the late 1980s of what is arguably a new form of organisation, which may be termed the segmented form.

4.3.1 From the U-Form to the M-Form

From the 1920s a major change occurred in the organisation of the American large corporation, although the existence, significance, and causes of this change were only appreciated from the early 1960s. The change referred to was the transformation from the centralised, functionally departmentalised, or unitary form of organisation—the U-Form—to the multidivisional form based on semiautonomous operating divisions organised along product, brand, or geographic lines, the M-Form. This widespread transformation affected large corporations in industries such as electrical and electronics, power machinery, automobiles, and chemicals. The first companies to adopt the M-Form included Du Pont and General Motors. The distinction between the U-Form and the M-Form is shown in Fig. 4.1.

Why did the transformation form the U-Form to the M-Form occur? The classical answer to this question was given by the Harvard business historian, Alfred Chandler, in his seminal book *Strategy and Structure* (1962) which was the first book to analyse this transformation in detail. Chandler explained the transformation in terms of the weaknesses of the U-Form which he summarised in the following way:

The inherent weakness in the centralised, functionally departmentalized operating company... became critical only when the administrative load on the senior exec-

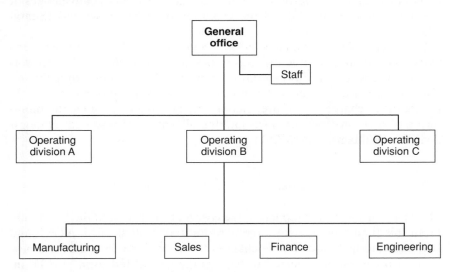

Fig. 4.1 The unitary and multidivisional forms

utives increased to such an extent that they were unable to handle their entrepreneurial responsibilities efficiently. This situation arose when the operations of the enterprise became too complex and the problems of coordination, appraisal, and policy formulation too intricate for a small number of top officers to handle both long-run, entrepreneurial, and short-run operational administrative activities (Chandler 1962, 382–3).

The M-Form, on the other hand as Chandler noted, was able to deal effectively with these shortcomings:

The basic reason for its success was simply that it clearly removed the executives responsible for the destiny of the entire enterprise from the more routine operational activities, and so gave them the time, information, and even psychological commitment for long-term planning and appraisal.... [The] new structure left the broad strategic decisions as to the allocation of existing resources and the acquisition of new ones in the hands of a top team of generalists. Relieved of operating duties and tactical decisions, a general executive was less likely to reflect the position of just one part of the whole   (Chandler, 1962, 382–3)

There were two major features of the M-Form which enabled it to overcome the weaknesses of the U-Form. The first entailed the *decomposition* of the corporation into a number of semiautonomous units—the divisions—which were relatively independent of one another. The relative independence of the divisions meant that a change could be made in their activities without having to change the rest of the corporation. In this way the efficiency and flexibility of the corporation was increased. In the 1960s the Nobel Prize laureate, Herbert Simon, had elaborated on the advantages of decomposition in his study of the evolution of complex systems (Simon 1981).

However, as Oliver Williamson—an economist who has used Chandler's work to develop economic theories of organisation—has noted, there was more to the M-Form of organisation than the decomposition of activities. The second feature of the M-Form was the establishment of a general corporate office charged with three major tasks: strategic planning, the monitoring of divisional performance, and the allocation of resources amongst divisions (Williamson 1985, 281).

4.3.2 From the M-Form to the S-Form

The M-Form served the modern large corporation well until the late 1980s. From this time a number of large corporations, such as IBM, AT&T, and ICI, began to make qualitative changes to the M-Form introducing a new form of organisation, referred to here as the segmented form or S-Form. The shortcomings of the M-Form and the transition to the S-Form can be illustrated by the case of IBM.

The case of IBM

One of the main advantages of the M-Form arose from its liberation of the senior executives running the corporation from involvement in the day-to-day activities of the operating divisions. By delegating responsibility for these activities to managers in charge of the operating divisions, the senior executives were able to avoid becoming overloaded by the information processing needs of the corporation as a whole. The decomposition of the corporation implied by the M-Form meant, therefore, that much of the information could be processed by the operating divisions, leaving the senior executives free to concentrate on strategy, monitoring, and resource allocation. In short, in Williamson's terminology, the M-Form allowed the corporation to 'economise on bounded rationality', that is to reduce the demands made on the limited information processing capabilities of the senior executives. Furthermore, Williamson argued, the reservation of strategic decisions to the general corporate office 'reduced partisan political input into the resource allocation process' (Williamson 1985, 296).

By the late 1980s, however, IBM discovered that the information processing advantages of the M-Form were insufficient to prevent the company from suffering a dramatic reversal in its profitability and growth. At the beginning of 1993, IBM announced what was then the biggest loss in corporate history. Why did IBM suffer this reversal in its fortunes? The reason was not excessive demands made on the limited information processing capabilities of the company's senior executives. The reversal had more to do with the *beliefs* of the dominant senior executives which led them to *interpret* the information at their disposal in ways that later turned out to be erroneous. More concretely, until as late as 1991 these executives believed that IBM's performance continued to rest on the mainframe computer as it had in the past. Paradoxically, IBM, the information processing company *par excellence*, was unable to interpret correctly the increasing information which provided evidence for the substitution of smaller, more powerful computers for mainframes. This substitution, based on the availability of increasingly powerful microprocessors, undermined the high profit margins that IBM earned on mainframes and thus undercut the company's profitability and growth.

The belief in the mainframe, together with IBM's failure to maintain its overwhelming technological lead, resulted in the company's senior executives becoming ever more reactionary. (For the evidence see the recent books on IBM by Ferguson and Morris (1993), Carroll (1994), and Heller (1994).) After the failure of IBM's Future Systems project, which was intended to produce a great leap forward in computer technology rendering obsolete the company's existing System 370, the senior executives became increasingly conservative. System 370 mainframes were now seen as the company's workhorses and new technologies and products which might compete were frustrated and even discouraged.

As a result new technologies such as RISC (reduced instruction set) microprocessors, which are currently launching a challenge to become the standard in this area, were not given the support they merited. Ironically, RISC, invented in IBM, was exploited by other companies, notably Sun, which used the technology for its workstations which competed with IBM's large computers at the bottom end of the market. Although after it introduced its own personal computer IBM rapidly captured the major share of the market, it was nevertheless a late entrant. The company's belief in the mainframe led it to contract out the key components of the personal computer, the operating system and the microprocessors, which in turn facilitated the triumph of two of IBM's most successful competitors, Microsoft and Intel.

From an *organisational* point of view (the main concern of this chapter), it is clear that the M-Form, contrary to the assertions of Chandler and Williamson, did not prevent a partisan bias on the part of the corporation's senior executives. While these executives were freed from the routine activities of the operating divisions, the 'mainframe lobby' and the corresponding belief in the mainframe exerted a dominant influence in the corporation. Since strategy was formulated centrally, this group and its thinking dominated the company as a whole to the detriment of a focus on new, increasingly important products and technologies. The centralised strategic decision-making process and its emphasis on mainframes meant the IBM lacked the flexibility and speed of response that was necessary to take advantage of the new opportunities.

In an attempt to deal with these shortcomings which were a by-product of the M-form John Akers, Chairman of IBM, introduced a major organisational change in December 1991. This was perhaps the most important legacy that he left IBM after he was forced out of office in 1993. Lou Gerstner, who replaced him, has not yet made any major modifications to this reorganisation. (It is worth stressing, however, that the weakness of the M-Form was not a necessary shortcoming. Although the centralisation of strategic decision-making in the M-Form allowed an incorrect set of beliefs—beliefs in the mainframe—to dominate the entire corporation, this was not inevitable. It was possible that senior management, with or without the assistance of members of the Board, could have given greater encouragement to new products and technologies which challenged mainframes. In the event, however, this did not happen.)

From M-form to S-form in IBM　　What are the main differences between the multidivisional form and the segmented form, the M-Form and the S-Form? The major difference is a tilt in the balance of power between the corporation and the divisions (or business units as they are sometimes called) in favour of the latter. While under the M-Form it was the general office which assumed sole responsibility for strategy formulation, monitoring, and resource allocation between divisions, in the S-Form the first of these functions is shared to a significantly greater extent with the divisions.

In the case of IBM the shift in the balance of power was clearly intended to increase the focus and hence the competitiveness of the businesses. As stated in 'IBM Management System', a company document published in June 1992 to clarify the details of the 'fundamental re-definition of IBM' announced by John Akers in December 1991, the aim of the reorganisation is 'to create an IBM that is a family of more focused . . . more competitive businesses' (IBM Management System 1992, 5).

The shift in the balance of power is evident in the company's new self-definition as 'an array of increasingly autonomous businesses and independent companies' (IBM Annual Report, 1994). Under the reorganisation this 'array' consists of thirteen relatively autonomous operating units. These operating units are divided into two main types: business units, of which there are nine, which are in charge of the manufacture and development of various parts and kinds of computer systems; and geographic units, of which there are four, which deal with sales in different parts of the world.

The balance of power change is most clear in the strategic functions that have now been delegated to these operating units. While, according to 'IBM Management System', the corporation's Management Committee retains the responsibility to 'develop and communicate IBM's vision, business definition, and worldwide strategies' (20), the business and geographic units are expected to 'prepare and execute worldwide plans' (10) to achieve their objectives in support of the corporation's vision and strategies.[1] While the change in the balance of power compared to the M-Form is apparent, the document emphasises that although the units have been given greater autonomy, they remain a part of, and are subordinated to, the corporation as a whole: 'While the management system provides significant autonomy to the operating units, its principal purpose is to assure that the goals and objectives of the IBM Corporation are achieved' (6). The Management Committee also retains the other corporate functions of monitoring of performance and allocation of resources.

In this way, by tilting the balance of power to some extent to the operating units, the corporation hopes to give greater authority to the units to pursue their own markets in their own ways, less encumbered by the central strategic decisions of the corporation as a whole. The intention is that this will enable the units to seize the opportunities provided by new products and technologies and therefore compete more effectively with other independent companies.

The case of AT&T

AT&T also arrived at the S-Form although via a very different route compared to IBM. Indeed, AT&T introduced its S-Form reorganisation in November 1988, some three years earlier than IBM.

In August 1982 the agreement between the US Justice Department and AT&T was signed which divested the company. This separated AT&T from the seven newly created regional operating companies, the so-called Baby Bells. Divestiture left AT&T with three main areas of activity: long lines, which provided long-distance telecommunications services; the former Western Electric, which produced telecommunications equipment; and Bell Laboratories, which undertook research and development.

The pre-divestiture form of organisation of AT&T is probably best characterised as U-Form since the company was organised largely on the basis of function. It was a form of organisation that reflected the monopolistic position in telecommunications that the company had enjoyed since shortly after its inception. With its focus on products, brands, or geographical markets, the M-Form was more adapted to competitive conditions.

At the time of divestiture, two weaknesses of the company's existing organisational structure soon became apparent. The first, again a reflection of AT&T's former monopolistic status, was that costs could not be readily assigned to the company's activities. The second weakness was that AT&T lacked a focus on customer segments and was therefore not geared up to deal with the competition that was to come from the new competitors such as MCI and GTE Sprint.

In order to deal with these shortcomings, in May 1983 AT&T announced that it would be reorganised on the basis of seven 'lines of business'. These lines of business were mainly defined in terms of products—such as network systems, components and electronic systems, and information systems—and represented AT&T's first move to an M-Form of organisation. However, it was only after Robert E. Allen took over as Chairman of AT&T in April 1988 after the sudden death of his predecessor, James E. Olson, that AT&T made its decisive move to the S-Form.

Allen wasted no time in moving to fundamentally reorganise the company. Shortly after he was installed, a major review of organisational and management issues began. By as soon as 4 November 1988 Allen met with AT&T's senior officers and presented them with his document, 'A Direction For AT&T'. This document spelled out what Allen saw as the main weaknesses in AT&T's existing form of organisation and outlined the new organisational directions that he envisaged for the company, referred to here as an S-Form.

From M-form to S-form in AT&T   Allen's diagnosis of AT&T's shortcomings was brief but incisive:

Today we are too interdependent; responsibilities are not clear cut; too many businesses must 'sign off' before decisions are made, much less carried out. Worship at the altars of centralisation, economies of scale and vertical integration—all matters worthy of consideration but not blind adherence—has split accountabilities. It has saddled business unit managers with sizeable costs they cannot control. It has occasionally blurred achievement, sometimes veiled failure and frequently left managers frustrated   (Allen, '*A Direction for AT&T*', 1988).

Despite its introduction of M-Form 'lines of business' more than 5 years earlier, AT&T in Allen's view was still too 'interdependent' and 'centralised'. This was a similar problem to that being encountered in IBM where the M-Form allowed the 'mainframe lobby' to dominate the company.

What was Allen's solution to the problems he had diagnosed? Allen made clear that it was only through an increasing segmentation of the corporation that the benefits of focus, increasing accountability and responsibility, and hence greater competitiveness could be achieved: 'I believe we must *focus our businesses*. We must create customer- or market-focused business units whose leaders have as much control as possible over their destiny. They must be both acountable *and* responsible—with as much freedom as possible—with the resources required to succeed . . . or fail'.

Indeed, Allen went so far as to drive the segmentation principle below the level of the business units (something that IBM also proposed in its 1991 document): 'And, to the extent feasible, we should push this principle below the business unit—focusing sub-units on discrete customer groups, market segments or product families'.

It is clear from these statements that Allen was envisaging a greater degree of segmentation than was conventional in the M-Form. He proposed a further departure from the M-Form when he suggested turning the organisation of AT&T 'on its head', with the customers on top, the business units and subunits on the next level responding to the needs of the customers, and the corporate headquarters one level lower, supporting the businesses and their strategies, rather than leading them.

In pursuit of this organisational vision, AT&T established four Groups containing an initial total of nineteen business units. The four groups are: Communications Services, which sells telecommunications services provided from AT&T's network; Network Systems, which sells the equipment needed to operate the network such as switches; Communications Products, which sells end-user products such as telephones, videophones, and personal communicators; and NCR, which sells computers and computing services.

4.3.3 U-Form, M-Form, and S-Form Compared

The U-Form, M-Form, and S-Form are compared in Fig. 4.2. These three forms of corporate organisation are compared along two dimensions, represented on the Y and X axes respectively. The first dimension is the degree of autonomy granted to the company's operating units. In the terminology of Herbert Simon, this is a measure of the degree of decomposition of the company. The second dimension is the degree of centralisation of strategy formulation.

As Fig. 4.2 shows, the U-Form is located in the bottom-left quadrant. In the U-Form the (functionally-defined) operating units have little autonomy since decision-making is centralised in the corporate office. Similarly, strat-

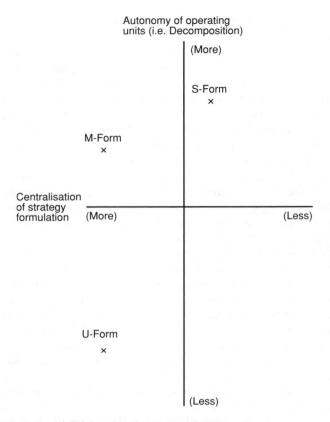

Fig. 4.2 Unitary, multidivisional and segmented forms

egy formulation is a centralised corporate function. The M-Form is located in the top-left quadrant. Strategy formulation remains a centralised corporate function since one of the main objectives of the M-Form was to free the company's top executives from the routine activities of the operating units in order to concentrate their energies on strategy, monitoring, and resource allocation. However, in the M-Form the operating units enjoy significantly more autonomy than under the U-Form.

The S-Form is located in the top-right quadrant. As emerges clearly from the studies of IBM and AT&T above, under the S-Form the operating units enjoy a greater degree of autonomy (as well as responsibility and accountability) than under the M-Form. It may be that the units are also smaller and focused on more narrowly defined market segments than in the case of the M-Form. At the same time, the S-Form strategy formulation, though still a central function for the corporation as a whole, is shared to a greater extent with the operating units than in the case of the M-Form. In this way the units are given greater responsibility for their destiny. In turn, it is hoped, the S-Form will yield a greater focus and responsiveness to the demands of unit customers than could be provided through the M-Form with its more centralised strategic function.

The case of NEC

NEC provides an interesting contrast to IBM and AT&T. NEC is an information and communication company *par excellence* being the only company in the world to hold positions in the top ten (in terms of global sales) in each of the three key markets of computers, telecommunications equipment, and semiconductors (see Chapter 2). By contrast, IBM has failed to establish itself in telecommunications equipment despite an attempt in the 1980s, while it is only with its recent acquisition of NCR that AT&T has established itself in the computer industry.

NEC is significantly smaller than IBM and AT&T. While in 1993 the latter two had sales of around $65 billion, NEC's sales were $33 billion. Despite its smaller size, however, NEC has been significantly more decentralised than the two American companies with an S-Form of organisation since 1965.

Up to 1965 NEC had a plant-based form of organisation with functions such as finance, marketing, and personnel concentrated in the corporate office. This form of organisation presented two major problems. The first, in line with Chandler's analysis of the shortcomings of the U-Form, was the overloading of the company's top executives as NEC grew in size and complexity. Secondly, the centralisation of the marketing function meant that the operating units were unable to efficiently receive feedback from, and respond to, the requirements of their markets.

In order to deal with these problems, Koji Kobayashi, who became President of NEC in 1964, introduced the company's most important reorganisation in 1965. NEC was divided into fourteen divisions which in turn were aggregated into four product groups: telecommunications equipment, computers, semiconductors, and home electronics. Each division was given the same kind of autonomy assigned by IBM and AT&T to its business units in the early 1990s. In Kobayashi's words, the head of each division 'would have the same authority and responsibilities as the head of an independent company' (Kobayashi 1991, 19) Division heads reported to a Group, likened to a holding company.

NEC's fourteen divisions in 1965 were obviously significantly smaller than AT&T's nineteen groups established in 1989 and IBM's nine business units set up in 1991. But NEC's decentralisation in 1965 went even further with the spinning-off of a number of wholly-owned, but semi-autonomous, subsidiaries outside the greater Tokyo area. These subsidiaries, grouped for organisational purposes with divisions in the same product area, were run as relatively independent companies under their own executive officers.

Semi-autonomous subsidiaries have continued to be important in NEC which in 1992 had 66 consolidated subsidiaries in Japan and a further 20 consolidated subsidiaries overseas.

It is clear, therefore, that NEC has been, and remains, a significantly more decentralised company than its Western counterparts, justifying the claim that it has been an S-Form company since the mid-1960s. And it is worth noting that in this respect NEC is similar to the other major Japanese companies such as Fujitsu, Hitachi, and Toshiba although there are some important organisational differences between them.

However, just how this greater degree of segmentation in Japanese companies is to be *explained* is a difficult question. One possible explanation is that life-time employment, and the tighter degree of integration and co-ordination that it facilitated, meant that there was less need for centralised monitoring and control and therefore greater opportunity for decentralisation.

4.4 The Problem Of Interdependence

As the above studies show, IBM, AT&T, and NEC have become an 'array' (in IBM's terminology) of more focused, more independent, business units. At the same time, however, the activities of these units have become more interdependent as a result of the integrative nature of the technologies and products that comprise the information and communication industry. This integrative nature is clear from the increasing connectivity and networking of products and technologies that previously stood alone. The replacement of large mainframe computers by distributed networks of personal computers, the networking of these personal computers into local area networks, and their connection to national and international switched communication networks based on optical fibre and microwave radio, provide an example.

The organisational dilemma presented by the coexistence of relatively independent business units and the need to coordinate them in order to realise the benefits of interdependence, or synergies, was well expressed by Bob Allen in his 1988 memorandum on AT&T's reorganisation:

Where synergy among business units exists, it must be leveraged—or at least examined—not ignored. Business unit conflicts and the allocation of finite resources must be managed to optimize AT&T's bottom line. These are just some of the obvious responsibilities and issues that are superimposed on a 'focused' business. But let me be clear, the bias is to place responsibility and accountability with the business unit. Centralization will have to meet the test of corporate necessity within this context.

What are the implications for the large company caught between these two contradictory tendencies: on the one hand, increasing internal segmentation into smaller, more independent, business units; on the other hand, increasing interdependence between the activities of these business units?

The main implication is that the company needs to find an effective way of *coordinating* the activities of its business units if it is to provide competitive integrated systems that meet the needs of its customers. What alternative modes of coordination are available to the company?

4.4.1 Alternative Modes of Coordinating Interdependent Business Units

The alternative modes of coordination are shown in Fig. 4.3. At the one extreme, the *external market alternative*, the company has the option of becoming fully decomposed, that is breaking itself up into a number of totally independent companies. These companies are free to enter into market contracts with each other or with other companies in order to realise the commercial opportunities that are available through the sale of integrated systems.

It is significant, however, that none of the large companies in the global information and communication industry has resorted to this option, although after Lou Gerstner assumed the leadership of IBM in 1993 it was seriously considered as an alternative. Logically, the external market alternative can only be rejected if the company believes that the returns produced by keeping all the businesses in the same corporate organisation will exceed the sum of the returns produced by each of the businesses if they became totally independent companies. Since the external market alternative has been rejected by these companies, it can be inferred that they hold this belief. What is the basis for this belief?

The basis is the further belief that coordination within the company, rather than coordination through the external market, will be more effec-

EXTERNAL COORDINATION		INTERNAL COORDINATION	
External market	**Internal market**	**Direction**	
1. Market contracting	2. Internal contracting	3.	Corporate management committee
		4.	Group organisation
		5.	Integrated systems organisation

Fig. 4.3 Modes of coordinating interdependent business units

tive in realising the total potential value of the company's resources. This raises two questions. First, why might the external market fail to provide the necessary coordination as efficiently? Second, what internal modes of coordination are available (i.e. within the company) and what are their strengths and weaknesses?

The answer to the first question hinges on the notion of 'positive externalities', that is where a company's activities produce potential benefits for other companies but the company is unable to reap sufficient reward in return for providing these benefits. As a result it does not produce these external benefits. For example, a company producing microprocessors might accumulate knowledge that would benefit producers of computers, but might be unable to sell this knowledge to the latter. The reason may be that computer producers lack information regarding the existence of this knowledge. Or it may be that the computer producers are unable to assess the value of this knowledge without possessing it in the first place. They are therefore unable to offer a price for the knowledge. But if they were given the knowledge in order to value it, it would have been given without any charge and therefore without any return to the microprocessor producer.

Difficulties such as this may prevent the external market mode of coordination from producing all the benefits that are potentially available. On the other hand, coordination inside a company may be able to realise these benefits by circumventing the need to conclude a contract. For example, a company may encourage the exchange of information between its business units without having first to calculate the costs and benefits to the units of the exchange. It is this kind of reasoning that underlies the argument that *synergies* provide the justification for maintaining the coherence of the company and not breaking it up into several completely independent companies.

We turn now to the second question, internal modes of coordination.

4.4.2 Internal Modes of Coordination

As Fig. 4.3 shows, there are four main internal modes of coordinating the activities of interdependent business units: internal contracting; the corporate management committee; the group layer of organisation; and the integrated systems form of organisation. In this section we will examine the use made by IBM, AT&T, and NEC of these modes.

Internal contracting

One important mode used by all the companies involves reproducing within the company the external market mechanism of contracting in order to facilitate coordination between the business units, while simultaneously requiring the units to behave in ways that will require them to generate the desired positive externalities. For example, IBM's Management System states that 'Relationships among units are established by agreements which reflect marketplace practices. . . . These [contracts] are business, not legal, instruments which summarize performance objectives, measurements, deliverables, prices, etc. Their terms and conditions and commitment enforcement are to, in general, conform to prevalent industry practice' (IBM Management System, undated, 15–17).

However, the document goes on to assert that 'Contracts and agreements are not the only conditions of acceptable and expected behavior' (19). For instance, in a section titled 'management system considerations' it is stated that each unit 'has the need to be a citizen of the company and balance . . . its own performance and potential impact on other operating units or the corporation as a whole' (8).

More concretely, the responsibilities assigned to business units include that they will 'continue to support certain cross-business product synergy activities and internal/external standards' (11). Furthermore, it is stated that business units 'generally will not compete with other business units, although overlaps may exist' and that the business unit 'is the preferred supplier to other operating units with the right of first refusal' (10). In this way IBM's management system tries to use internally the market-like mode of coordination while attempting through central direction to obviate its shortcomings.

Corporate management committee

All three companies also have corporate management committees with powers to override the internal market mechanism in the interests of the company as a whole. For example, AT&T has a Management Executive Committee, which is responsible for the company's overall vision and strategic direction, and an Operations Committee which oversees implementation. It is the latter committee, consisting of the executives of the four groups and the Chief Finance Officer, which is charged with the realisation of synergies from the interdependencies of the business groups. As expressed in a recent feature article on AT&T in *Fortune*:

The idea is that none of these guys can possibly make the right operational decisions for the company without thoroughly understanding what each of the others is doing. From that will flow the elusive virtue synergy, as well as carefully considered tradeoffs among groups when conflicts arise. The committee members' bonuses are based in roughly equal proportions on the performance of their group and of AT&T as a whole   (*Fortune*, May 17, 1993).

Group layer of organisation

Both AT&T and NEC have selected to have an additional layer of organisation for the purposes of internal coordination, namely their Groups which aggregate divisions within the same group of products. IBM, however, does not have such a layer, relying solely on the Management Committee to provide the necessary coordination. In IBM's view, evidently, the costs of an additional layer of organisation are not sufficiently compensated for by the benefits of coordination and monitoring that the groups provide.

Integrated systems form of organisation

In its most important reorganisation since 1965, begun in July 1991 and completed in July 1992, NEC went significantly beyond AT&T and IBM by reorganising its groups on the basis of *integrated information and communications systems* rather than stand-alone products. These integrated systems are called C&C systems (computer and communications systems) in NEC. In this way it is hoped that the activities of the company's relatively autonomous divisions will be better coordinated so as to produce more customer-friendly integrated systems. The thrust of the reorganisation is shown in Fig. 4.4.

4.5 Conclusion

This chapter has shown how IBM, AT&T, and NEC, three of the largest and most important diversified companies in the global information and communication industry, have dealt with the problems of decentralisation and interdependence. It has been shown that none of them has resorted to the radical step of breaking the company up into a number of smaller, completely independent companies. Rather, through their reorganisations of the 1990s and in somewhat different ways, they have attempted to increase focus, flexibility, speed of response, and efficiency by segmenting their activities to a greater extent while developing internal modes of coordination to reap the potential benefits of interdependence, or synergies, between the activities of their business units.

Will their efforts succeed? The answer to this crucial question depends on two factors. First, will the process of segmentation, a process that is still occurring *within* the confines of a large company, produce as much focus, flexibility, speed of response, and efficiency as that possessed by their competitors? Second, will the costs of internal coordination (implied by the activities of additional layers of organisation such as the group structure and corporate management committees) be more than outweighed by the benefits of internally generated interdependence, or synergy?

Over time the answers to these two further questions will become evident in the outcome of the competitive battles being waged by the three com-

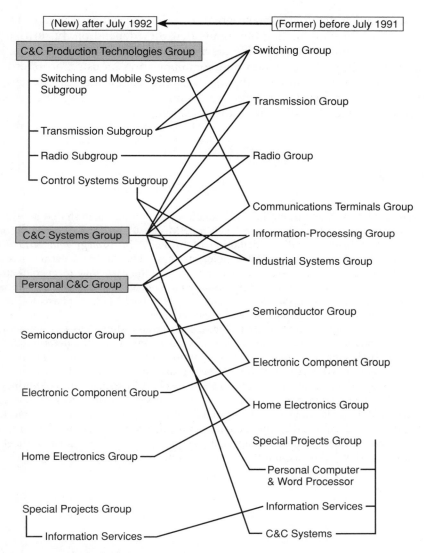

Fig. 4.4 Comparison of NEC's former and new organisation

panies with their smaller competitors—for example, IBM with Compaq and Dell in personal computers, Sun in workstations, Intel in microprocessors, and Microsoft in software for smaller computers; AT&T with MCI in telecommunications services and Ericsson and Northern Telecom in telecommunications equipment; and NEC with a similar group of competitors. These smaller competitors, concentrating on a narrower range of markets and technologies, make greater use of the external market as a mechanism for coordinating the inputs that they depend on. In turn, this competitive outcome will provide the answer to one of the great outstanding debates in the information and communication industry: do interdependencies, or synergies, justify the size and complexity of the large diversified companies that have so far dominated this industry? The jury, it must be concluded, is still out on this question.

NOTE

1. The extent to which the strategy formulation function has been shared between the corporate and operating unit levels in IBM's post-1991 form of organisation is evident from Chandler's definition of 'strategy' in *Strategy and Structure* (Chandler 1962). According to Chandler, strategy, which in the M-Form is a corporate function, is defined as 'the determination of the basic long-term goals and objectives of an enterprise, *and the adoption of courses of action and the allocation of resources necessary for carrying out these goals*' (13, emphasis added). While in IBM the first part of the definition remains a corporate function, the second part—given here in italics—has been largely shifted to the operating units. Chandler continues, elaborating on what he means by 'the determination of the basic long-term goals' and 'the adoption of courses of action': 'Decisions to expand the volume of activities, to set up distant plants and offices, to move into new economic functions, or become diversified along many lines of business involve the defining of new basic goals. New courses of action must be devised and resources allocated and reallocated in order to achieve these goals and to maintain and expand the firm's activities in the new areas in response to shifting demands, changing sources of supply, fluctuating economic conditions, new technological developments, and the actions of competitors' (13).

5

A Vision of the Japanese Innovation System and How It Works

5.1 Introduction

What influence has the Japanese government had on the innovation and competitiveness of Japanese companies? Is the process of innovation in Japan and the institutions which influence this process similar to that in Western countries or is it distinctive?

A significant amount of interpretive ambiguity surrounds these questions as is evident in the very different answers that have been constructed by different analysts. For example, some have argued that the Japanese government has had a major impact on the innovation and competitiveness of Japanese companies in particular industries through its influence on the priorities set by these companies and the resources allocated to them. According to this view, Japan has had a 'strong' state which has intervened decisively to promote the development of the country through the significant degree of influence that it has wielded over Japanese companies. Other analysts, however, have constructed a very different vision of how the innovation process in Japan works. Contradicting the first view, they emphasise the importance of Japanese companies com-peting through innovation in strongly competitive markets. According to the latter vision, the Japanese government plays primarily a market-conforming role and in doing so spends relatively small amounts on research and development compared with the governments of the other major Western countries.

In view of this interpretive ambiguity, the aim of this chapter is not to attempt to produce 'the' definitive account of the innovation process in Japan. Rather, an effort is made to examine the roles played by three key institutions that are central to the innovation process in Japan (as in any other country), namely, companies, government, and universities. These three interacting institutions form a crucial part of what is referred to as the Japanese Innovation System.

An earlier version of this chapter was prepared as a background paper for a conference on Japan organised by the British Parliament's Science Committee held at the Royal Society, November 1992. See *Science in Parliament*, 49/4 (October 1992), 23–8. This chapter was originally published as 'The Japanese Innovation System: How it works', *Prometheus*, 1994, 12(1), 36–45.

5.2 Chapter Overview

The chapter begins with a summary of the innovation process in Japanese companies. Here particular attention is paid to several distinctive Japanese forms of organisation, such as the life-time employment system (referred to in the Japanese context as the assumption of no exit) and the importance of committed shareholders. The effects of these forms of organisation on the innovation process are examined.

The influence of the Japanese government on the innovation process is then analysed. It is argued that, while the 'engine' of innovation is located in Japanese companies, organs of the Japanese government have played an important supportive role in facilitating the innovation process. Attention is then turned to the part played by the Ministry of International Trade and Industry (MITI). While it has often been argued that MITI is the most important organ of the Japanese government in terms of impact on the process of industrial innovation, MITI's expenditure on R&D is dwarfed by that of the Ministry of Education and the Science and Technology Agency. How is this paradox to be explained? This question is answered in terms of MITI's location at the center of a vast information processing network.

Finally, attention is turned briefly to the role of universities in the Japanese Innovation System. It is argued that, although Japanese universities are often weaker than their leading counterparts in the other major industrialised countries in terms of their contribution to frontier research, the Japanese university system nevertheless makes an important contribution to the innovation process in Japan.

5.3 Background

It is now widely accepted that innovation drives competition at both the corporate and national levels. And in order to survive in a market-interdependent world, it is essential to become and remain competitive. This paper is concerned with the innovation process in Japan and with the major factors that influence it. Questions such as the following are examined: To what extent is innovation and the competitiveness that follows from it the result of the activities of the private sector in Japan? What role is played by the Japanese government and its various ministries? How great is the contribution of Japanese universities to the innovation process?

The examination of these questions hinges on the notion of the Japanese Innovation System (JIS). JIS is a complex system comprising processes, institutions, and forms of organisation. These include the market process, intra- and inter-corporate organisation, government regulation and intervention, and university teaching and research.

As with any complex system, the analysis of JIS involves a simplification, an abstraction of some of the major factors which influence the system and its behaviour and performance. This chapter accordingly will examine some of the major features of JIS without delving into some of the complexities that would require more space than is available here.

Before proceeding with the analysis, however, a word of caution is necessary. Like the proverbial elephant, JIS can be all things to all people. For example, those who see market forces as the motor of capitalism see in JIS: cut-throat competition between Japanese companies and a government which spends a relatively small proportion of national income while ensuring that its interventions are exclusively of a market-conforming kind. On the other hand, those who believe in the virtues of government intervention see in JIS: a strong state which is oriented to the development of the nation's economy and which is prepared to put considerable pressure on Japanese companies to move in the directions which the government feels are desirable. The result has been a vigorous debate between the proponent of these two views (or versions of them) on the effects of industrial policy in Japan which shows little sign of abating.

5.4 Japanese Companies' Role in the Innovation Process

One measure of the role of private industry in Japan in the innovation process is its contribution to total expenditure on R&D. According to this measure private industry contributes about 76 per cent, to the total, while government contributes about 18 per cent, and universities about 5 per cent.

From the point of view of competitiveness, however, this considerably underestimates the role of Japanese companies since much innovation which has an important positive effect on competitiveness is of an incremental kind and takes place on the factory floor (sometimes referred to as 'blue collar R&D') and therefore is not recorded in R&D statistics. (The absolute size of R&D expenditures of the major Japanese companies is worth emphasising. To get this into perspective, the R&D expenditures of the top five Japanese R&D spenders—Hitachi, Toyota, Matsushita, NEC, and Fujitsu—is as great (in terms of purchasing power parity) as the total R&D expenditure of the entire private sector in Britain.)

It may accordingly be concluded that the bulk of expenditure on innovation is undertaken by the private sector in and for this sector. This is particularly true with respect to the 'downstream' portion of R&D, that is the applied research and development portion where the Japanese government and its various organs have little influence. In the following section more will be said about the role of the Japanese government in the innovation process.

Since innovation in JIS is largely the responsibility of Japanese companies, it is necessary to say a little more regarding the factors that influence the innovation process in these companies. Before doing so, however, another caveat is necessary. That is that, as Michael Porter has emphasised in his book, *The Competitive Advantage of Nations* (Porter 1990), while Japan has produced some sectors that have been outstandingly successful in terms of international competitiveness, this by no means applies to all or even most sectors of the Japanese economy. Thus, while consumer electronics, machine tools, motor cars, and memory semiconductors are included in the outstandingly successful sectors, microprocessors, complex telecommunications equipment, chemicals, and pharmaceuticals must be excluded. To stamp all Japanese companies and sectors with the 'success stamp' would be to miss an essential part of the Japanese story.

In most sectors, however—including microprocessors, complex telecommunications equipment, chemicals and pharmaceuticals—Japanese companies tend to be committed and patient innovators. This commitment and patience is attributable to a number of interrelated factors. One of these factors is the generally intense competition that Japanese companies face in both the domestic and international markets. Competition through innovation is a common response on the part of the Japanese companies to this competitive pressure.

The Japanese market, however, does not only provide a source of pressure which motivates innovation. It also provides users of products and processes who are extremely sophisticated and demanding regarding what they are willing to accept and who generally have alternative sources of supply if a supplier is unwilling or unable to comply with their demands. This demanding environment also generates feedback for companies and gives them the opportunity to learn how to improve their products and processes, in addition to creating the pressure for innovative change.

But why, in those cases where Japanese companies have been internationally successful, have they managed at times to out-innovate their Western rivals? Surely these Western rivals also exist in the same intensely competitive domestic and international markets and therefore should be similarly motivated to innovate like their Japanese counterparts?

One factor which has at times assisted Japanese companies is their possession of what may be referred to as 'committed shareholders'. Committed shareholders may be defined as those who will remain loyal to the company in which they hold shares by retaining their shares in that company even in the face of expected share price differentials which would leave them better off in the short run if they were to sell their shares and switch to another company.

Why do these shareholders choose to 'stay and fight' rather than switch?

The reason is that, unlike pension fund managers who are attempting to maximise the short run value of their portfolios and who therefore have an arm's length relationship with the companies in which they hold shares, committed shareholders usually have close business relationships with these companies.

Committed shareholders, for instance, are often banks or other financial institutions which deal with the company, or major customers or suppliers who buy from or sell to it. They therefore have a longer term stake in the health of the company. Their commitment has removed many (though by no means all) of the pressures that Western companies face when short term profitability does not meet with the expectations of arm's length shareholders, pressures that frequently impede the process of innovation.

Japanese companies have also been helped in their attempts to innovate by organisational practices that have evolved over time in their companies. One of the key determinants behind these practices has been the institution of lifetime employment for most white and blue collar workers in larger firms. More accurately, the assumption of 'no exit' has had a number of extremely important consequences which have influenced organisational practices which, in turn, have been conducive to innovation.

The difference between the assumption of continuing employment in the same organisation or life-time employment on the one hand and the assumption of no exit on the other hand must be stressed. While some Western firms have traditionally offered life-time employment, this does NOT mean that their employees operate on the assumption of no exit. The functioning of labour markets in Western countries typically means that employees, particularly those with sought-after skills, do have the option of exit through employment by another organisation.

The no-exit assumption has facilitated innovation in Japanese companies in a number of ways. First, this assumption has given Japanese companies a strong incentive to train their employees since, by ensuring that these employees do not leave, it has allowed them to reap the returns from investment in training. Secondly, the no-exit assumption has encouraged the companies to provide more general and flexible skills since these allow employees, who have been provided with long term employment, to be more easily redeployable in different parts of the company. Redeployment may be necessary when a company faces a downturn in some of its business areas. Thirdly, the possession of more general and flexible skills on the part of the workforce has facilitated the widespread practice of job rotation within the company. One major benefit of this practice has been more efficient flows of information within the company which has allowed more effective coordination across corporate functional and other boundaries. This has encouraged innovation in activities such as new product development, the interfacing of R&D, production, and marketing, and just-in-time and quality control activities which depend on information flows and cross-functional coordination.

The no-exit assumption has also benefited the innovativeness and competitiveness of many Japanese companies in another more indirect way. By requiring companies not only to provide continuing jobs for its employees but also to provide opportunities for promotion and other incentives, the no-exit assumption has made it more difficult for Japanese companies to engage in merger and acquisition activities. In turn, this has encouraged Japanese companies to 'stick to their knitting' and concentrate on those activities where they have already acquired distinctive competences, a tendency that has been further encouraged by the engineering background of many Japanese corporate leaders who are often keener than their Western counterparts with financial backgrounds to keep to areas which they know and understand. This has often meant that Japanese companies have been able to focus their limited attention on where they have established distinctive competences and have deepened these competences while some of their Western rivals, lured by the hope of financial gain through merger, acquisition, or competence-unrelated diversification, have had their attention diverted to other concerns. The result has been that over time some Western companies have not been able to keep up with the innovation of their more focused Japanese competitors.

These are some of the factors which have generated an innovative dynamic in some Japanese sectors which has resulted in strong international competitiveness and rapid growth in sales and market share both in Japan and abroad. But what role is to be attributed to the Japanese government in accounting for the innovative performance of Japanese companies? It is to this question that we now turn.

5.5 Japanese Government Influence on the Innovation Process

One measure of the influence of government on the national innovation process is its share of total expenditure on R&D. According to this measure the Japanese government plays a significantly smaller role than its Western counterparts. The figures show that in 1988 the Japanese government was responsible for 18 per cent of total R&D. This compared with about 50 per cent in France, 45 per cent in the USA, and 35 per cent in West Germany. In 1989 the figure for the UK was 37 per cent. If defence-related R&D is excluded, the figures become 18 per cent for Japan, 34 per cent for France, 26 per cent for the USA, and 30 per cent for Germany.

What is the significance of the figure for Japan? The first point to make, underscoring that made in the last section on the role of Japanese companies, is that private Japanese companies undertake 76 per cent of R&D in

Japan, a significantly higher proportion than in the other industrialised Western countries. Since a greater proportion of R&D is undertaken in companies in Japan which are 'closer' to the point of production and marketing, it follows that a larger proportion of R&D is commercially targeted. (It is worth noting, however, that the Japanese government and the ministries responsible for science and technology expenditure are committed to increasing government's share of total R&D and raising it to a proportional level more commensurate with that of the other Western industrialised countries. With Japan's fiscal commitments in its recession-bound economy, however, this will take some time to achieve.)

Secondly, it is necessary to get the relatively low figure of 18 per cent into perspective. It would be wrong to conclude from this figure that the Japanese government has had a negligible influence on the innovation process. This is so for a number of reasons. To begin with, as will be reiterated in the following section on the role of universities, the Japanese government has had a major impact on the process of innovation through its education and training activities which have supplied Japanese companies with a high-quality, literate, numerate, and cooperative work force. This work force, with its high level of general skills, has then been further enhanced by the corporate organisational practices referred to in the last section which have facilitated the development of competitive distinctive competences.

Furthermore, although the Japanese government has had a negligible impact on the 'downstream' part of R&D—namely, applied research and development which constitutes some 90 per cent of total R&D—its influence on the 'upstream' part has been significantly greater. This upstream part relates to basic research and, extremely important in Japan, what may be referred to as 'oriented basic' research. In these areas the Japanese government has directly and indirectly had a greater impact, largely as a result of the degree of uncertainty in this kind of research and the reduced incentive that companies accordingly have to engage in such research.

What impact have Japanese ministries had on innovation and competitiveness? While in answer to this question much Western policy and academic analysis has focussed on the role of the Ministry of International Trade and Industry (MITI), it is necessary not to ignore the distinctive role of some of the other ministries. One example is the Ministry of Posts and Telecommunications which is currently, independently of MITI, playing an extremely important role in shaping the whole of the Japanese telecommunications sector in the post-liberalisation era. Another example is the role of the Science and Technology Agency and the Ministries of Health and Welfare and Agriculture, Forestry and Fisheries which, together with MITI and the Ministry of Education, Science and Culture, have exerted influence in the area of biotechnology.

Having said this, some concentration on MITI's role is justifiable in view of the influence which this ministry has had, and continues to have although in changing ways, on the largest parts of the Japanese manufacturing and distribution sectors. Historically, MITI's influential role has derived from Japan's position as a latecoming industrialising country with a strong state committed to the development process. Until the late 1960s MITI's power *vis-à-vis* the companies which fell within its sphere stemmed largely from its control of foreign exchange allocations and its ability to influence the extension of credit to the sectors and companies which it prioritised. Through the exercising of this power MITI was able to influence the allocation of resources within Japan, although analysts continue to debate the extent to which this influence benefited the Japanese economy.

Most analysts now recognise, however, that since the 1960s MITI's influence has changed considerably. This has followed for several reasons. Firstly, from the late 1960s MITI lost most of its direct influence over foreign exchange and credit. Secondly, Japanese companies grew in size and strength and their increasing globalisation gave them access to international capital markets thus reducing their dependence on the government for finance. Thirdly, as they grew Japanese companies also began allocating larger absolute and often proportional amounts to R&D and as a result came to depend less and less on government research institutes which formerly played a significant role in transferring advanced technologies to these companies.

In terms of total expenditure on science and technology, however, MITI's role is dwarfed by that of the Ministry of Education, Science and Culture and the Science and Technology Agency which spend 46 per cent and 26 per cent respectively of total government expenditure on science and technology compared with MITI's mere 12 per cent. In view of these figures, is it justifiable to argue, as usually is argued, that MITI has a greater influence on the innovation process in Japan than these other ministries?

In my view, MITI's relatively great influence derives largely from its central nodal position in a vast and complex information network that crisscrosses not only Japan but also the world. This information network provides MITI's decision-makers with outstanding high-quality information over a broad range in the areas of science, technology, industry, and trade. On the basis of the information which it possesses MITI is able to make maximum impact, not only with the direct resources which it commands, but also with the influence that it wields through indirect contacts and connections.

The close links that MITI has forged over the years with the Japanese companies in the sectors of manufacturing and distribution that are under its influence reinforce both the information flows which the ministry receives and the influence which it exerts. This information network, it is worth noting, was developed originally as a useful resource to help MITI in its efforts to enable Japanese industry to catch up with the more advanced Western countries.

While the costs of collecting, storing, analysing, and recalling information were and are substantial, MITI as an organisation became committed to these costs in view of the policy-making benefits which it derived from the information collected. While other ministries also have their own information networks, and while there are important cross-connections between the networks of the different ministries, these are not as extensive as MITI's. The Ministry of Finance, for example, relates closely to the private sector financial institutions, the Ministry of Health and Welfare to the pharmaceuticals companies, the Ministry of Construction to the construction companies, the Ministry of Agriculture, Forestry and Fisheries to the agriculture and food processing sectors, etc.

How is MITI's information network constructed? MITI's internal organisational structure consists of a matrix of vertical units, which correspond to the main industrial sectors in the economy, and horizontal units which deal with issues that cut across the various sectors. Examples are the vertical Machinery and Information Industries Bureau which deals with areas such as computer hardware and software and electronics and the horizontal Industrial Policy Bureau which has responsibility for questions of overall industrial policy. Regular rotation of senior MITI staff between the various units, while sacrificing some of the benefits of specialisation, helps to improve knowledge and information flows within the ministry. MITI also has a number of formally constituted Advisory Councils the membership of which includes company representatives and academics and which constitute important channels of information flow.

Equally important are the informal networks that exist between MITI officials and the corporate and academic sectors which provide similar information. Furthermore, industry associations, often set up originally with MITI's assistance and staffed by MITI personnel, such as the Electronics Industry Association of Japan, serve as subnodes which collect and process information at industry level and form an important link between that industry and the corresponding units in MITI. Abroad, the well-staffed JETRO (Japan External Trade Research Organisation) provides information about markets and technologies in other countries. It is common for MITI officials to be seconded to JETRO offices abroad in order to accumulate international experience. (Ironically, JETRO, originally established to aid Japan's export drive, now, in view of Japan's large trade surplus, assists the attempts of foreign organisations to export to Japan.)

But this account of MITI's role in a vast information network raises further questions. Why do Japanese companies continue to cooperate so closely with MITI? Do they need the information that MITI has at its disposal or would they be better off going their own way?

These questions are difficult, and within the large companies which have close relationships with MITI there are contradictory answers that are given. Nevertheless, there are a number of considerations that have a bearing on these questions which would probably be fairly widely accepted. To begin with, it is accepted by the companies themselves that the government (in this case MITI) must do for private industry what needs to be done and what industry cannot do for itself.

One important example is the resolution of international trade conflicts. As the study of cartels shows, it is extremely difficult for autonomous players to coordinate their actions so as to act in their collective self interest. This is so for the simple reason that an incentive often exists for individual players to break ranks in the hope of increasing individual gain but to the detriment of the collective interest. Relating this to Japan's international trade conflict, an individual semiconductor or motor car company has an incentive to increase its exports when its counterparts in the industry are voluntarily restricting theirs in order to reduce trade conflict.

Another example is environmental protection where MITI is playing an expanding role. Here too the incentives facing private firms may not be compatible with the socially desired outcome thus justifying involvement by MITI. It is widely acknowledged in Japan that MITI's intervention is necessary in these kinds of situations in the interests of all the companies concerned as well as in the national Japanese interest. Here the information that MITI has at its disposal is an invaluable aid in both policy-making and implementation.

Secondly, and more closely related to innovation, MITI is able to play an extremely constructive role in facilitating cooperative research between competing companies that in the absence of MITI's interventions would be less likely to cooperate. Here the information at MITI's disposal has been invaluable in facilitating the choice of research projects in strategic technology areas that will increase the competitive strength of Japanese companies, in selecting appropriate companies to participate in the cooperative research, and in securing the right kind of participation from these companies. Examples include the Fifth Generation Computer Project, its successor the Real World Computer Project that is still in its formative stage, and the Protein Engineering Research Institute which MITI established through the Japan Key Technology Center which it controls together with the Ministry of Posts and Telecommunications. The role that MITI has played in cooperative research has been analysed in detail (Fransman 1990; Fransman and Tanaka 1995, reprinted here as Chapter 7).

Thirdly, the rich information available to MITI's decision-makers has enabled the ministry to complement the 'bounded vision' of private companies which tend to have good information in the areas in which they are involved but which are often unable to perceive the importance of emerging new technologies and markets in hitherto unrelated areas. On the basis of its broad detailed information MITI has been able to identify new technology areas with important commercial potential which have not received the attention they deserve in Japan and take steps to encourage companies to more actively develop these technologies and related markets. Recent examples include biotechnology and new materials where MITI has played an extremely important (though not very costly) role in facilitating entry by a large number of Japanese companies.

This discussion on MITI and information provides an answer to the question regarding how MITI is able to exert significant influence on the innovation process while accounting for only a relatively small proportion of the Japanese government's expenditure on science and technology. Drawing on work by Chihiro Watanabe, one of MITI's leading younger theorists, it may be concluded that for the reasons analysed in this section MITI has been able to 'induce' innovation in Japanese companies on the basis of relatively modest financial sums. The information network which MITI orchestrates has been a crucial resource facilitating its inducement role (Watanabe 1992).

But how important are Japanese universities in the Japanese Innovation System? It is to this question that we now turn.

5.6 Importance of Japanese Universities

A common judgement by analysts of Japan is that Japanese universities tend not to measure up to their Western counterparts in terms of research and that most advanced research is found, not in universities, but in the research laboratories of the leading companies. As it stands, this judgment, though with some evidence to support it, obscures the role that Japanese universities play in the innovation system. The aim of this section is to briefly elaborate on this role.

The first point to make is that one of the most important functions played by the universities in the innovation system is to provide graduates with good general levels of education to private companies. These graduates are then given company-specific training as outlined in the first section of this chapter. University professors, with close informal links with numbers of companies, frequently play an important role in helping to allocate their students to places in companies. This allocation mechanism with its tight networks of personal contact and information stands in strong contrast to the more impersonal labour market mechanism which is often used in Western countries.

Secondly, while there is some evidence suggesting that in many areas Japanese universities tend not to be as strong as their Western counterparts in frontier research, judgment of the role of Japanese universities based on this evidence overstates the importance of such research for innovation and competitiveness. The reason is simply that what counts immediately for most companies is not frontier research but intra-frontier research. And Japanese universities are often an important source of this kind of research for Japanese companies. My own research on Japanese biotechnology, for example, suggests that Japanese universities are a more important source of knowledge for some of the major Japanese biotechnology companies than are other companies and non-Japanese universities. Supporting this, a recent study based on publication citations has concluded that the scientific research of Japanese companies 'draws most heavily on Japanese, not foreign sources, universities being the most important Japanese source' (Hicks *et al.* 1992).

5.7 Conclusion

In this brief account of the Japanese Innovation System it has been possible to do no more than provide an analysis of some of the main characteristics of this system. While it has been stressed that the 'engine' of the system lies in the Japanese companies and the competitive processes of which they form a part, the important role of both government and universities in encouraging innovation and competitiveness has also been emphasised. Returning finally to the proverbial elephant, while the 'true nature' of the beast may still be subject to debate, a satisfactory analysis of innovation and competitiveness in Japan will have to take account of the Japanese Innovation System as a whole and many, if not all, of the points raised in this chapter.

6

Is National Technology Policy Obsolete in a Globalised World?: The Japanese Vision

6.1 Introduction

It is increasingly being argued, both in the USA and Europe, that national technology policy, designed to give national firms a competitive edge based on superior technology, has become obsolete in a globalised world. The reason, the argument goes, is that in a world where trade, business and finance, and science and technology cross national borders, attempts by national governments together with their firms to appropriate the fruits of national technology programmes are doomed to fail.

A significant degree of interpretive ambiguity, however, surrounds this argument. The aim of this chapter is to examine the vision of Japanese government policy-makers regarding the role that government technology policy should play in an increasingly globalising Japan. Although Japan began to globalise later than its Western counterparts, and although Japan has been globalising at a slower rate, the Japanese economy has become significantly more globalised over the last two decades. This is seen in indicators such as increased outward and inward direct foreign investment, the increase in foreign R&D laboratories in Japan, the growing number of international strategic technology alliances involving Japanese and Western firms, increased (temporary) outflow and inflow of researchers and engineers, and greater international co-authoring of science and technology research papers.

However, despite the increased globalisation of the Japanese economy, Japanese policy-makers, as shown in detail in this chapter, have responded, not by abandoning national technology policy, but by internationalising it while retaining national objectives. Does this mean that the Japanese are following obsolete policies that are doomed to fail, as the above argument implies, or is there an acceptable justification for current Japanese technol-

This chapter was originally published as 'Is National Technology Policy Obsolete in a Globalised World?: The Japanese Response', *Cambridge Journal of Economics*, 1995, 19, 95–199.

ogy policy? If the latter is true, is the Japanese case special, or is it at least to some extent valid for other large Western countries? These two questions are at the heart of the present chapter.

6.2 Chapter Overview

This chapter begins with a brief discussion of the convergence hypothesis, which argues that there has been a convergence in the economies of the major industrialised countries in the post-Second World War period. It then goes on to examine a corollary that has been derived from this hypothesis, namely that national technology policy has become obsolete.

The globalisation of the Japanese economy and science and technology system is then documented on the basis of several selected indicators, including international imitation, international strategic technology alliances, the international movement of researchers and engineers, direct foreign investment, foreign research laboratories in Japan, technology trade, and internationally co-authored science and technology papers.

The role of the Japanese government in science and technology is then considered, beginning with an account of the rationale given by the Ministry of International Trade and Industry (MITI) for its involvement in the science and technology area. This is followed by a detailed account of MITI's response to globalisation, a response which reveals the vision which guides MITI's policy-makers in their interventions in the field of science and technology within the context of the globalising Japanese and world economies. The implications of the Japanese response to globalisation for other large Western countries are then examined. Finally, the sources of MITI's influence in the Japanese economy are analysed.

6.3 The Convergence Hypothesis

In a number of important recent articles several authors have put forward the argument that there has been a convergence in the economies of the major industrialised countries in the post-Second World War period (see, for example, Abramovitz 1986, Baumol 1986, Baumol *et al.* 1989, Nelson 1990, and Nelson and Wright 1992). According to one strand of this argument, convergence has resulted from the increasing internationalisation of trade, business, and technology. In Nelson and Wright's words, 'the convergence model looks more and more plausible. In our view, it is the internationalization of trade, business, and generic technology and the growing commonality of the economic environments of firms in different nations that have made it so' (Nelson and Wright 1992, 1961).

The convergence hypothesis itself, however, is not the concern of this chapter. Of interest, rather, is a corollary that has been derived from this hypothesis, namely that convergence also implies that national technology policy has become obsolete.

6.4 The Corollary: National Technology Policy Has Become Obsolete

Why has it been argued that national technology policy has become obsolete? According to Nelson and Wright, 'national borders mean much less than they used to regarding the flow of technology, at least among the nations that have made the new needed social investments in education and research facilities' (ibid. 1961). Governments, however, have been slow to comprehend these important changes: 'National governments have been slow to recognize these new facts of life. Indeed, the last decade has seen a sharp increase in what has been called 'techno-nationalism', policies launched by governments with the objective of giving their national firms a particular edge in an area of technology' (ibid).

'Techno-nationalist' policies, however, are unlikely to succeed in a globalised world: 'Our argument is that these policies do not work very well any more. It is increasingly difficult to create new technology that will stay contained within national borders for very long in a world where technological sophistication is widespread and firms of many nationalities are ready to make the investment needed to exploit new generic technology' (ibid). In other words, while national governments may assist national firms to create new technologies, these firms are unlikely to be able to appropriate the benefits of the technologies through increased competitiveness. The reason is that their counterparts elsewhere in the global economy, having made the necessary investments in training and research and development and therefore having accumulated the required 'social capabilities' (Abramovitz 1986), will also have access sooner rather than later to these technologies.

6.5 The Leaks in the Japanese System

Japan is a late globaliser, but a globaliser nonetheless. As a globaliser Japan confronts the same 'leaks' in its national science and technology system as do the other industrialised countries. Although a greater proportion of advanced research is done in Japan in the corporate sector rather than the public sector (universities, public research institutes, etc), where it is subject to normal corporate control, there is little evidence that this control has resulted is a significant 'knowledge lead' for Japanese companies.

Even in those sectors where Japanese companies have enjoyed an over-whelming international dominance, such as consumer electronics, memory semiconductors, and cameras, their competitiveness has been based more on quality and in some cases characteristic advantages than on superior underlying knowledge. The dramatic rise of Korean companies such as Samsung and Gold Star in international markets for memory semiconductors, and the resurgence in these same markets of American companies like Motorola and Texas Instruments, bears testimony to the absence of a significant technology lead on the part of the Japanese companies.

These cases of comparative Japanese success, therefore, do not constitute a refutation of the convergence hypothesis which allows for competitive divergences between firms and nations and even a process of 'falling behind'. To quote Nelson and Wright (1992) once more, 'While we argue that the principal factor driving convergence over the last quarter of a century has been internationalization, we do not dismiss the possibility that the United States may be in the process of slipping into second, third, or fifth rank in productivity and per capita income, and in terms of mastering the application of several important technologies. Although the forces that now bind together nations with sufficient "social capabilities" are far stronger than they were in the past, there is certainly room for variance within that group' (1961).

6.5.1 International Imitation

A major source of leakage from the Japanese system which has contributed to convergence is the competitive process of imitation as other companies, on the basis of the capabilities which they have accumulated, have emulated Japanese success. The case of semiconductors just referred to, and the closely related case of semiconductor process equipment, the production of which has been encouraged by the Sematech Programme in the United States, provide striking examples of the imitation process.

At the same time, however, the case of automobiles provides a more cautionary tale of the difficulties and costs that may arise in the attempt to imitate. The latter case is of particular interest because, despite a good understanding of the reasons for Japanese superiority in productivity and quality in the automobile industry aided by several excellent studies, and despite the possession of similar underlying knowledge, Western competitors have nevertheless found it extremely difficult to close the gap (see, for example, Womack *et al.* 1990 and Clark and Fujimoto 1991. The reason for the difficulty in the automobile case is that the problem stems not from the lack of knowledge on the part of Western companies, but from the difficulty of *implementing* both intra- and inter-firm organisational innovations such as the just-in-time and subcontracting systems. This case illustrates, therefore, the competitive divergences that may continue to exist between converging firms that have similar 'social capabilities' in Abramovitz's sense).

6.5.2 International Strategic Technology Alliances

A more direct channel for the leakage of knowledge from the Japanese system has been the spate of international strategic technology alliances that have been concluded between Japanese companies and Western competitors. Again, the case of semiconductors provides a useful illustration of the phenomenon, as is shown in Table 6.1.

Table 6.1 shows some of the recent technological alliances that have been established between Japanese companies and Western competitors. The main motivation behind these alliances has been the growing R&D costs in developing next generation semiconductor products and processes. These costs are now so high that few companies can afford to pay them alone. Table 6.1 also shows that the general pattern has been for Japanese companies, threatened more by competition from their Japanese rivals than from Western companies, to form alliances with the latter. These alliances, however, imply a further leakage from the Japanese system as Japanese companies pass on knowledge, acquired from their internal R&D as well as from Japanese government programmes in which they have participated, to their Western partners.

More generally, data from MITI shows a cumulative total of 135 international research joint ventures involving Japanese companies between the years 1982 and 1987 (Mowery and Teece 1992, 125). Of these, thirty-two were in electrical machinery (including computing and telecommunications), twenty-four in chemicals, and ten in transport machinery.

Table 6.1 International Strategic Technology Alliances in Semiconductors involving Japanese Companies

Companies	Area
1. Toshiba-Siemens-IBM	265M DRAM
2. NEC-AT&T	Semiconductor manufacturing
3. Fujitsu-AMD	Flash memories
4. Intel-Sharp	Flash memories
5. Hitachi-Texas Instruments	DRAM
6. Mitsubishi Electric-SGS-Thomson	Flash memories

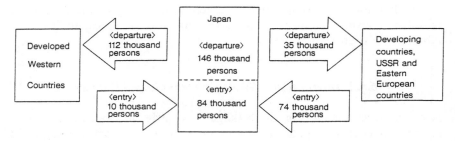

Fig. 6.1 Researcher/engineer exchanges between Japan and other countries (1989)
Source: Ministry of Justice: 'Annual Report of Statistics on Legal Migrants for 1989'.

6.5.3 *International Movement of Researchers and Engineers*

While the leakage of knowledge from Western countries to Japan as Japanese companies have learned from their Western counterparts has been well documented, a reverse flow of knowledge has begun to increase in significance. One channel for this reverse flow is the (usually temporary) migration of foreign engineers and researchers to Japan where they are employed in government and company laboratories and factories. This migration is shown in Fig. 6.1.

Although the flow of engineers and researchers into Japan is increasing, and although this constitutes an increasingly important source of leakage from the Japanese system, Fig. 6.1 also shows that there is still a significant 'deficit' in Japan's 'trade' in this area. While in 1989, 112,000 engineers and researchers departed for Western industrialised countries, 10,000 entered Japan, an out–in ratio of 11. Japan's relationship with developing countries is to some extent the mirror image of this, with 74,000 engineers and researchers entering Japan and 35,000 departing, an out-in ratio of 0.5.

Further details are provided in Fig. 6.2 on the source and destination of the engineers and researchers who come to and go from Japan. Of all those who entered Japan, 12 per cent came from the industrialised Western countries 6.2 per cent of the total number of entrants came from the USA, while 2.1 per cent came from the UK and 0.9 per cent from France. Korea sent the largest proportion of engineers and researchers to Japan, 24 per cent of the total, followed by Taiwan and China, with 18 per cent and 14 per cent respectively.

6.5.4 *Direct Foreign Investment*

Increasing direct foreign investment in Japan is also a growing source of leakage from the Japanese system as foreign companies based in Japan 'tap

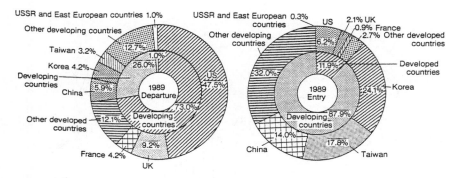

Fig. 6.2 Breakdowns of researchers/engineers going out from and coming into Japan

Source: Ministry of Justice: 'Annual Report of Statistics on Legal Migrants for 1989'.

into' Japanese science and technology. Here too, however, there remains a substantial imbalance, with outflows greatly exceeding inflows. The overall picture is shown in Fig. 6.3.

This figure reveals that in 1989 direct investment from Japan to the USA totalled $17.3 billion, while that in the opposite direction was $1.2 billion, an out-in ratio of 14. In the same year, direct investment from Japan to the EC was $9.8 billion, while the figure for flows from the EC to Japan was $327 million, an out–in ratio of 30. Between 1985 and 1989, Japanese direct investment to the USA increased 5.1 times while US direct investment to Japan increased 2.5 times. (For comparative purposes it is worth noting that the out–in ratio for direct investment from the EC to the USA in 1989 was 3.)

6.5.5 Foreign Research Laboratories in Japan

A further source of leakage of knowledge from the Japanese system comes from the activities of the R&D laboratories of foreign companies located in Japan. How extensive are these laboratories? Data from MITI indicate that in 1990 there were a total of 137 foreign R&D laboratories in Japan (Mowery and Teece 1992, 115). Interestingly, the bulk of these laboratories were in areas where Japanese industry is weakest in international comparative terms rather than where it is strongest, namely in chemicals and pharmaceuticals rather than electrical machinery. In chemicals there were fifty-nine laboratories, in pharmaceuticals twenty-five, and in electrical machinery eleven. However, it is unclear from this data how extensive were the research activities undertaken by these laboratories or what kind of development work was being done.

Data from the Science and Technology Agency, however, suggests that

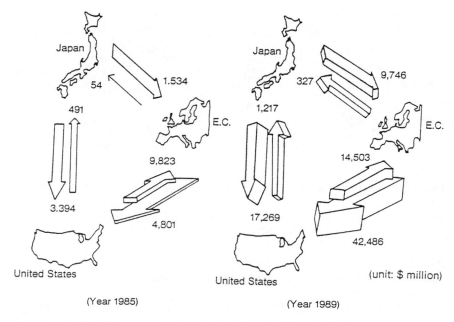

Fig. 6.3 Flow of direct investment between Japan, USA, and EC

Note: Figures for EC: sum of ten countries for 1985 and twelve countries for 1989.

Compilation: Science and Technology Agency.

Sources: US Department of Commerce, 'Survey of Current Business' for the flows between the USA and Japan, and between the USA and the EC; Japan's Ministry of Finance, 'Monthly Statistics of Finance' for the flow between Japan and the EC.

most foreign laboratories in Japan had located in the country primarily to adapt their products to local conditions rather than to 'tap' into the Japanese science and technology system. An STA survey concluded that just over 90 per cent of the foreign laboratories located their operations in Japan 'to plan and localize new products meeting host country needs'. Only about 30 per cent located because 'Japan [was] seen as leader in R&D in my field'; just under 30 per cent 'to monitor technological developments and activities [in Japan]'; just under 20 per cent because 'Japan [was] seen as leader in production technology in my field'; and just over 10 per cent because of the 'existence of outstanding research personnel [in Japan]' (STA 1991).

6.5.6 Technology Trade

A further direct 'leakage' occurs when Japanese companies sell their technology abroad. This leakage is picked up in figures for technology trade which takes account of items such as the sale abroad of patents and other know-how. Fig. 6.4 and Table 6.2 shows that Japan's exports of technology increased significantly between 1975 and 1990, although so have its imports.

This figure also shows the ratio of exports to imports of technology for some of the other major large industrialised countries. As can be seen, the USA is the only country with a surplus in its balance on technology trade, a significant surpius. While Japan remained in deficit throughout this period, the deficit has decreased. According to Bank of Japan figures, the Japanese ratio of export to import increased from 0.13 in 1970 to 0.41 in 1990 (Table 6.2).

Further information is provided in Fig. 6.5 on the ratio of exports to imports of technology by the Japanese sector. Here it can be seen that it is only construction and iron and steel that have enjoyed a clear surplus. The three most important sectors, namely electrical machinery, transport equipment, and chemicals have been in deficit over the period from 1975 to 1989, although for all three the deficit narrowed sharply towards the end of the period, while for transport equipment and chemicals the deficit had almost disappeared by 1989.

Table 6.2 Changes in Japan's technology trade amounts (¥100 m.)

	Export (A)	Import (B)	Ratio A/B
1970	197	1,479	0.13
1971	213	1,638	0.13
1972	212	1,655	0.13
1973	231	1,850	0.12
1974	324	2,153	0.15
1975	421	2,069	0.20
1976	519	2,373	0.22
1977	548	2,647	0.21
1978	594	2,460	0.24
1979	703	2,791	0.25
1980	803	3,011	0.27
1981	1,063	3,775	0.28
1982	1,392	4,369	0.32
1983	1,351	4,707	0.29
1984	1,651	5,401	0.31
1985	1,724	5,631	0.31
1986	1,527	5,454	0.22
1987	1,870	5,515	0.34
1988	2,098	6,429	0.33
1989	2,782	7,347	0.38
1990	3,589	8,744	0.41

Note: Figures are values in each calendar year.

Source: Bank of Japan, *Balance of Payments Monthly*.

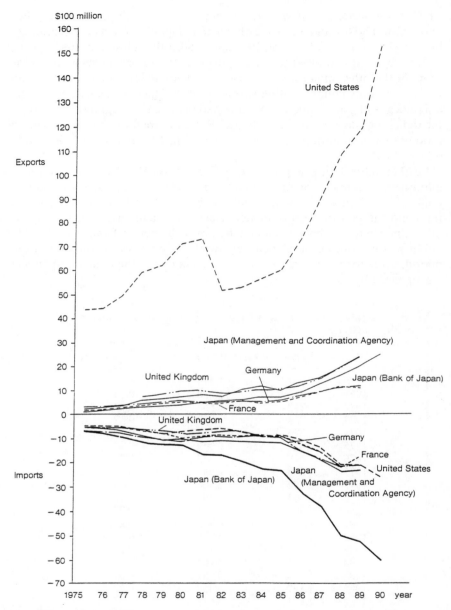

Fig. 6.4 Trends in technology trade of selected countries

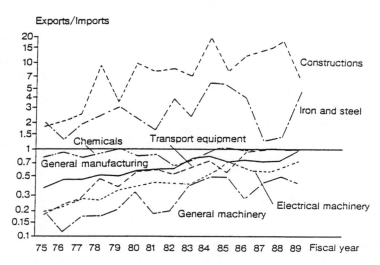

Fig. 6.5 Trends of technology trade balance in major industry sectors

Source: Statistics Bureau, Management and Coordination Agency, 'Report on the Survey of Research and Development'.

6.5.7 Internationally Co-Authored Papers

'Leakages' also take place from the Japanese system as Japanese researchers exchange information and knowledge with their counterparts abroad. One indicator of this exchange is internationally co-authored papers. Figure 6.6 provides data on the growing proportion of Japanese papers (included in the Science and Engineering Literature Database) which are internationally co-authored.

This figure shows that the proportion of Japanese papers included in this data base which were internationally co-authored increased from around 5 per cent in 1981 to 7.5 per cent in 1986. This compared with about 10 per cent in the USA. The European countries, smaller and in closer geographical proximity, had a higher proportion. In the UK the proportion was 17 per cent while in France and Germany, where there has been a greater internationalisation of the science and technology system, the proportion was 21 per cent.

Conclusion

From the above data it can be seen that although Japan still lags behind in many respects in terms of the globalisation of its science and technology system, the degree of internationalisation has increased significantly over

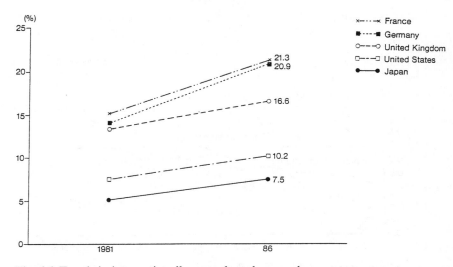

Fig. 6.6 Trends in internationally co-authored papers by country
Compilation: Science and Technology Agency.
Source: Computer Horizons, Inc., 'Science & Engineering Literature Data Base 1989'.

the last decade. This implies that the 'selfcontainedness' of the system has decreased in line with the convergence hypothesis outlined above. Does this mean, however, that the corollary of this hypothesis, that national technology policy has increasingly become obsolete, also applies in the Japanese case? This question will now be examined.

6.6 The Role of the Japanese Government

6.6.1 Some General Considerations

To begin with, it is worth stressing that the Japanese government since the Meiji Restoration of 1868 has *always* taken the position that it has an important necessary role to play in strengthening the science and technology base for Japanese companies. The role that the government has played, however, has changed as Japan has moved through the 'early catch-up', 'late catch-up', and 'frontier-sharing' stages of its economic development. (See Chapter 2, and for a detailed study of this role in the case of the computer and semiconductor industries, see Fransman 1993.)

In the current frontier-sharing stage, the Japanese government, specifically the Ministry of International Trade and Industry (MITI), believes that it must continue to play a pro-active role by encouraging the development of those areas of science and technology that are important for the future global competitiveness of Japanese companies. This and the following points regarding MITI's involvement in the science and technology system are based on detailed interviews with senior MITI officials closely involved in the policy-making process in the area of science and technology held from July to December 1992.

6.6.2 Market Failure

MITI officials stress, however, that the criterion of 'market failure', which has long been used in the Ministry, is of overriding importance in deciding on where and when to act in the area of science and technology. In other words, where private companies either do or can take care of necessary scientific and technological development, MITI will steer clear of these areas.

MITI identifies two areas where market failure is possible. The first is where there is significant 'risk' and where companies as a result do not undertake sufficient R&D. Several further points must be made here. MITI does not argue that wherever there is significant risk there is insufficient corporate R&D. The Ministry accepts that in some cases where there is substantial risk there may be sufficient or even excessive R&D. One reason for this may be that the expected pay-off from R&D is sufficient to compensate the company for the risk that it is taking. Accordingly, MITI will only consider acting where it judges (*a*) that the degree of risk results in insufficient R&D and (*b*) that more R&D is necessary to increase the competitiveness of Japanese companies. (It is worth noting that in economists' jargon MITI really is referring to uncertainty. For economists, risk is probabilistically predictable, and therefore insurable, while uncertainty is not.)

The second reason why private companies might fail to develop the needed area of R&D follows from the size of investment that is required. Once again MITI accepts that even extremely large investments might be justified by the private company without government involvement, or by companies acting in cooperation, as a result of the satisfactory payoff expected, and that in these cases government action may therefore be unnecessary. A case in point may be the international strategic technology alliances in the field of semiconductors referred to earlier where governments have not been involved. Clearly, although these two reasons for market failure might be distinct, they may interact. Thus, an expensive area of R&D may also be highly uncertain in terms of payback. On the other hand, there may be little uncertainty, but the investment required may still be too large for private companies to contemplate in the light of the expected pay-off.

6.6.3 Basic Research

A further priority has become important since the mid to late 1980s for MITI and the other organs of the Japanese government involved in science and technology, such as the Science and Technology Agency and the Ministry of Education, Science, and Culture. This is the area of basic research which the Japanese government believes it must play an increasingly important role in fostering. Although the government acknowledges that Japan has managed to perform extremely well globally in a number of industries without a particularly strong basic research base in Japan, and although in this sense the linear model of technology development which emphasises the sequential movement from basic through applied research to development and commercialisation is rejected, it nevertheless feels that it is increasingly important for Japan to strengthen its capabilities in basic research.

Why is basic research being given high priority in Japan? This question poses something of a puzzle since, as just mentioned, the Japanese authorities acknowledge that they have done extremely well so far with little basic research. Furthermore, although basic research is not a global free good and there can be substantial costs involved in exploiting basic research, it remains that basic research is more 'open' and therefore less appropriable than more applied research. Why, then, have the Japanese attached increasing priority to basic research?

There are several answers to this question. The first is that, having gradually moved 'upstream' from efficient production and commercialisation through development to applied research, the link to basic research is the last one to make. While many Western companies, as documented in numerous case studies, have failed to commercialise adequately the fruits of their significant basic research, the Japanese hope that with the 'downstream' portion of the value chain working effectively, a productive interface can now be forged with basic research. It is this hope that lies behind the establishment of basic research laboratories such as Hitachi's Advanced Research Laboratory and NEC's Princeton, New Jersey, and Tsukuba laboratories. Companies like NEC nevertheless emphasise that their 'basic' research is in effect 'oriented basic research'. The orientation of the research is partly determined by the ultimate commercial objectives of this research, and partly by the research's corporate context which emphasises the 'downstream' part of the value chain.

While many large Japanese companies have felt the expected return from oriented basic research to be sufficiently attractive to allocate a portion of their R&D funds to this research without government involvement, both companies and the government in Japan are in agreement that the latter has an important role to play in encouraging this kind of research. To begin with, it is felt that although generally speaking Japanese universities have not been as good as many of their Western counterparts in *frontier* research, these universities have nevertheless been a far more important source of external knowledge for Japanese companies than is usually acknowledged in academic analysis and policy-oriented discussion of Japan. The reason, simply, is that in most cases companies are not interested in frontier research but rather on more pragmatically-oriented research which is more easily and rapidly commercialisable. This kind of research tends to be *intrafrontier* research and, furthermore, many Japanese universities are good at this kind of research. Supporting this view, a recent study based on publication citation has concluded that the scientific research of Japanese companies 'draws most heavily on Japanese, not foreign sources', universities being the most important Japanese source (Hicks *et al.* 1992, 1).

One role for government, therefore, is to help upgrade both the quantity and quality of basic research undertaken in Japanese universities and also government and semigovernment research institutes. Not only do Japanese companies plug in directly to research in Japanese universities, they also recruit their researchers and developers from these universities. Strengthening basic research in the universities will therefore help companies in at least two ways. [While the Japanese Management and Coordination Agency estimates that about 6.4 per cent of the R&D of Japanese companies is basic research, the figure for national research institutions is 27.1 per cent, and that for universities and colleges 53.2 per cent (STA 1991, 126). ('Basic research' was defined as 'research undertaken primarily for the advancement of scientific knowledge, where a specific practical application may be indirectly sought' (ibid. 124)].

A second reason for the high priority now being given to basic research is that, having reached the international frontier in many areas of research, many Japanese companies no longer have the option of following their Western counterparts as they did before. They therefore have no option but to play a greater role in charting the future scientific and technological directions that they will follow through basic or oriented basic research.

Thirdly, Japan's government, and to a lesser extent companies, now acknowledge that they are becoming internationally obligated to make a significantly larger contribution to the global stock of knowledge from which in the past they have so usefully drawn. This consideration has been an important force further motivating the prioritising of basic research. However, in the absence of the first and second reasons for the greater emphasis on basic research, it is unlikely that the third reason alone would have resulted in as great a commitment in Japan to basic research.

6.6.4 *The Japanese Government's Contribution to S&T Expenditure*

The Japanese government's share of total R&D expenditure is far lower than that of the other large Western countries' as is shown in Fig. 6.7. The contribution of the government is 18.6 per cent compared with 33.2 per cent

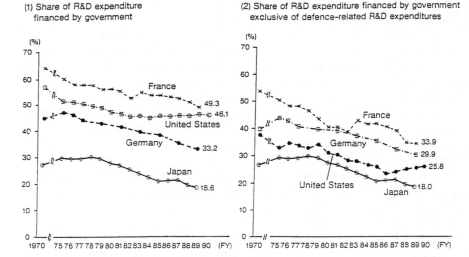

Fig. 6.7 Trends in government finance for R&D expenditures in selected countries

Notes: 1. For comparison, statistics for all countries include research in social sciences and humanities.
2. Government percentages exclusive of defense-related research expenditures are calculated by the following equation:

$$\frac{(\text{Government financed R\&D expenditures}) - (\text{Defense-related R\&D expenditures})}{(\text{R\&D expenditures}) - (\text{Defense-related R\&D expenditures})}$$

3. The 1989 data for the USA are provisional and the 1990 data are an estimate.
4. The defense-related expenditures for Germany for 1989 are provisional.
5. The years for which German data are not available are indicated on a straight line.
6. The 1989 and 1990 data for France are provisional.

Source: Science and Technology Agency (1991), p. 115.

for Germany, 46.1 per cent for the USA, and 49.3 per cent for France. If defence-related R&D expenditures are excluded, the Japanese figure becomes 18.0 per cent compared with 25.8 per cent for the USA, 29.9 per cent for Germany, and 33.9 per cent for France.

It should be noted, however, that although these figures are frequently quoted, it is the declared intention of the Japanese government to increase its share of national R&D expenditure to a proportion more commensurate with that of these other Western countries. It is not yet clear how long it will take to achieve this as a result of the other priorities that are taking precedence in the current fiscal attempts to stimulate the recession-bound Japanese economy.

While Japanese companies undertake a slightly smaller proportion of

Table 6.3 The flows of R&D funds between industry, universities and colleges, and government sectors in selected countries

Financing sector	Performing sector	Japan (1989)		United States (1990)		Germany (1989)		France (1983)		United Kingdom (1988)	
		Amount ••	Share %	Amount ••	Share %	Amount ••	Share %	Amount ••	Share %	Amount ••	Share %
Government	Government	8,827	92.6	33,400	100.0	6,590	92.7	7,227	95.6	4,278	84.2
	Government	707	7.4	0	0	393	5.5	52	0.7	472	9.3
	Industry	1,028	1.2	71,300	33.0	4,526	11.5	3,646	22.4	3,888	16.5
Industry	Industry	81,161	98.6	145,000	67.0	34,771	86.8	11,867	73.0	16,799	71.4
	Universities and Colleges	10,921	51.3	28,860	68.6	7,115	92.5	4,424	97.6	4,222	77.9
	Universities and Colleges	458	2.2	2,300	5.5	575	7.5	58	1.3	322	5.9

Notes: 1. For comparison, statistics for all countries include research in social sciences and humanities.
2. Percentages show the share of the R&D expenditures of financing by sector against the total R&D expenditures of performance by sector.
3. The amounts are converted based on OECD purchase power parity.
4. The US data are estimated.

Source: Science and Technology Agency (1991).

total R&D than companies in the USA and Germany as will shortly be shown, they receive a significantly smaller proportion of their R&D expenditures from their government than do companies in the USA, Germany, France, and the UK. This is seen in Table 6.3 which shows the flow of R&D funding between government, industry, and universities. A number of points emerge from this table. First, in Japan industry only receives 1.2 per cent of its R&D expenditure from government. This compares with 33.0 per cent in the USA, 22.4 per cent in France, 16.5 per cent in the UK, and 11.5 per cent in Germany. The reason for the high US figure is the large amount of defense R&D undertaken by industry, but funded by government. In the largest Japanese industrial electronics companies approximately 5 per cent of total R&D is funded by the Japanese government (see Fransman 1993).

Second, 2.2 per cent of the research undertaken in Japanese universities is funded from industry. This compares with 7.5 per cent in Germany, 5.9 per cent in the UK, and 5.5 per cent in the USA.

The fact that the Japanese Government finances a smaller proportion of total R&D than its Western counterparts, however, does not mean that a greater proportion of R&D in Japan is undertaken in industry compared with Western countries. Fig. 6.8 shows that while 69.7 per cent of total R&D is performed by industry in Japan, the corresponding figure for Germany is 73.5 per cent, for the USA 72.1 per cent, for the UK 66.4 per cent, and for France 59.5 per cent.

However, Table 6.3 shows that Japanese industry finances a substantially greater proportion of the R&D that it undertakes compared with the large Western countries. This implies that a far greater proportion of the R&D of Japanese industry is targeted at the objectives of industry, rather than the objectives of non-industrial funders of R&D, notably, in the case of the USA, France, and the UK, government funders of defence-related R&D.

While in Japan 98.6 per cent of R&D undertaken is financed by industry, in the USA the figure is 67.0 per cent, in the UK 71.4 per cent, in France 73.0 per cent, and in Germany 86.8 per cent.

6.7 The Role of MITI

6.7.1 MITI's Share of Total Expenditure on Science and Technology by the Japanese Government

While the Ministry of International Trade and Industry is usually held up as the major government influence on science and technology in Japan, the Ministry only accounts for a relatively small proportion of expenditure on science and technology by the Japanese government. This is shown in Table 6.4 which shows that in 1991 the Ministry of Education was the largest

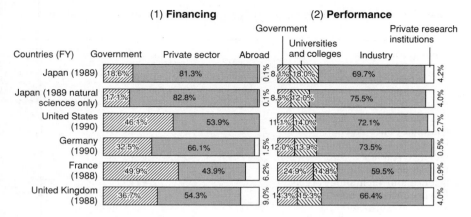

Fig. 6.8 Share of R&D expenditure financing and performance sector in selected countries

Notes: 1. For comparison, statistics for all countries include research in social sciences and humanities. The figures for Japan also show the amount for natural sciences.
2. In the financing column, the private sector includes any sector other than the government and abroad.
3. In the performance column, government means government research institution as defined by the OECD.

Source: Science and Technology Agency (1991), p. 114.

spender on science and technology, accounting for almost half of total government expenditure in this area. The Science and Technology Agency came next with just under half of the Ministry of Education's budget. MITI came third with just under half of the Science and Technology Agency's budget. Fourth came the Defence Agency with just under half of MITI's budget.

These figures raise a puzzle: how can MITI be as influential in Japanese science and technology as is usually claimed by analysts if it only accounts for a relatively small proportion of the expenditure by the Japanese government in this area? This puzzle will be examined in more detail later.

6.7.2 MITI's Expenditure on Science and Technology

A breakdown of MITI's expenditure on science and technology is given in Table 6.5. A number of important points emerge from this table. The first is that energy R&D accounts for 52 per cent of MITI's science and technology expenditure. This means that non-energy industrial R&D—which includes the so-called hi-tech industries such as computers, semiconductors, biotechnology, and new materials, which MITI has been credited (and sometimes blamed) with fostering—accounts for only 48 per cent of MITI's science and technology budget.

Table 6.4 Science and technology budget breakdown by ministries and agencies (¥m.)

Ministry or agency	Fiscal year	
	1990	1991
Diet	533	533
Science Council of Japan	951	1,051
National Police Agency	1,055	1,143
Hokkaido Development Agency	149	148
Defence Agency	104,268	115,045
Economic Planning Agency	809	850
Science and Technology Agency*	494,775	522,561
Environment Agency	9,217	10,900
Ministry of Justice	939	1,006
Ministry of Foreign Affairs	7,095	8,160
Ministry of Finance*	1,087	1,193
Ministry of Education*	894,301	936,324
Ministry of Health and Welfare*	51,242	56,144
Ministry of Agriculture, Forestry and Fisheries*	70,108	73,557
Ministry of International Trade and Industry*	251,548	255,913
Ministry of Transport*	17,402	20,514
Ministry of Posts and Telecommunications*	30,657	33,904
Ministry of Labour*	4,190	5,046
Ministry of Construction	5,979	6,624
Ministry of Home Affairs	565	616
TOTAL	1,920,871	2,022,631

Notes: 1. All amounts represent initial budgets or appropriations for the respective fiscal year.
2. Since amounts have been rounded off, the sum of the amounts for each column, and the totals shown above do not necessarily agree.
3. Some amounts include appropriations for humanities.
4. The amounts for the ministries and agency marked with asterisks include the Science and Technology Budget appropriations from Special Accounts.

Second, MITI-initiated cooperative R&D programmes involving the cooperation of competing Japanese companies, which many in the West have seen as the most important way in which MITI has fostered the generation and diffusion of new advanced technologies, account for a relatively small proportion of MITI's total science and technology budget.

Most of MITI's funding for non-energy 'high-technology' cooperative R&D projects comes from four programmes. The first of these is the Large-Scale R&D Programme which began in 1966 and which is now under the control of MITI's Agency of Industrial Science and Technology (AIST) and MITI's New Energy & Industrial Technology Development Organization (NEDO). The second programme is the R&D Programme on Basic Technologies for Future Industries. This programme began in 1981 and is also under the control of AIST and NEDO.

Table 6.5 Miti's industrial technology R&D expenditures, 1987 (¥100m.)

	Expenditures	Total R&D (%)
1. Energy R&D	1,145.7	52
	1,068.4	48
2. Non-energy R&D of which:		
Large scale (A)	(139.3)	
Future tech. (A)	(60.4)	23
Key tech. centre (A)	(250.0)	
Information tech. (M)	(57.9)	
3. MITI's total R&D	2,214.1	100

Note: (A) = AIST/NEDO; (M) Machinery and Information.
Source: Watanabe (1992).

The third programme is that undertaken by the Japan Key Technology Center (Kiban Gijutsu Kenkyu Sokushin Senta). This Center was established in October 1985 at the time when NTT, the largest domestic telecommunications carrier, was privatised. In fact the Key Technology Center represented part of the politically negotiated compromise which emerged from the fierce battles which raged between the Ministry of Posts and Telecommunications (MPT) and MITI in the early 1980s over regulatory control over the converging area of computers and communications. The Center is funded largely from dividends from government-owned shares in NTT and Japan Tobacco Inc. This brings the important advantage of funding for research which is relatively independent of the financial strictures of the Ministry of Finance. Although formally under the joint control of MITI and MPT, there is a *de facto* split down the middle of the Center, with the two ministries taking sole charge for the areas under their own jurisdiction. Typically, research projects are set up for a fixed period of time with research participation from companies, universities, and government. Usually 70 per cent of the funding comes from the Center with the remaining 30 per cent provided by the companies. Intellectual property rights usually remain with the participants in the project. In MITI the Key Technology Center falls under the responsibility of AIST and NEDO. (For an analysis of the Protein Engineering Research Institute, a biotechnology project funded from MITI's part of the Key Technology Center, see Fransman and Tanaka 1995.)

The fourth programme in MITI that funds cooperative R&D is that run by the Ministry's Machinery and Information Industries Bureau. Projects funded by this Bureau in the area of information technology include the Fifth Generation Computer Project and, currently, the Real World Computing Project.

From Table 6.5 it can be seen that these four programmes, which together represent most of MITI's non-energy cooperative R&D funding, account for only about 23 per cent of this Ministry's total spending on R&D. Assuming that the proportions remained the same in 1991, this would mean that these four programmes, which many have seen as having an important impact on the international competitiveness of Japanese companies, accounted for a mere 2.9 per cent of the total spending of the Japanese government on science and technology.

6.8 MITI's Response to Globalisation

MITI's response to the globalisation of the Japanese science and technology system can be characterised in three ways.

First, MITI has retained its use of cooperative R&D projects as an important policy tool aimed at strengthening the international competitiveness of Japanese companies. This national objective is reflected in MITI's use of the term 'National R&D Programmes'. (It should be noted, however, that MITI's international competitiveness objective is to some extent counterbalanced by another important MITI objective, namely achieving harmonious international trade relations.)

Second, MITI has acknowledged the importance of globalisation, not by attempting to insulate its national R&D programmes from global influence, but by internationalising them. This has been done by not only allowing foreign companies to join national R&D programmes, but by positively encouraging them to do so. This was facilitated by a new law which MITI drafted and which was passed in 1988, the *Law For Consolidating Research & Development Systems Relating To Industrial Technology*. This law had two major aims: to internationalise Japan's industrial technology, and to increase Japanese competences in the areas of basic and scientific R&D. At the same time NEDO, established in 1980, was reorganised and an Industrial Technology Department was set up within NEDO in order to help achieve these two aims. From 1989 foreign companies were allowed to join national R&D programmes.

It is important to emphasise, however, that while foreign companies were both allowed and encouraged to join MITI's national R&D programmes from 1989, these programmes continue to be set with national objectives in mind. The objectives include strengthening the competitiveness of Japanese companies and increasing basic and scientific research capabilities in Japan. In other words, while foreign companies are encouraged to join these programmes, they are not allowed to influence the choice of programme in the first place nor the objectives of the programme. In this way it may accurately be said that MITI has internationalised its national R&D programmes.

The third 'plank' in MITI's response to globalisation has been to establish purely internationalised cooperative R&D programmes. While the original broad area of research has been chosen by MITI through its consultation procedures, these programmes have been opened to international negotiation in order to establish precise objectives and *modus operandi*. Examples of these internationalised programmes include *The Human Frontier Science Program*, *The Space Station Program*, and *The Intelligent Manufacturing System Program*.

In general it is true to say that MITI's approach to its internationalised cooperative R&D programmes is still evolving. A significant amount of suspicion on the part of Western policy-makers greeted MITI's launching of both its Human Frontier and its Intelligent Manufacturing System programmes. Many originally argued that these programmes represented attempts by MITI to further strengthen the competitiveness of Japanese companies by tapping more effectively into advanced Western research. The result was that strong pressure was put on MITI, on the whole rather successfully, to give a greater role to Western policy-makers in shaping both the objectives and *modus operandi* of these programmes.

As MITI acceded to these pressures and opened the programmes to international consultation, so much of the suspicion changed into somewhat greater enthusiasm for the programmes and optimism regarding the benefits that will be received by all the participating countries. The main lesson that MITI has probably derived from its experience in launching these programmes is that it will have to begin consulting with Western policy-makers at a far earlier stage in the programme definition process but that significant progress in cooperative international research can be achieved with this international consultative process in place.

To summarise, MITI has responded to the globalisation of science and technology by retaining its objectives of strengthening both the competitiveness of Japanese companies and Japanese competencies in basic research and science; by internationalising its national cooperative R&D programmes by allowing and encouraging the participation of foreign companies; and by taking the initiative in establishing fully internationalised cooperative research programmes whose objectives and *modus operandi* are negotiated with the other participating countries.

6.9 National Objectives versus Globalisation?

From the above it is clear that MITI is attempting to internationalise its national R&D programmes while retaining their national objectives, and to establish purely internationalised programmes partly with the aim of furthering national objectives. But this contradicts the corollary of the convergence hypothesis discussed above. To quote Nelson and Wright once more:

[P]olicies launched by governments with the objective of giving their national firms a particular edge in an area of technology... do not work very well any more. It is increasingly difficult to create new technology that will stay contained within national borders for very long in a world where technological sophistication is widespread and firms of many nationalities are ready to make the investment needed to exploit new generic technology (Nelson and Wright 1992, 1961).

So is MITI attempting to do the impossible? I believe that MITI's nationally oriented policies in a globalising world are not only consistent but are sensible. This is so for the following reasons. The corollary of the convergence hypothesis *assumes* that 'new technology will not stay contained within national borders for very long' and then *deduces* from this that 'policies launched by governments with the objective of giving their national firms a particular edge in an area of technology... do not work very well any more'. The problem with this argument, as is suggested by MITI's current policies, is that while the assumption of the corollary may be true, this deduction does not necessarily follow.

More specifically, MITI's policies suggest that it is possible to formulate and implement programmes that give Japanese companies a competitive edge in particular technologies, even though some of the new generic technologies created under the programmes 'leak' to non-Japanese competing companies. How can this be? Are there reasons for believing that MITI's policies are appropriate, or are they simply misguided?

The following are the reasons for believing that MITI's policies are indeed appropriate. First, not all the technology acquired by the participants in the national R&D project will leak to non-participating competing companies, even those that have the necessary 'social capabilities'. The reason is that technology created under these projects is not a public good which is freely available. A good deal of this technology will remain tacit and untransferable. Accordingly, a significant amount of the technology will remain with the participants who have undertaken the research and development. (Polanyi (1967) defined tacit knowledge as existing when someone knows more than they can tell. In the case of the national R&D projects under discussion here—such as those referred to below—while the *results* of the project are usually publicised at internationally open conferences, the *ways in which these results were obtained* are usually not disclosed in detail. Typically, there is a significant degree of tacitness, in Polanyi's sense, regarding these ways.)

MITI's national R&D projects are all oriented to the research and development of practical implementable technological systems, rather than to the production of pure ideas or theories. They therefore have a high degree of tacitness. To substantiate this important point, further details are provided in Fransman (1993), *The Market And Beyond*, for several of MITI's national R&D projects which illustrate in detail the substantial degree of tacitness involved in these projects. The projects analysed include the High-Speed Computing System for Scientific and Technological Uses, the Optical Measurement and Control System, and the Pattern Information Processing System, which are part of MITI's national Large-Scale R&D Program; and the Superlattice Devices, and Three-Dimensional ICs projects that are part of MITI's R&D Program on Basic Technologies for Future Industries. Three other projects under the latter program in the area of biotechnology, the Bioreactor, Large-Scale Cell Cultivation, and the Utilization of Recombinant DNA projects are analysed in detail in Fransman and Tanaka (1995).

An additional point regarding the implications of tacitness was made in *The Market And Beyond* to explain why the dominant Japanese companies in a particular technology area were willing to send some of their researchers to a MITI-initiated cooperative R&D project even though this would mean the leakage of some of their knowledge to weaker Japanese companies. The willingness of the dominant companies, it was shown, was partly attributable to the existence of a significant degree of tacitness within the cooperative R&D project. The fact that the dominant companies generally assigned a greater number of researchers to the project in the areas where they were dominant ensured, given the tactiness that existed, that they were able to derive a greater degree of benefit from the project than the weaker companies.

The implication of this point for MITI's national projects where non-Japanese companies participate is that the participation of these companies does not imply that they receive as much knowledge from the project as the Japanese companies (taken collectively and in some cases individually). Accordingly, while there may be some 'leakage' abroad from the national R&D project, the amount of knowledge which actually leaks is significantly constrained by the tacitness involved.

The second reason for the appropriateness of MITI's policies is that even if all the knowledge created in national R&D projects and internationalised projects were to leak, that is even if there is no tacitness, it will still take time for the knowledge to leak. This implies that the creator of the knowledge will enjoy a *lead* in that knowledge for as long as it takes the knowledge to diffuse to other competitors with the necessary social capabilities to acquire that knowledge.

Furthermore, in a world where 'underlying' core knowledge is widely diffused and where social capabilities are evenly distributed amongst competitors, competitiveness may be driven primarily by the lead that a company has, even if the lead is short-lived. For example, even a short lead of several months in processing power and price for a PC producer such as Compaq or Dell may mean a great deal in terms of competitiveness. This implies that to the extent that MITI's national R&D projects are able to provide Japanese companies with even a short term lead, they may be able to help achieve the national objective of increasing the competitiveness of these companies.

Third, as is widely acknowledged, the competitiveness of Japanese firms is often determined by strong comparative competencies in the downstream parts of the value chain. In some cases it may be possible for Japanese firms to increase their competitiveness by linking the upstream technology that is derived from their participation in a national R&D project (e.g. technology which is the outcome of oriented-basic and applied research) with their existing downstream competencies. Accordingly, in those cases, where Japanese firms are able to acquire new technologies through national R&D projects, even where there is no tacitness or lag in the diffusion of these upstream technologies to competitors (a highly unrealistic assumption), they may still derive a competitive advantage from these projects relative to their competitors with weaker downstream competencies.

Fourth, although there may be leakages of technology from the national R&D project, these may be adequately compensated for by inflows of technology (leakages to Japan from other national science and technology systems) that occur as a result of the activities of the project. For example, the participation of foreign companies in a Japanese national R&D project may constitute a leakage, but this leakage may nonetheless be compensated for by the knowledge that the foreign companies bring into the project. Furthermore, the goodwill that both the project and possibly the Japanese system more generally may earn from opening to foreign participation may result in compensating inflows elsewhere in the system.

Fifth, Nelson and Wright refer to 'policies launched by governments with the objective of giving their national firms a particular [competitive] edge in an area of technology' (1992, 1961). However, the criterion that should be used in deciding whether technology policies with national objectives are viable or not is less demanding. The appropriate criterion is not whether participating national firms derive a competitive edge, but whether they are better off with the project rather than without it and whether this benefit exceeds the cost of the project. Under this criterion, some national R&D projects may be viable under internationalised conditions even if they do not give participating national companies a competitive edge.

The area of protein engineering, one of the core generic technologies in biotechnology, provides an example. In a report on biotechnology in Japan published in 1985 by the US-sponsored Japanese Technology Evaluation Program it was concluded that 'Japan currently ranks fourth to the United States, United Kingdom, and Western Europe in protein engineering. There is not much activity at the present time [in Japan] at either the universities or industries'.

To remedy this situation, MITI established the Protein Engineering

Research Institute (PERI) in April 1986 under the auspices of the Japan Key Technology Center. Companies and universities sent researchers to PERI where generic protein engineering technologies were generated in areas such as protein structural analysis and computer graphics. The commercialisation of these technologies was undertaken outside the project in the individual participating companies under normal conditions of commercial secrecy. Many of the major Japanese companies in the biotechnology field and in related fields joined. In addition, two foreign companies joined, Nihon Roche, the Japanese subsidiary of the large Swiss pharmaceutical company, and Digital Equipment. (This was one of the earliest examples of foreign companies joining a Japanese national R&D project.)

By 1989 there was strong evidence that the research at PERI was of international frontier standards. (See Fransman and Tanaka 1995 for details.) From the Japanese national point of view it seems clear that this project was viable (and in Japan it is acknowledged as being one of the most successful undertaken by the Key Technology Center). This is so even though it is unlikely that the Japanese companies participating were able to derive a 'competitive edge' from the project in terms of better protein engineering technology than their Western competitors.

For these five reasons it may be concluded that MITI's cooperative R&D projects oriented to national objectives are viable in the internationalised world of the 1980s and 1990s. But if this argument is true for Japan, does it also hold for other large Western countries?

6.10 The Implications for Other Large Western Countries

With the exception of the fourth argument in the last section (which is based on the assumption of the comparative strength of Japanese companies in the downstream parts of the value chain), all the arguments given apply also to other large Western countries.

Let us take, for example, the fifth argument, that the benefits of the project may exceed its costs and make the national participating companies better off than they would have been. The case of protein engineering that was given in support of this argument may indeed be paralleled by the US case of Sematech. The Sematech project, funded by DARPA, was ultimately oriented largely to the development of semiconductor equipment competencies at a time when Japanese companies such as Nikon had begun to establish an international competitiveness in this field. Current reports indicate that the Sematech cooperative R&D project has succeeded insofar as it has allowed many US semiconductor manufacturers to buy competitive US-produced semiconductor equipment where before the project Japanese equipment was more likely to have been the only viable alternative.

Since four of the five arguments may also apply to large Western countries then, to the extent that these arguments are valid, it must be concluded that R&D projects oriented to the achievement of national objectives may be viable in an internationalised world. It is important, however, to note the assumptions on which these arguments are based, such as the assumption of tacitness, since these assumptions constrain the instances when such nationally oriented projects will be viable. It is certainly not being argued in here that there is necessarily very wide scope for nationally-oriented R&D projects.

6.11 The MITI Paradox

While the Ministry of Education controlled 46 per cent of the Japanese government's science technology budget in 1991, and the Science and Technology Agency 26 per cent, MITI's proportion was only 13 per cent. How then can MITI be the most powerful ministry in the technology area, as many argue?

My answer to this intriguing question is that MITI is indeed the most powerful ministry in this area but that its power and influence comes, not from its budget, but from two critical related sources: the companies which fall under its jurisdiction, and the highly effective global information network that it controls. These two sources require some elaboration.

Although MITI is not responsible for the whole of the manufacturing sector, the most dynamic parts of this sector fall under this ministry's jurisdiction. More specifically, the transportation, electronics (which includes semiconductors, computers, and telecommunications), and chemicals sectors, which account for the bulk of Japan's manufacturing value added and exports, are under MITI's jurisdiction, as are other less important or dynamic sectors such as textiles.

Until the late 1960s, MITI's direct control over foreign exchange allocations meant that manufacturing companies wanting to import needed inputs, including technology, had to get permission from this ministry. Furthermore, MITI also had a significant degree of control over capital allocations through its influence over the loans extended by the Japan Development Bank, which in turn influenced the extension of credit by the city banks. By selecting particular industries for promotion, MITI had an important impact on the fortunes of the companies included in these industries. In addition, MITI's laboratories and cooperative R&D projects provided an important boost to companies that were only just beginning to catch-up with their Western counterparts. In this way MITI was able to wield a significant degree of influence over its companies in the manufacturing sector.

Two decades later, MITI's influence had changed substantially. Japanese companies—far larger, with much stronger technological capabilities, and with access to international capital markets often with high credit ratings—needed MITI far less than they had previously. Having lost many of its direct controls, including control over foreign exchange allocations, MITI came to rely on 'administrative guidance' in order to pursue its industrial, technology, and trade policies.

Japanese companies, however, continued to rely on MITI to do those things which they could not do adequately for themselves. These included the following. First, in the area of science and technology, MITI began increasingly to look to the longer term future as Japanese companies successfully closed the technology gap with their foreign competitors. Japanese companies, while possibly 'longer-term oriented' than many of their Western counterparts, were nevertheless still significantly constrained by their need to generate profits and by the factors which bounded their corporate visions. These constraints meant that they were frequently unwilling to venture into new technology areas where future returns were highly uncertain. Understanding these constraints, MITI, as was seen earlier in this paper, began increasingly to emphasise its role in helping to generate, and later diffuse, new technologies which were not receiving the attention that they possibly deserved from Japanese companies. In this way MITI has been able to ensure its continued relevance in the area of technology for many Japanese companies.

Secondly, with the growing importance of international trade conflict, MITI has come to play an indispensable role in mediating Japan's international economic relations with its trading partners. This is an area where by definition Japanese companies, driven by profit and market considerations, are unable individually or collectively to resolve the problems that arise. In the field of international trade, therefore, MITI's role has been crucial.

Thirdly, MITI has also in the last few decades come to play an important role in the fields of energy and environment. In the case of energy, the oil shocks of the 1970s revealed dramatically how important energy was to the Japanese economy. Once again, MITI, with its watchguard brief for the whole of the manufacturing sector, stepped in to develop a set of energy-related policies. The legacy of MITI's role in the field of energy is evident in the fact, referred to earlier, that over half of its expenditure in R&D currently relates to energy. In the area of the environment it is also acknowledged that for-profit companies are unable to deliver the activities that are necessary for the environmental protection and enhancement that is needed. Here too MITI has come to play an important role.

For these reasons, although MITI's power over Japanese companies has undoubtedly diminished, the ministry continues to play an indispensable role. This has ensured that MITI continues to have political 'clout', including in the science and technology area where its influence far exceeds its share of the Japanese government's budget.

However, MITI's influence comes, not only from the important role that it continues to play in Japanese industry and trade, but also from the substantial global information network that it controls. The 'nodes' in this network extend out from MITI to include the formal and informal advisory and consultative committees that the ministry has established; the industry associations that have been established, often under MITI's guidance, in the sectors over which MITI has jurisdiction which, as noted, are the most dynamic in the Japanese economy; the links that MITI has forged with other ministries and agencies, often through the secondment of MITI staff; and the activities of JETRO which provides detailed information on industry, technology, and markets abroad.

MITI's global information network has given the ministry unparalleled high quality information regarding both Japan and the rest of the global economy. This information, crossing countries, technolgies, companies, industrial sectors, and markets, has given MITI's decision-makers an enormously broad 'vision' on the basis of which to identify the strengths, weaknesses, and opportunities facing the Japanese manufacturing sector. While this information network has not necessarily been particularly expensive to run, it has put MITI's bureaucrats in a strong position to identify what needs to be done and how (although MITI officials do not always 'get it right'— see Fransman 1995*a*).

6.12 Conclusions

This chapter has been primarily concerned with two closely related issues. The first is the question of whether national technology policy, oriented to increasing the strength of national companies, is now obsolete in a world of global business, trade, and science and technology. The second issue has been the role of the Japanese government, and in particular its Ministry of International Trade and Industry, in the area of trade and technology.

Regarding the first issue we have seen in this chapter that MITI has responded to the fact of the globalisation of the Japanese science and technology system (a globalisation that has been documented in detail) in two ways. The first is by internationalising its national cooperative R&D programmes while retaining their national objectives, while the second has involved establishing new fully internationalised programmes that are also oriented towards national objectives. It has been shown, furthermore, that although there are over time significant 'leakages' of knowledge from the Japanese science and technology system, MITI's policies aimed at strengthening Japanese companies through these programmes are nonetheless appropriate. Furthermore, it has been argued that most of the reasoning justifying MITI's policies is also relevant for other large Western countries.

With regard to the role of the Japanese government in science and technology it has been shown that, although its proportion of total national R&D expenditure is significantly smaller than in similar Western countries, the government continues to play a crucial role in strengthening the science and technology base for Japanese companies which are the main 'engine' of the Japanese economy. This chapter also deals with the 'MITI Paradox' which asks how MITI can have as much influence in the field of Japanese science and technology as is alleged if it only controls 13 per cent of the Japanese government's budget in this area. This paradox was resolved with reference to MITI's continuing important role *vis-à-vis* companies in the most dynamic sectors of the Japanese economy and its role as controller of a vast information network that criss-crosses not only Japan but also the other major economies of the world.

APPENDIX 6.1

R&D Projects under Large-Scale R&D Project

Table A1.1 Completed twenty-one projects

Name of project	Duration of R&D	R&D expenditure (¥100 m.)
1. Super high-performance electronic computer	1966–1971	10,100
2. Desulfurization process	1966–1971	2,700
3. New method of producing olefin	1967–1972	1,200
4. Remote-controlled undersea oil-drilling rig	1970–1975	4,500
5. Sea-water desalination and byproduct recovery	1969–1976	6,700
6. Electric car	1971–1976	5,700
7. Comprehensive automobile control technology	1973–1978	7,300
8. Pattern information-processing system	1971–1980	21,900
9. Direct steelmaking process using high-temperature reducing gas	1973–1980	13,700
10. Olefin production from heavy oil	1975–1981	13,800
11. Jet aircraft engines	1971–1981	19,700
12. Resource recovery technology	1973–1982	12,600
13. Flexible manufacturing system complex using laser	1977–1984	13,500
14. Subsea oil production system	1978–1984	18,200
15. Optical measurement and control system	1979–1985	15,700
16. C_1 chemical technology	1980–1986	10,500
17. Observation system for earth resources satellite-1	1984–1988	10,900
18. High-speed computing system for scientific and technological uses	1981–1989	17,500
19. Automated sewing system	1982–1990	8,200
20. Advanced robot technology	1983–1990	15,600
21. New water treatment system	1985–1990	9,400

Source: Watanabe (1992).

Table A1.2 Ongoing nine projects

1. Manganese nodule mining system	1981–1994
2. Interoperable data base system	1985–1991
3. Advanced material-processing machining system	1986–1993
4. Fine chemicals from marine organisms	1988–1996
5. Super/hyper-sonic transport propulsion system	1989–1996
6. Underground space development technology	1989–1995
7. Advanced chemical-processing technology	1990–1998
8. Human sensory measurement application technology	1990–1998
9. Micro-machine technology	1991–

Source: Watanabe (1992).

APPENDIX 6.2

R&D Projects under R&D Programme on Basic Technologies for Future Industries

Table A2.1 Completed eleven projects

Name of project	Duration of R&D	R&D expenditure (¥100 m.)
New materials		
1. Advanced alloys with controlled crystalline	1981–1988	3,903
2. Advanced composite materials	1981–1988	4,649
3. Synthetic membranes for new separation technology	1981–1990	4,179
4. Synthetic metals	1981–1990	2,883
5. High-performance plastics	1981–1990	2,441
Biotechnology		
6. Bioreactor	1981–1988	2,987
7. Large-scale cell cultivation	1981–1989	3,362
8. Utilization of recombinant DNA	1981–1990	3,084
New electron devices		
9. Fortifield ICs for extreme conditions	1981–1985	1,315
10. Superlattices devices	1981–1990	3,666
11. Three-dimensional ICs	1981–1990	6,488

Source: Watanabe (1992).

Table A2.2 Ongoing eleven projects

Super conductivity	
1. Superconducting materials, superconducting devices	1988–1998
Advanced materials	
2. Fine ceramics	1981–1992
3. High-performance materials for severe environments	1989–1996
4. Photoactive materials	1985–1992
5. Non-linear photonics materials	1989–1998
6. Silicon-based polymers	1991–
Bio technology	
7. Molecular assemblies for functional protein systems	1989–1998
8. Production and utilization technology of complex carbohydrates	1991–
New electronic devices	
9. Bio-electronic devices	1988–1995
10. Quantum functional device	1991–
Software	
11. New models for software architecture	1990–1997

Source: Watanabe (1992).

7

Visions of Future Technologies: Government, Globalisation, and Universities in Japanese Biotechnology

7.1 Introduction

Which groups of technologies will drive industrial output, productivity, and global competitiveness in the next century? What role should governments and universities play in connection with these technologies?

Significant interpretive ambiguity surrounds both these questions. This chapter goes beyond the previous two chapters, which also deal with aspects of the Japanese Innovation System, by examining in detail how organs of the Japanese government and Japanese universities have responded to the advent of a particular group of technologies which many believe will have important pervasive effects in all economies, namely biotechnology. What steps have been taken by government and universities in Japan in the area of biotechnology? Why have these steps been undertaken and with what effect? The answers to these questions are explored in this chapter.

7.2 Chapter Overview

The chapter begins by outlining several influential views regarding to role of the Japanese government and universities in the area of new technologies. The role of the Japanese Ministry of International Trade and Industry (MITI) in biotechnology is then examined in detail. Attention is next focused on some of the major cooperative research programmes initiated by MITI in the field of biotechnology and the outcomes of these programmes. Some of the biotechnology projects undertaken under the auspices of the Science and Technology Agency (STA) are then analysed and evaluated.

But why did the policy-makers make the policies that they did? What are the main influences that shaped their policies? These questions are tackled

This chapter was written with Shoko Tanaka. It was originally published as 'Government, Globalisation and Universities in Japanese Biotechnology', *Research Policy*, 1995, 24, 13–49.

next through an examination of the relationships between business, bureaucrats, and politicians in Japan. The role of some of the other Japanese ministries involved in biotechnology is then discussed, including conflicts between ministries that have arisen in this area.

In the next section the role of Japanese universities in biotechnology is analysed. The analysis includes evidence from a study on the importance of research in Japanese universities for some of the leading Japanese biotechnology companies, as well as the case study of a leading biotechnology research laboratory at Tokyo University.

How is advanced research in biotechnology distributed in Japan between company laboratories and universities and does this pattern of distribution differ from the major Western countries? This question is examined next on the basis of a study of patents in biotechnology-related pharmaceuticals. The chapter ends with a summary of some of the main features of the Japanese system in biotechnology.

7.3 Background

The question regarding the appropriate role for government in encouraging industrial growth remains vexed. While the tide of popular sentiment regarding this question has changed markedly in the US with the advent of the more pro-active Clinton Administration, academic opinion still remains sharply divided regarding the effect that government can have on industrial growth. Expressing this academic ambivalence, Nelson (1992) summarises the findings of a study of a number of national innovation systems: 'what distinguishes systems where firms are strong and innovative from systems where they are not . . . has somewhat less to do with aggressive 'technology policies' than current fashion might have one believe'.

This chapter is concerned with three main questions. What role has been played by the various organs of the Japanese Government in strengthening the technological base of Japanese companies through cooperative research in biotechnology? How important are Japanese universities for Japanese companies involved in biotechnology? How has the 'globalisation' (increasingly opening) of the Japanese innovation system affected the role of the Japanese Government in biotechnology?

All these questions remain controversial within the Japanese context, as are similar questions asked of other national innovation systems. They nevertheless remain central for the simple reason that industrial growth and competitiveness is a high priority in all countries and a key issue that naturally follows relates to what, if anything, the government can do to help achieve these objectives.

Progress towards answering this question must begin with careful studies of the efforts made by governments to influence industrial growth and competitiveness in their countries. On the basis of these studies an attempt can then be made to tackle the crucial question: what difference has the government's efforts made, that is, what would have been the outcome had the government not intervened in the way it did? This is the approach adopted here. While this counter-factual question is inherently difficult to examine, some progress can be made in answering it, as is shown in the last section.

7.4 Background

7.4.1 The Role of the Japanese Government in Biotechnology

The seminal 1984 report on biotechnology by the US Office of Technology Assessment (OTA) concluded that 'Japan is likely to be the leading competitor of the United States [in biotechnology]' (OTA 1984, 7). Two reasons were given for this conclusion. The first was that

Japanese companies in a broad range of industrial sectors have extensive experience in bioprocess technology. Japan does not have superior bioprocess technology, but it does have relatively more industrial experience using old biotechnology, more established bioprocessing plants, and more bioprocess engineers than the United States   (OTA 1984, 7).

The second reason hinged on the role of the Japanese Government:

[T]he Japanese Government has targeted biotechnology as a key technology of the future, is funding its commercial development, and is coordinating interactions among representatives from industry, universities, and government   (OTA 1984, 7–8).

We will examine here whether there is compelling evidence to support the latter argument regarding the alleged role of the Japanese Government in fostering the competitiveness of Japanese companies in biotechnology.

7.4.2 The Role of Japanese Universities in Biotechnology

According to the conventional wisdom, Japanese universities are a source of weakness in the Japanese innovation system, at least relative to their Western counterparts. According to the OTA report, 'Neither Japan nor the European competitor countries identified in this assessment have as many or as well-funded university/industry relationships as the United States does' (ibid. 17).

A leading Japanese economist, Masahiko Aoki, has arrived at the following rather defensive conclusion regarding the role of Japanese universities:

Japanese universities have been downgraded by foreign observers as less dynamic and less innovative in comparison with the advanced industrial laboratories. I recognize that Japanese national universities lag behind firstrate American research universities both in research and graduate-level education except in a few fields (Aoki 1988, 252).

Aoki, however, qualifies his conclusion in two respects:

First, the Japanese have made substantial progress in some scientific fields in recent times, and the role of the university in it (sic) is not entirely negligible . . . Second, under the condition of low mobility of researchers and engineers between firms, laboratories of university professors have been playing non-negligible roles as information clearinghouses. Professors of major faculties of engineering have decisive roles in allocating new graduates among leading firms   (Aoki 1988, 252).

In order to test this conventional wisdom more directly we interviewed six of the largest Japanese biotechnology-related companies in order to establish how important Japanese universities were as an external source of knowledge. Furthermore, we had detailed discussions with a leading biotechnology researcher at Tokyo University in order to establish the kinds of university–industry linkages that can be realised in Japan under the current institutional and legal conditions.

The results given in this chapter suggest that Japanese universities are a far more important component of the Japanese innovation system than is commonly acknowledged.

7.4.3 Globalisation, and the Role of the Japanese Government

In recent years, increasing prominence has been given to the argument that government policies, aimed at giving national firms an edge in particular technology areas, are being undermined by the 'globalisation' of technology. For example, Nelson and Wright argue that

National borders mean much less than they used to regarding the flow of technology, at least among the nations that have made the new needed social investments in education and research facilities. National governments have been slow to recognize these new facts of life. Indeed, the last decade has seen a sharp increase in what has been called 'technonationalism', policies launched by governments with the objective of giving their national firms a particular edge in an area of technology (Nelson and Wright 1992, 1961).

According to Nelson and Wright, 'technonationalist' policies are unlikely to succeed in a globalised world:

Our argument is that these policies do not work very well any more. It is increasingly difficult to create new technology that will stay contained within national borders for very long in a world where technological sophistication is widespread and firms of many nationalities are ready to make the investments needed to exploit new generic technology (Nelson and Wright 1992, 1961).

Applying this argument to Japanese biotechnology, the efforts of the Japanese Government to strengthen Japanese companies in this field are doomed to fail. But is this indeed the case? Or, are there reasons to suggest that the Japanese Government's programmes in biotechnology are having the desired effect of strengthening Japanese companies? More generally, how has the Japanese Government responded to 'globalisation' in the area of biotechnology? These questions are examined later in this paper.

7.5 The Role of MITI in Biotechnology

7.5.1 Introduction

Although the Japanese Government is responsible for a smaller share of total R&D expenditure than its major Western counterparts, it is committed to playing an important role in its national innovation system. As Figure 6.7 shows, in 1990, the contribution of the Japanese Government to total R&D was 18.6% compared with 33.2% for Germany, 46.1% for the USA, and 49.3% for France. If defence-related R&D expenditures are excluded, the Japanese figure becomes 18.0% compared with 25.8% for the USA, 29.9% for Germany, and 33.9% for France. The Japanese Government, however, has publically stated its intention to double its expenditure on R&D as soon as financial circumstances permit.

In this section, the overall role of the Ministry of International Trade and Industry (MITI) in biotechnology is examined. In the following section, four of MITI's most important biotechnology projects are analysed and evaluated, three in the Future Industries Programme, the fourth being the Protein Engineering Research Institute. The next section examines the biotechnology part of the ERATO programme established under the auspices of the Science and Technology Agency (STA). In the succeeding section the biotechnology programmes of the other ministries with an interest in biotechnology are examined.

7.5.2 The Life Sciences in Japan in the 1970s and New Emerging Trends in Biotechnology

The government machinery in Japan first began to highlight the industrial strategic significance of the life sciences in the early 1970s. In April 1971, the Prime Minister's Council for Science and Technology recommended the promotion of the life sciences. In 1973, the STA established its Office for Life Science Promotion.

At the same time, global events began to highlight the potential significance of the life sciences in general and the emerging new biotechnology in particular. Drawing on Watson and Crick's model of the double helix in 1953, the first gene was cloned in 1973 by Boyer and Cohen giving birth to the new genetic engineering technique of recombinant DNA, while in 1975 the first hybridoma (fused cell) was created by Milstein and Kohler.

In 1976, the first so-called new biotechnology firm was set up to exploit recombinant DNA technology, Genentech, a spin-off from university-based research. When Genentech shares were first sold on Wall Street in 1980, they set the record for the fastest price increase, rising from $35 to $89 in 20 minutes. In 1981, the initial public sale of shares by Cetus, another new biotechnology firm, established a new Wall Street record for the highest amount raised in an initial offering, amounting to $115 million.

By the end of 1981 over 80 new biotechnology firms had been established in the US. In the same year, Du Pont, the largest American chemicals company, allocated $120 million to R&D in the life sciences, followed by Monsanto, the third largest, which committed a similar amount. While events such as these emphasised the opportunities that were perceived to exist in the field of new biotechnology, the changes that were beginning to occur in the property rights regime signalled the potential threats that faced companies which delayed entry into this new technology area. In 1980, in Diamond vs. Chakrabarty, the US Supreme Court ruled that microorganisms could be patented under existing law and in the same year the Cohen/Boyer patent was issued for the technique relating to the construction of recombinant DNA.

7.5.3 The Response of MITI and the Large Japanese Chemicals Companies

Japanese relative failure in the chemicals industry

In order to understand MITI's response to the advent of new biotechnology in the early 1980s it is necessary to be aware of the standing of the Japanese chemicals industry at this date and MITI's previous attempts to bolster its fortunes.

In some senses the Japanese chemicals industry is a case of 'relative failure', at least insofar as the size and international activity of Japan's largest chemicals companies go, relative to that of the largest Western chemicals companies. As Itami (1991) has recently noted in one of the best available studies of the Japanese chemicals industry, the largest Japanese chemicals companies spend significantly less on R&D and employ far fewer staff in this area than their Western counterparts.

Bayer, Hoechst, BASF, Du Pont, and ICI, for example, spend approximately 2,500, 1,320, 1,020, 1,320, and $980 million respectively on R&D. The corresponding figure for the two largest Japanese chemicals companies, Mitsubishi Chemical and Sumitomo Chemical, is $310 and $220 million respectively. While Hoechst, Bayer and Du Pont employ 13,000, 12,700, and 5,000 in R&D, the corresponding figure for Mitsubishi Chemical and Sumitomo Chemical is 1850 and 1800 respectively.

Furthermore, Japanese chemicals companies are far more dependent than their Western counterparts on their domestic market. While the ratio of exports to local production in 1987/88 was 58, 51, 28, and 27% for Bayer, ICI, BASF, and Du Pont respectively, the corresponding figure for Mitsubishi Chemical was 2.7.

Despite these figures, according to other criteria the Japanese chemicals industry is more successful. The total value of output of the Japanese chemicals industry in 1988, for example, was $160,200 million. This compared with $240,500 million for the USA and $89,500 million for West Germany. While the West German chemicals industry accounted for 8.9% of GNP in this year, the corresponding figure for Japan was 6.2% compared with 6.0% for the USA. In 1987, the Japanese chemicals industry accounted for 14.1% of world output of chemicals. The figures in this section come from Itami (1991).

Explaining Japan's relative failure in chemicals

While the definitive explanation of Japan's relative failure in chemicals remains to be provided, Itami (1991) gives some of the important reasons. His account stresses the weakness of the industry immediately after World War II, MITI's promotional activities at this time to cultivate the chemical fertilizer industry, the re-focus of the chemical industry with the advent of petrochemicals, and the effect of the two oil shocks in the 1970s and early 1980s. According to Itami, these changes had the effect of keeping the chemicals companies dependent on government support and limiting inter-company competition. By contrast, in the case of Japanese success stories such as electronics, automobiles, and steel, companies outgrew their dependence on government far sooner and had to confront strong competition both domestically and in international markets.

While these factors doubtless were important, further account needs to be provided of the reasons for the failure of the Japanese chemicals companies to reap the economies of scale which were important at the time. In the more recent period an understanding is also needed of the growing significance of economies of scope and of the benefits to Japanese chemicals companies of their close supplier–user interactions with sophisticated user industries such as electronics and automobiles (see Freeman 1990).

Whatever the reasons for the relative failure of the Japanese in the chemicals industry may be, for present purposes the main point is that MITI officials responsible for the chemicals industry saw in the advent of new biotechnology a new set of opportunities for an industry which they had long tried to nurture without any particular success.

The response of MITI and large Japanese chemicals companies to the advent of new biotechnology

Like their American and European counter-parts, Japanese chemicals companies were 'pushed' into biotechnology by falling rates of profit in their traditional areas of business as much as they were 'pulled' into this new technology area by expected rates of return. For many of these companies the concentration on oil-based products such as bulk chemicals and plastics led to difficulties when the level of international competition in petrochemicals began increasing. Profitability was further hit by the oil price rises in 1979 and 1980 and the subsequent global economic downturn.

In 1980, a Biotechnology Forum, with the objective of consolidating interest in biotechnology, was established by five Japanese chemicals companies: Asahi Chemical, Kyowa Hakko, Mitsubishi Chemical, Mitsui Toatsu, and Sumitomo Chemical. At around this time, these and other Japanese companies began to do their first research in new biotechnology-related areas.

In 1981, MITI entered the field of biotechnology, reflecting both the increasing sense in Japan of the importance of biotechnology and this ministry's traditional role in helping to strengthen the performance and competitiveness of those industries under its jurisdiction. Further factors which motivated MITI's entry into biotechnology were the recession which existed at the time in the international chemicals industry, MITI's long concern at the relative weakness of Japanese chemicals companies, and the Ministry's preoccupation with energy policy in the wake of the second 'oil shock'.

After initial discussions with around 50 companies, MITI in 1981 eventually invited 14 companies to join in the biotechnology part of the Programme on Basic Technologies for Future Industries. (The other parts of this Programme dealt with future electronic devices and new materials. See Fransman (1993) for a detailed analysis of the future electronic devices part of the Programme.) The companies eventually chosen were Ajinomoto, Asahi Chemical, Daicel Chemical, Denki Kagaku Kogyo, Kao Soap, Kyowa Hakko, Mitsubishi Chemical, Mitsubishi Chemical Institute of Life Sciences, Mitsubishi Gas Chemical, Mitsui Petrochemical, Mitsui Toatsu, Takeda, Toyo Jozo, and Sumitomo Chemical. Reflecting MITI's jurisdiction over the chemicals industry, all of the companies had important interests in the chemicals area, while 12 of them (that is, èxcept Ajinomoto and Toyo Jozo) were primarily chemicals companies. (This Programme is analysed in detail below.)

To consolidate further its link with Japanese companies with an interest in biotechnology, MITI established its Bioindustry Office in 1982, located within the Basic Industries Bureau of the Ministry which had long held responsibility for the chemicals, steel, and non-ferrous metals sectors.

In June 1982 the Bioindustry Office established the Committee for the development of Bioindustry, a government-industry consultative committee charged with surveying the situation in the industry and producing a 'vision' for the future. In the same year the Bioindustry Office established a new industry association, the Bioindustry Development Center (BIDEC), initially under the auspices of the Japanese Association of Industrial Fermentation (itself established in 1943). BIDEC would gather information on the biotechnology industry, facilitate the flow of non-proprietary information between its member companies, coordinate the presentation of the industry's views to government, and provide feedback on government programmes. Of BIDEC's approximately 150 members in the mid-1980s (including several foreign-owned companies), 28% were from the chemicals sector, 23% from the electrical, machinery, and construction sectors, and 20% from the food sector.

Industry–government information flows and cooperative research

It is clear from the above historical account that there were two main components to MITI's attempts to strengthen and increase the competitiveness of Japanese chemicals companies by encouraging them to adopt new biotechnology. The first involved adding a new strand to MITI's existing vast information network linking the Ministry with the companies and sectors under its jurisdiction and their technologies and markets. This new strand would serve the purpose of improving industry–government information flows in the area of new biotechnology. On the basis of this improved information, MITI, in consultation with the industrial interests involved, would be in a better position to appraise the strengths and weaknesses of the Japanese companies and research institutions that might be affected by this new set of technologies and decide where government intervention might be productive.

The second component of MITI's programme of action in biotechnology involved the establishment of a number of cooperative research projects. These projects were designed to strengthen the technological competencies of the participating companies and other research institutions in areas where, left to their own devices, they would not do sufficient research as productively. Participation in these projects often involved competing companies. This second component drew on the experience that MITI had already accumulated in promoting the development of other industries, such as computers and semiconductors analysed in detail in Fransman (1993).

7.5.4 MITI's Cooperative Research and Development Projects in Biotechnology

MITI's cooperative R&D projects in the area of biotechnology up to 1992 are shown in Table 7.1. MITI's biotechnology projects fall under seven main programmes. The first, the R&D Programme on Basic Technologies for Future Industries which began in 1981, has already been referred to. It is under the control of MITI's Agency of Industrial Science and Technology (AIST) and MITI's New Energy and Industrial Technology Development Organization (NEDO). The second is the Large-Scale R&D Programme which was started in 1966 and which is also under AIST and NEDO's control.

The third programme is run by the Japan Key Technology Center (Kiban Gijutsu Kenkyu Sokushin Senta). This Center was established in 1985 at the time that NTT, the largest domestic telecommunications carrier, was partly privatised. In fact, the Key Technology Center represented part of the politically negotiated compromise which emerged from the fierce battles which raged between the Ministry of Posts and Telecommunications (MPT) and MITI in the early 1980s over regulatory control over the converging area of computers and communications.

The Key Technology Center is funded largely from dividends from government-owned shares in NTT and Japan Tobacco Inc. This brings the important advantage of funding for research which is relatively independent of the financial strictures of the Ministry of Finance. Although formally under the joint control of MITI and MPT, there is a *de facto* split down the middle of the Center, with the two ministries taking sole charge for the areas under their jurisdiction. Typically, research projects are set up for a fixed period of time with research participation from companies, universities, and government. Usually 70% of the funding comes from the Center with the remaining 30% provided by the companies. Intellectual property rights usually remain with the participants in the project.

The remaining programmes are the NEDO Research Base Facilitating Programme, the R&D Programme for Global Environment, the Human Frontiers Programme, and the R&D on Biomass Programme.

Many questions are raised, however, regarding these projects, questions that have not been dealt with adequately in the existing literature on Japanese biotechnology. For example, what are the objectives of the projects? Which companies participate? More significantly, what kind of 'research cooperation' exists in the project? Specifically, to what extent is the knowledge generated under the project shared amongst the participants of the project, particularly the competing companies which take part? How precisely is knowledge shared and what are the constraints, if any, on the knowledge-sharing process? What benefits do the participating companies

Table 7.1 MITI's biotechnology programmes

Programme	Type of support[a]	R&D theme	Research period	Main participating institution
The next generation basic technology programme	C	Bioreactor	1981–1988	Research association for biotechnology
	C	Large-scale cell cultivation	1981–1989	,,
	C	Recombinant DNA technology	1981–1990	,,
	C	Application technology of functional protein complex	1989–1998	,,
	C	Production and application technology of polysaccharide	1991–2000	,,
Large scale industrial technology research development programme	C	Water reutilization system (aqua-renaissance)	1985–1990	Research association for aqua-renaissance technology
	C	Manufacturing methods of chemicals, using marine biology	1988–1996	The Marine Biotechnology Institute Co.
The Japan key technology centre	I	R&D on manufacturing of peptides using rDNA and chemical synthesis technology as well as screening methods	1985–1990	M.D. Research Co.
	I	Protein engineering	1986–1995	Protein Engineering Research Institute
	I	Engineering of plant cells to	1986–1992	PCC Technology Co.
	I	R&D on bio-active material	1987–1993	Bio Material Research Institute
NEDO research base facilitating programme	I	Building a large-scale research facility for research on marine biology	1988–	R&D Centre for Marine Biology for Mining and Industry Co.

Table 7.1 *Continued*

Programme	Type of support[a]	R&D theme	Research period	Main participating institution
The R&D programme for global environment	C	R&D on fixation of carbon dioxide utilizing bacteria and algae	1990–1999	Institute for Industrial Technologies for Global Environment
	C	R&D on plant functions (CO_2 fixation)	1991–1999	Research Association for Biotechnology
	C	R&D on biodegradable plastics	1990–1997	Institute for Industrial Technologies for Global Environment
	C	R&D on bioreactor for chemical synthesis	1990–1997	”
	C	R&D on environmentally benign hydrogen production technologies	1991–1998	”
The human frontier science programme		Basic research on brain functions	1989–	The Organisation for International Human Frontier Science Programme
		Basic research on molecular approach to living organism		
The R&D on bio-mass	S	R&D on fuel alcohol technology	1983–1990	Research Association for Fuel Alcohol Technology
	S	Development of new fuel	1980–1987	Research Association for New Fuel Technology
	C	R&D on efficient fermentation technology for productive yeast	1987–1993	The Alcohol Association
	C	Research cooperation for the use of eucalyptuses	1989–1993	BIDEC
	S	Development of new use of petroleum	1983–1991	Research Association for New Use Technology of Petroleum
	S	R&D on new production technology of chemicals using organism function	1983–1987	Research Association for Production Technology of Chemicals with Organism Function

[a] C: Contract R&D; I: Investment; S: Subsidy.
Source: [Karube (1992), p. 264].

derive from the project? And, most difficult, what 'additionality' has resulted from the project, that is, what benefits have resulted which would not have occurred had the project not been undertaken?

In order to answer these kinds of questions we selected four of MITI's most important biotechnology projects for closer analysis. These are the three initial projects established under the R&D Programme on Basic Technologies for Future Industries, namely the bioreactor, large-scale cell cultivation, and recombinant DNA projects. The fourth project is the Protein Engineering Research Institute (PERI) established under the Japan Key Technology Center. In the following section the biotechnology projects of the ERATO programme, established under the jurisdiction of the Science and Technology Agency (STA), are analysed.

7.6 MITI's Initial Biotechnology Projects Under the R&D Programme on Basic Technologies for Future Industries

7.6.1 Objectives of the Projects

The objectives of the three projects reflect MITI's concern to promote the growth and competitiveness of the Japanese chemicals companies in a context where government planners were still wrestling with the effects of the 1979/80 oil shock. The objective of the Bioreactor Project was to develop new energy-saving biological technologies using bioreactors that would facilitate the cost-effective manufacture of commodity (bulk) chemicals. These technologies, it was hoped, would substitute for the more energy-intensive conventional processes.

The objective of the Large-Scale Cell Cultivation Project was to develop large-scale cell culture technologies which would make the cost-effective manufacture of fine chemicals possible. More specifically, the project aimed at developing the basic technologies for the high density cultivation of cells in a serum free medium.

The Recombinant DNA Project's objective was to further refine the newly developed rDNA technologies for use in industrial applications. This objective related to industrial usage generally, thus going beyond the chemicals-related objectives of the other two projects.

7.6.2 Participating Companies

The 14 companies that took part in the R&D Programme on Basic Technologies for Future Industries (henceforth the Future Industries, FI, programme) were divided, on the basis of consultation with the companies, as follows. The Bioreactor Project consisted of six companies and MITI's Fermentation Research Institute based in Tsukuba which had extensive bioreactor facilities. The companies were Daicel Chemical, Denki Kagaku Kogyo, Kao Soap, Mitsubishi Chemical, Mitsubishi Gas Chemical, and Mitsui Petrochemical.

The Large-Scale Cell Cultivation Project consisted of five companies; Ajinomoto, Asahi Chemical, Kyowa Hakko, Takeda, and Toyo Jozo. The Recombinant DNA Project had three member companies, Mitsubishi Chemical Institute of Life Sciences (a research institute belonging to Mitsubishi Chemical, dedicated to basic research), Mitsui Toatsu, and Sumitomo Chemical.

Formally, as indicated in Table 7.1, the companies undertook their research under contract to MITI, with resulting intellectual property rights being shared between MITI and the producing company.

7.6.3 Output from the Projects

In 1992, two years after the termination of the last of the three projects, the Research Association for Biotechnology, the MITI-established organisation responsible for the biotechnology part of the FI Programme, published a summary of the achievements of the three projects. This summary is reproduced here as Table 7.2.

Several points are worth highlighting from Table 7.2. The first is the large number of researchers involved in these three projects, a total of 385, although it is unclear from the data whether these are full-time equivalents.

Table 7.2 Achievements of MITI's Future Industries Programme

	Bioreactor	Large-scale cell culture	rDNA
Period (years)	8	9	10
R&D subsidy (billion Yen)	2.43	3.23	2.46
No. of firms	6	5	3
No. of researchers	156	143	86
No. of articles produced	15	32	64
No. of conferences presentations			
(domestic)	75	87	147
(overseas)	17	12	42
Patents applied			
(domestic)	124	69	66
(overseas)	6	7	10

Sources: Research Association for Biotechnology, Baiotekunoroji kaihatsu gijutsu kenkyu-tukmiai no gaiyo (Research Association for Biotechnology, Tokyo, 1992).

Secondly, the data on project output (namely articles produced, conference presentations, and patents applied for) are insufficient to provide a proper evaluation of the projects. The reasons are that the data do not provide any indication of quality of output. Furthermore, they do not provide criteria to decide on the adequacy of the quantity of output. The high ratio of patents applied for domestically compared with patents applied for overseas is, however, notable, even though without further information on patenting behaviour little can be inferred from this ratio.

In the light of the inadequacy of this data for evaluation purposes, it is worth providing more information on the research substance of the three projects.

The bioreactor project

A large part of the Bioreactor Project involved screening micro-organisms to be used as biocatalysts in bioreactors. Mitsubishi Chemical, for example, screened micro-organisms for the production of muconic acid from benzoic acid, an inexpensive raw material. Muconic acid is used in the production of high-performance resin polyesters such as nylon. Kao Soap was also involved in the selection of micro-organisms, in this case for the microbial oxidation of higher alkyl compounds. Similarly, Daicel selected micro-organisms for the production of acetic acid.

The Bioreactor Project was the only one of the three where researchers from several companies worked together in joint research facilities, namely in MITI's Fermentation Research Institute. Members of the project met every two months to report on their results, in addition to the annual conference held by each of the three projects to announce more formally research findings.

Unsurprisingly, MITI, the Bioreactor Project's initiator, concluded officially that the project was a success. According to the official account, the Project broadened the potential of bioreactor technologies by raising the productivity of bioreactor systems and methods for screening micro-organisms.

However, we encountered serious criticism of the project among some of the researchers participating in it. It was argued that the energy-saving objective of the project, conceived at the time of the second oil shock, became irrelevant when international oil prices began to fall and when it became clear that alternative biological-based technologies for the production of commodity chemicals were not going to become cost-effective relative to the conventional technologies. The critics argued that when these facts became clear, MITI ought to have terminated the project. In the event, the Project was terminated some two years earlier than originally intended, a highly unusual event for MITI's cooperative R&D projects. However, the termination came too late for the critics who argued that the absence of a mechanism for evaluating the cooperative projects independently from MITI which initiated them meant that MITI had a vested interest in 'proving' that the projects were successful. The early termination of the Bioreactor Project, nevertheless, does show that MITI was ultimately responsive to the changing circumstances and the criticisms that were made, although it might not have responded quickly enough.

The large-scale cell cultivation project

An example of the research done under this project is the work of Takeda, the largest Japanese pharmaceutical company. Under the auspices of this project, Takeda researchers developed hybridomas (fused cells) which could produce human monoclonal antibodies against tetanus toxin and the surface antigen of the hepatitis B virus. A major aim of this project was to produce these antibodies on an industrial scale in biofermentors.

This Takeda research illustrates an important characteristic of most of the work done under the Future Industries Programme, namely its pragmatic, applied nature. Rather than concentrating solely on basic research, these projects were all actively concerned with industrial application.

MITI and the participating researchers concluded that the Large-Scale Cell Cultivation Project achieved important results in three areas. The first is the development of a serum free medium which lowered the cost of cell cultivation to one-tenth of that using alternative methods, and guaranteed a stable supply of high-quality medium. This serum free medium is now produced commercially and has assisted research on cell cultivation. Further details are provided below on the development of this medium in the Project.

Second, through the large-scale cultivation of vein cells, a vein contracting peptide (endocrin) was discovered. This research, which has received a significant amount of international attention, was done in cooperation with Tsukuba University. Third, process innovations were achieved. These included the development of cell cultivation equipment using a cell deposition tube and the improvement of various cultivation methods. These process innovations, it is claimed, have improved the industrial production of peptides and other animal proteins.

The recombinant DNA project

Most of the research done under this Project involved the cloning of various types of DNA in host systems, such as *E. coli*, *B. subtilis* and yeasts, to produce proteins and peptides. For example, Sumitomo Chemical was involved in the genetic engineering of *E. coli* with enhanced monooxygenase activity with large-scale industrial applications in mind, in areas such as the oxidation process of various industrial chemicals and the removal of hydrocarbons from industrial waste.

According to MITI and the researchers involved in this project, success was achieved in developing vector systems to produce peptides such as human growth hormones, human nerve growth factor, and human β-endorphine. These techniques, it is claimed, will be of significant use in the industrial production of these substances. (Technical features of these three projects are discussed in more detail in Karube 1992.)

7.6.4 Knowledge-sharing Among the Competing Companies Participating in the Projects

The benefits of knowledge-sharing through cooperative R&D

It was noted earlier that a major plank in MITI's response to the advent of new technologies such as biotechnology or new materials has involved the establishment of cooperative R&D programmes. But in what sense are these programmes 'cooperative'? What is their rationale? In order to answer these questions it is necessary to delve more deeply into the economics of cooperative R&D (see also Fransman 1993).

The main reason for the government intervening in the R&D decisions of private companies is to influence the allocation of R&D resources in these companies, and therefore to influence the amount and/or the kind of R&D that is undertaken. It follows, therefore, that the government has reason for intervening in these decisions only if it has reason to believe that the existing allocation of resources by companies is inadequate.

In line with this reasoning, MITI officials claim that they only intervene where Japanese companies are not allocating resources appropriately to R&D. Reasons for inappropriate allocation include uncertainty regarding the outcome of R&D, expected difficulties in appropriating adequate returns from investments in R&D, and the scale of investment and time-frame that some areas of R&D require. All of these factors may result in a field not receiving the R&D attention that government officials feel is necessary, based on the information at their disposal and their judgments on the basis of this information.

To encourage companies to pay more R&D attention to selected areas, the government can provide particular companies with incentives of various kinds. To the extent that these policies are successful, more R&D will be undertaken by these companies in the targeted fields.

The effectiveness of government policies, however, may be enhanced where knowledge is shared by companies. Additional benefits will be provided by knowledge sharing for a number of reasons. For example, to the extent that knowledge is shared amongst competing companies, no individual company will be able to develop monopolistic positions on the basis of that knowledge even in the short run. This will enhance the degree of competition, in turn benefiting consumers of the products and services in which the knowledge is incorporated and possibly increasing the rate of innovation. In addition, the sharing of knowledge might lead to a saving of resources where it obviates the duplication of efforts to create knowledge in companies which do not share. Furthermore, companies may be able to add their own distinctive knowledge and competence to the shared knowledge, resulting in a greater variety of products and services than would otherwise occur. These may be referred to as *benefits of cooperative R&D*.

The potential benefits of knowledge-sharing through cooperative R&D, however, confront a major problem: for-profit companies have a disincentive to share knowledge where they expect that sharing will leave them worse off than they would be without sharing. The design of government policy therefore needs to take this problem into account by adding mechanisms where feasible to increase knowledge-sharing.

Knowledge-sharing in the FI programme's biotechnology projects

For these reasons, an important question relates to the degree of knowledge-sharing that occurred in the biotechnology projects just discussed. In order to deal with this question we obtained and analysed patent data for the three projects, as will shortly be explained.

In a widely quoted study, Herman Lewis of the US National Science Foundation passed judgment on the extent of research cooperation in the three projects:

. . . bringing about cooperative research or even getting the companies within each group to agree upon a common project has been the biggest problem of the [Biotechnology Research] Association. During the first two years of the association's history this has not been accomplished. Within each of the three research groups there has been what is generously labeled 'cooperative competition' which is a euphemism to describe consensus on the broadest general terms but disagreement on all specifics. Within this framework, the three research groups can be characterised with respect to the degree of communication within the group. The Recombinant DNA Group displayed the least desire to exchange information or ideas between the companies within the group, while the Large-Scale Cell Cultivation Research Group seems to be willing to exchange certain kinds of information. The Bioreactors Research Group gets an intermediate score   (Lewis 1984, 50–1).

Accordingly, Lewis concluded that 'the Research Association for Biotechnology has not yet succeeded in pooling the resources of the participating companies to carry out long term cooperative research' (ibid. 53).

Joint patents as a measure of knowledge-sharing Is there more substantial evidence to support Lewis' impressionistic conclusions? In order to examine this question more rigorously, we obtained a list of all the patents granted and applied for each of the three biotechnology projects up to January 1987. We then checked on each of these patents at the Japanese patent office in order to establish how many of them were joint patents, defined as patents where the inventors came from more than one of the companies which participated in the project. Joint patents, accordingly, serve as a quantitative indicator of the extent to which knowledge is shared by the R&D scientists and engineers of different companies.

The data are presented for the three projects in Tables 7.3, 7.4, and 7.5.

A number of points emerge from these tables. To begin with, it is only in the Bioreactor Project that joint patents (formally owned by MITI)

Table 7.3 Patents granted and pending for the bioreactors research group of MITI's next generation biotechnology programme, January 1987

Firm	No. of single Patents	No. of joint patents[a]	Joint patent holders[a]
Daicel Chemical	23	0	—
Denki Kagaku Kogyo (DKK)	0	12	MPI, FRI
Denki Kagaku Kogyo (DKK)	—	1	FRI
Fermentation Research Institute (FRI)	0	12	MPI, DKK
Fermentation Research Institute (FRI)	—	1	DKK
Kao Soap (KS)	13	0	—
Kao Soap (KS)	—	1	MGC
Mitsubishi Chemical Industries (MCI)	8	—	—
Mitsubishi Chemical Industries (MCI)	—	11	MGC
Mitsubishi Gas Chemical Co. (MGC)	4	—	—
Mitsubishi Gas Chemical Co. (MGC)	—	1	KS
Mitsubishi Gas Chemical Co. (MGC)	—	11	MCI
Mitsui Petochemical Industries (MPI)	0	12	DKK, FRI
TOTAL	48	25[b]	

[a] All patents in this programme are owned by MITI. 'Joint patents' here refer to patents where the inventors come from more than one company.
[b] There is 'double counting' in this column. This results from showing in the table the joint patent holders for each of the firms.

Source: information obtained by the author.

Table 7.4 Patents granted and pending for the Recombinant DNA research group of MITI's next generation biotechnology programme, January 1987

Firm	No. of single patents	No. of joint patents
Mitsui Toatsu Chemicals	9	0
Mitsubishi Chemical Institute of Life Sciences	5	0
Sumitomo Chemical	8	0
TOTAL	22	0

Source and notes: see Table 7.3.

Table 7.5 Patents granted and pending for the large-scale cell culture research group of MITI's next generation biotechnology programme, January 1987

Firm	No. of single patents	No. of joint patents
Ajinomoto Co.	8	0
Asahi Chemical	8	0
Kyowa Hakko Kogyo	6	0
Takeda Chemical	3	0
Toyo Jozo Co.	5	0
TOTAL	30	0

Source and notes: see Table 7.3.

resulted. Neither in the Recombinant DNA nor in the Large-Scale Cell Cultivation Projects were there any joint patents. Second, in the Bioreactor Project the joint patents were granted to two groups of companies. The first consisted of Mitsui Petrochemical, Denki Kagaku, and the Fermentation Research Institute which received 12 out of a total of 25 joint patents held by the Bioreactor Project. The second group consisted of Mitsubishi Chemical and Mitsubishi Gas Chemical which received 11 of the 25 joint patents. Of the two remaining joint patents, one was held by Denki Kagaku and the Fermentation Research Institute, and the other was held by Kao Soap and Mitsubishi Gas Chemical.

Third, the ratio of single to joint patents is almost 2:1. Fourth, the firm holding the highest number of patents, Daicel Chemical, was engaged in only a limited amount of joint research (to the extent that patents serve as an accurate indication of joint research). Fifth, most of the patents were from the Bioreactors Research Group which accounted for 73 or 58% of the total of 125 patents.

This analysis of patent data suggests a number of conclusions. The most important of these is that joint research, to the extent that this is indicated by joint patents, existed only in the Bioreactor Group. Furthermore, it may be concluded that joint research was facilitated by the complementary, rather than competitive, relationship that existed between the firms that engaged in joint research. On the basis of further interviews we established that neither Mitsui Petrochemical nor Denki Kagaku were involved in direct competition with each other and, in addition, that they were both closely related to the Mitsui group of companies. (Mitsui Petrochemical has an ongoing research programme in biotechnology with other Mitsui group companies, including Mitsui Toatsu, Oji Seishi, and Daiichi Engei.) Similarly, Mitsubishi Chemical and Mitsubishi Gas Chemical are complementary firms which are part of the Mitsubishi group.

In contrast, competitive relationships are more prevalent in the other two research projects. To take one example, all the eight firms in these two project were involved in the development of pharmaceuticals. It is reasonable to suppose that these competitive relationships provide at least part of the explanation for the absence of joint patenting, and by implication, the absence of joint research in these two groups.

Informal knowledge-sharing   However, joint patents provide only one indicator of the sharing of knowledge between firms. In particular, the patent data might well obscure more informal flows of knowledge between the participating firms. We therefore supplemented our patent analysis with interviews with several of the participant firms which revealed that there were indeed instances of more informal knowledge sharing which were regarded as important by the recipient firms.

For example, as an unintended spin-off from its research under the FI Programme, Takeda developed an innovative medium (brand-named GIT medium) for culturing animal cells. This medium, containing partially purified growth factors from the serum of adult cattle, was a highly economical substitute for the conventional medium, which contained expensive fetal-calf serum. Unlike the several serum-free media which were already being marketed and which were effective only in cultivating specific cell lines, the GIT medium is almost equivalent to that supplemented with fetal calf or bovine serum with respect to its applicability to a wide range of cells.

Ajinomoto also developed an innovative medium under the FI Programme, namely a non-serum medium for animal cell culture. Although there were similar media developed in the USA and Europe, the one developed by Ajinomoto was reported to be the first which could be heated and sterilised.

From the point of view of the concern with knowledge-sharing, it is significant that the data on the Takeda and Ajinomoto media were shared with all the other firms in the Large-Scale Cell Project before this knowledge was commercialised. Similarly, Toyo Jozo, Asahi, and Kyowa Hakko shared their findings on growth factors of cells under various conditions. Kyowa Hakko developed a new apparatus for cell culture under the programme and this was made available to, and was used by some of the other firms.

Conclusions

It may be concluded that although most of the research under the FI Programme was undertaken inside the individual participating companies rather than in joint research laboratories, and although there was a limited joint creation and sharing of the kind of knowledge that leads to patentable output, there was a fair amount of inter-firm flow of knowledge which benefited the participants.

These flows were facilitated by the regular meetings of both a formal and informal kind that took place under the auspices of the project. On the whole, it seems likely that a significantly greater inter-company flow of knowledge occurred as a result of the FI Programme than would have taken place in its absence. Nevertheless, the underlying competitive relationship between some of the companies grouped particularly in the Large-Scale Cell Culture and the Recombinant DNA projects, and the commercial implications of some of the research being done in these research projects, served to constrain the extent of knowledge flow between competing companies.

It may be concluded, therefore, that an important benefit which resulted from these project was the increased flow of knowledge between the participating companies. A further conclusion, as shown by the examples from these projects discussed here, is that the projects contributed to the improvement of the industrial application of biotechnology, rather than to fundamental advances in this field of research. It is these practical improvements, diffused to other participating companies through the sharing of knowledge which took place, which constitute the main benefit of these projects. It is in this practical applied area that the combined strength of MITI and the companies lies.

7.7 MITI's Protein Engineering Research Institute (PERI)

7.7.1 Introduction

In 1986, PERI was established under the auspices of the Japan Key Technology Center (JKTC), the background of which was discussed earlier. According to Nature (1992, 577), PERI is 'MITI's showpiece' among the many institutes set up under JKTC, totalling 83 by 1992. PERI's 10-year life will come to an end in 1996 by which time it is expected that a total of 17.1 billion Yen (about $137 million) will have been spent on the institute. Currently PERI has around 60 researchers. Since 1987 JKTC's annual budget, spent with the objective of encouraging research cooperation between companies, government, and universities, has been between 25 and 28 billion Yen (about $200 to $225 million).

7.7.2 The Origins of PERI

The original idea for a national research programme in the area of protein engineering came from a number of individuals in MITI who, in conjunction with various formal and informal advisory bodies, had responsibility for making policy in the area of biotechnology. They included Mr Hosokawa and Mr Masami Tanaka.

By 1985, it was acknowledged that (a) protein engineering was a potentially important new generic technology and (b) Japanese companies and universities lagged seriously behind their Western counterparts in this field. This was underlined in a report published in 1985 under the US-sponsored Japanese Technology Evaluation Program (JTECH) (see US Department of Commerce 1985). The report identified three technologies as being essential for protein engineering: recombinant DNA technology, protein structural analysis, and computer graphics.

It was concluded that the first technology was 'the easiest to acquire and [that] Japan has as good a capability in these areas as the United States' (p. 6). However, in the area of protein structural analysis, including crystallography, it was noted that 'Japan has a relatively small pool of trained experts ... and it is not easy to rapidly expand this base' (p. 6). There were only two major centers for protein structural analysis in Japan, the Institute for Protein Research in Osaka, and the Faculty of Pharmaceutical Sciences at the University of Tokyo.

The report concluded that 'Neither Director [of these two institutions] knew of any significant effort in protein engineering anywhere in Japan as of late 1984' (ibid.). In the case of both hardware and software it was concluded that the 'computer graphics equipment and programs are being imported into Japan and are usually a generation behind that now being used in the United States' (ibid.). The overall conclusion of the report was that 'Japan currently ranks fourth to the United States, United Kingdom, and Western Europe in protein engineering. *There is not much activity at the present time at either the universities or industries*' (p. 6, emphasis added).

In 1985, MITI officials began discussions with a number of companies and eventually, in April 1986, PERI was established by five companies:

Kyowa Hakko, Mitsubishi Chemical, Takeda, Toa Nenryo, and Toray. Of these companies, only the latter two had not taken part in the earlier Future Industries Programme. Later, a number of other firms joined, including Ajinomoto, Fujitsu, Kanegafuchi, Kirin Brewery, Showa Denko, Suntory, Toyobo and two foreign firms, Nihon Digital Equipment (DEC), and Nihon Roche, a subsidiary of the Swiss pharmaceutical company. An amount of 17.1 billion Yen was budgeted for the project over a period of 10 years with 30% provided by the mainly corporate membership. The original five company members own a slightly higher proportion of the equity and send a greater number of researchers to the Institute.

The first President of PERI was Dr Masakazu Ito, Chairman of Toray, while the General Manager was Dr Morio Ikehara, Professor Emeritus of Osaka University. PERI is divided into five departments which work jointly on topics of common interest. These are: 1. Structural analysis (13 researchers); 2. Structural-function correlation and design of new proteins (13 researchers); 3. Synthesis (12 researchers); 4. Purification and characterisation (9 researchers); and 5. Database analysis and computer system (11 researchers). Of the 58 researchers, 5 were post-doctorates, 43 researchers, and 10 assistants. Of the 43 researchers, one third had PhDs, 30 were from the participating companies, and 13 from universities. A number of the post-doctorates were from foreign countries.

7.7.3 The Organisational Characteristics of PERI

Unlike the Future Industries Programme, where research is done mainly inside each of the participating organisations, PERI is a case where research is done jointly in joint research facilities. Although it was not consciously modeled on the MITI Institute for New Generation Computer Technology (ICOT), PERI bears striking organisational similarities to ICOT. (See Fransman (1993) for a detailed analysis of ICOT.)

The following are the main features of PERI, analysed in terms of the creation, diffusion, and use of knowledge, which are illustrated in Fig. 7.1.

1. Structural separation of generic research and applications research The role of PERI itself is to undertake generic research into protein engineering. Although the boundary between generic research and applications research is sometimes difficult to draw, it is intended that the latter research is done inside the laboratories of the individual member companies, rather than in PERI. Typically, the researchers from the member companies spend about 3 years in PERI after which they rotate back to their companies and are replaced by other company researchers. At times, parallel research groups are established inside the companies whose research closely follows that being done in PERI, but with concentration on applications. In this

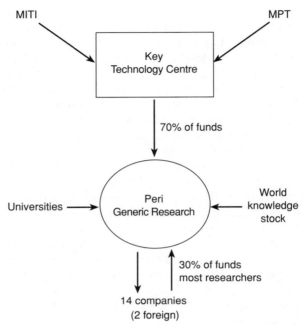

Fig. 7.1 Organisation of the Protein Engineering Research Institute (PERI)

way, there is a relatively smooth transfer of generic knowledge from PERI, where joint cooperative research is undertaken, to the member companies, where private applications-oriented research is done.

2. PERI's generic research and the world stock of knowledge   Like similar Japanese organisations such as ICOT, PERI is able to tap effectively into the world stock of knowledge. As the major centre for protein engineering research in Japan, and with a concentration of resources in a single location exceeding that of comparable research programmes in other Western countries, PERI has an extremely high international profile. This has greatly facilitated knowledge exchanges with the other major centres, and with individual researchers, elsewhere in the world. These exchanges are assisted by the open nature of PERI, where research publications and results are made easily available and where visitors are readily received and PERI researchers sent to other international centres. However, the applications research, which is done inside the member companies and draws on the generic research done in PERI, as in the case of research done in any private company in any country, normally remains private.

3. Interfacing with Japanese universities PERI also provides a suitable vehicle for interactions with Japanese universities. In Japan, one of the constraints on the contribution of universities results from the restriction preventing employees of Japanese national universities from taking up full-time although temporary employment in companies and government research institutes. However, Japanese university researchers can be involved in the research programmes of institutes such as PERI. In addition, university academics also play an important role in the review committee which regularly reviews the output of PERI and provides feedback and suggestions.

4. Subsidising the development and diffusion of new generic technologies With 70% of the research funds of PERI coming directly or indirectly from government, the companies participating in this organisation receive a significant research subsidy. Although, in view of the centrality of protein engineering, it is likely that the companies would in any event, even without this or similar subsidies, have acquired protein engineering capabilities, it is probable that they have done so faster and more cost effectively as a result of PERI. The lag in Japanese protein engineering in 1985, relative to other Western countries described in the JTECH report above, bears testimony to the degree of uncertainty that individual companies would have faced in deciding to invest in developing capabilities in this area. The subsidy that in the event they have received is likely to have significantly speeded their entry into protein engineering.

7.7.4 Other Benefits Provided by PERI

PERI has also provided the following additional benefits.

1. Avoidance of overlap In the absence of a cooperative project like PERI, it is likely that the individual companies would have engaged to a considerable extent in overlapping research. One of the main benefits of PERI, however, has been the avoidance of some overlap in developing capabilities in the companies in protein engineering technologies.

2. Combining distinctive competences A further benefit has resulted from the combining in PERI of the distinctive competences of researchers from various companies, universities, and government research laboratories, with their idiosyncratic strengths and skills. It is unlikely that research, done in isolation inside these different kinds of organisations, would have achieved the same synergistic result.

3. Sharing expensive skill-intensive equipment   One of the major benefits provided by PERI has followed from the sharing of expensive equipment, such as a supercomputer and nuclear magnetic resonance (NMR) equipment, and the shared development of generic software tools for protein modeling. This sharing has reduced significantly the cost per company or research laboratory of access to equipment and software, thus providing a significant benefit.

4. Increased diffusion of generic protein engineering technology   In the absence of this joint research there would have been a strong tendency for the companies to privatise their knowledge and limit its spread to other companies. In PERI, however, with the joint participation of companies (which in some cases are competing) in the joint research laboratories, the diffusion of generic protein engineering technologies has been increased.

5. Focusing national attention on protein engineering as a strategic technology   One of the important spin-off benefits from the PERI project has been the raising of awareness in Japan of the significance of protein engineering as a strategic technology. It is likely that a number of other companies, together with the members of PERI, have as a result of this project devoted additional attention and resources to protein engineering.

6. Overcoming some of the problems of technology transfer   With the current absence of a rigorous theoretical underpinning for protein engineering, there is a significant degree of tacitness in this area of research. In general, the greater the degree of tacitness, the greater the difficulty in transferring knowledge from one location to another. The interdisciplinary nature of protein engineering, which necessitates cooperation between researchers from diverse areas such as molecular genetics, protein structural analysis, and computer science, further complicates the problem of knowledge transfer. The organisation of PERI, however, with company researchers who have been involved in the generic research returning to their companies after their secondment to the Institute, provides an effective solution to this difficult problem.

7.7.5 Assessing the Benefits of PERI

It is still too early for a final assessment of PERI's output. There are, however, three indirect indications which are of some use. The first is the assessment made by the JKTC's academic committee which is charged both with the selection and the assessment of Center projects. This committee uses an 'internal' method of assessment whereby the performance of the project is judged according to the extent that the objectives of the project, stated in the project proposal, have been achieved. According to information informally supplied to us by a senior member of this committee, PERI has been very positively assessed and is regarded as one of the most successful of all the Center's projects.

The second indication comes from two senior British academics, closely involved in British national research programmes in protein engineering, who have on two occasions been exposed to the research results of PERI. In their opinion, the research currently being done in PERI is of the same standard in many fields as the frontier research being undertaken in Britain.

Third, at least one of PERI's researchers has been suggested as a possible Nobel Prizewinner. He is Dr Kosuke Morikawa, a department director in PERI, who has devised techniques using X-ray crystallography which enable the precise drawing of DNA and RNA molecules (see *Financial Times*, Survey of Japanese Industry, 3 December 1990, p. 3).

Together, these indirect sources of assessment suggest that significant progress has been made in PERI since the project started. To the extent that this is indeed correct, a substantial revision is needed to the assessment of the state-of-the-art in Japanese protein engineering summarised in the 1985 JTECH report.

7.8 The Science and Technology Agency's ERATO Programme

7.8.1 Introduction

Although the Science and Technology Agency's main activities involve policy in the area of science and technology in addition to direct involvement in policy and research in the nuclear and space fields, the agency has been involved in the area of biotechnology since the 1970s. In 1973, the STA established its Life Science Office and it is closely linked to the Life Science Committee of the Council for Science and Technology.

The STA was established in May 1956. At this time, there was a good deal of discussion in Japan regarding the country's dependence on foreign technology. Amongst the many steps that were taken to redress this dependence were proposals put forward by Keidanren (the Japanese federation of companies) and the Science Council of Japan. These proposals eventually resulted in the establishment of the Research Development Corporation of Japan (JRDC) in May 1961 under the supervision of the STA. The birth of JRDC was accompanied by a tough battle for control between the STA and MITI, which argued that it had responsibility for projects aimed at increasing technological capabilities in the country. Keidanren, the Ministry of Finance, and politicians from the Liberal Democratic Party were involved in the battle which was ultimately resolved in the STA's favour. According to one of the participants in the battle 'MITI was extremely nasty to JRDC for several years after the decision was made'.

The evolution of JRDC's activities mirror the growth of science and technology in Japan. Until the late 1970s, the JRDC's main activity involved commercialising technologies that were 'incubated' in universities and government research institutions. From the late 1970s, however, the role of JRDC began to change significantly. With basic research a much higher priority in Japan, JRDC launched its Exploratory Research for Advanced Technology (ERATO) Programme. By the early 1990s about half of JRDC's expenditure went to the development of new technology, while about a third was allocated to the ERATO programme.

From the point of view of the concerns of this chapter, the ERATO programme derives its significance from two factors. First, it is a programme designed to bring university science and industrial technology closer together, thus increasing the connections between these two important parts of the Japanese innovation system. Second, the programme aims at funding some projects which are highly uncertain, and which may therefore otherwise be underfunded, and furthermore aims to provide researchers with a considerable degree of freedom in carrying out their research. It is these two factors which give the programme its significance, even though in total financial terms the programme is not particularly large.

Each ERATO project lasts five years and receives approximately $2–8 million per year. The plan is to have four new projects beginning each year so that there are approximately twenty running at any time. The ERATO programme is also of interest in terms of the methods used for project selection and evaluation of results. A major criterion in the selection of projects is the creativity and scientific standing of the project leader or leaders. While the overall aim of the ERATO programme is to support uncertain research which may yield returns only in the longer run (although the programme does have a portfolio of projects which vary in terms of the degree of uncertainty involved), at the project selection stage, more attention is given to the creativity and standing of the project leader than to the details of the proposal which they put forward.

In making a judgment on questions of creativity and standing, particular attention is paid to the assessments of younger scientists. The ERATO staff of six have their own networks to collect information and make judgements, they regularly attend scientific conferences in order to gather further information, and they conduct surveys for the same purpose.

At the time the ERATO programme was established in 1981 its founder, Mr Genya Chiba, waged some tough battles, particularly with the Ministry of Finance, in order to establish the principle that there should be no evaluation of the project after its completion at the end of the five year period. In Chiba's view, which ultimately prevailed, evaluation at project completion stage did not make sense in the case of oriented-basic research of the kind the ERATO programme was designed to support. By definition, he argued, the importance of these kinds of projects only becomes apparent in the longer term. Furthermore, it was feared that the pressures resulting from early evaluation might deflect the researcher's attention from the longer term goals. The refusal to evaluate on project termination, however, placed increased importance on the correct initial choice of project leader.

7.8.2 *Evaluation of the ERATO Programme's Biotechnology Projects*

In 1988, the ERATO Programme was evaluated by the US National Science Foundation sponsored Japanese Technology Evaluation Program (JTECH 1988). The evaluation panel noted that the ERATO programme 'has a tendency to select high-risk, adventuresome areas that are not in vogue but that would become highly visible if successful' (ibid. 10). The general conclusion of the panel was that the programme was 'a success' and that the 'overall scientific quality of the . . . programme was high, but varied considerably from project to project' (10).

In the area of biotechnology, the panel evalutated three projects. The Bioholonics Project (1982–1987), directed by Professor D. Mizuno, involved parallel processing with many units (holons) working synergistically. The aim of this project was 'to simulate and utilize the organization of information and processes found in biological systems to develop novel approaches to the treatment of diseases, such as cancer and atherosclerosis' (7). The general conclusion of the panel was that the 'quality of this research is comparable to similar efforts in the United States'. Furthermore, the development of improved tumor necrosis factor (TNF-S) under this project 'is something of a breakthrough' (47).

The second project was the Superbugs Project (1984–1989) directed by Professor K. Horikoshi. The purpose of this project was 'to search the world for unusual microorganisms such as those which thrive under extreme conditions of pH, temperature, salinity, or in the presence of biotoxic materials. The aim of the project is to establish a 'new biotechnology' using knowledge acquired in studies of the unique properties of these superbugs' (54). A notable feature of this project was the substantial participation by 16 Japanese companies, five Japanese universities, and foreign researchers from six countries. In evaluating this project the panel concluded that it was 'a guaranteed success project . . . The area of research was well chosen in the sense of gaining success. . . but we don't think that it is truly basic knowledge with a basic technology or technical impact, and it is certainly not a high-risk project' (62). The panel was of the opinion that the 'quality of the research is about comparable to that of the United States or elsewhere in Japan' (63).

The third project was the Bioinformation Transfer Project (1983–8) directed by Professor Osamu Hayaishi. The general aim of this project was 'understanding how the brain is wired and how information is processed, transferred, and stored' (49). It was hoped that this would lead to new 'information technology with important applications in the field of medicine, as well as computers' (49). More specifically, the project was concerned with a class of biological compounds called prostaglandins (which are produced by nearly every cell in the body) and their role in the cental nervous system. Seven pharmaceutical companies sent researchers to work on this project.

The panel concluded that this project 'has been extremely successful. It is being directed by one of the best known biochemists in the world, who has attracted an impressive group of productive scientists' (52). The panel noted that the ERATO directors had 'picked a strong leader with a good track record who had the respect of younger scientists, and then gave him the freedom and flexibility to pursue all aspects of a given research area. Serious evaluation of the project is to be delayed until five years after the termination of the five-year project' (53). It was concluded that this 'ERATO project has clearly established Prof. Hayaishi as the world's expert on prostaglandins, in general, and, more specifically, for their role in the central nervous system' (52).

More general comment is deferred to the concluding section on the role of the Japanese Government in biotechnology.

7.9 Business, Bureaucrats, Politicians and State Power in Japan

7.9.1 Introduction

Up to this point we have merely described the role that various organs of the Japanese state have played in the field of biotechnology. However, the missing dimension in this as in most other accounts of state policy is a convincing explanation of why the state does what it does.

Why is it important to explain as well as describe the state's interventions? The reason is that an explanation of the state's interventions provides information not only on why the state has intervened in the way it has, but also on the kinds of interventions that the state is unlikely to make. Without an explanation of state intervention, there is the danger of implicity imputing either rationality or irrationality to the state's activities. For example, MITI bureaucrats are often portrayed as omniscient administrators, correctly knowing what needs to be done, and doing it, while those around them by implication remain ignorant. Or in other accounts (or even later on in the same accounts) MITI bureaucrats are shown to be impotent administrators, for instance trying in vain to bring about mergers in automobiles or computers against the better judgments of the managers of the companies concerned.

In these cases, what is lacking is an explanation of state power based on an acceptable theory of the state. However, while for these reasons a strong case can be made for the need for such a theory of the state, the problem is that such a theory does not yet exist and there is little consensus among analysts regarding the outlines of such a theory. Nevertheless, despite the absence of consensus, some progress can be made towards an explanation of government intervention in Japan in the field of biotechnology, as will now be shown.

7.9.2 Bureaucrats and Politicians

An explanation of the role of government must come to grips with the politics underpinning this role. This requires, *inter alia*, an understanding of the political interactions between business, bureaucrats and politicians. In this section, we briefly examine the interactions between bureaucrats and politicians in Japan, while in the following section the relationship between business and bureaucrats is discussed. The succeeding section then relates the discussion to the role of different organs of the Japanese government in biotechnology.

One of the most succinct views of the relationship between bureaucrats and politicians in Japan has been put forward by Johnson (1985): 'the Diet reigns but the bureaucracy actually rules—or, to put it another way, the bureaucracy makes policy and the Diet merely rubber-stamps it' (p. 60). He expresses the same views in his well-known book: 'Although it is influenced by pressure groups and political claimants, the élite bureaucracy of Japan makes most major decisions, drafts virtually all legislation, controls the national budget, and is the source of all major policy innovations in the system' (Johnson 1982, 20–1). Dore, putting it rather more bluntly, is in substantive agreement: '*the Japanese do not much honour politicians, whose role in running the economy is small* . . . Politicians are more-or-less corrupt brokers for interest groups who have limited powers of veto over bureaucratic initiatives, but rarely take initiative of their own' (Dore 1987, 16, italics in original).

A somewhat different view is put forward by Muramatsu who argues that 'party politicians in Japan routinely have more impact than they are typically given credit for' (Muramatsu 1991, 287). Drawing attention to the role played by the Liberal Democratic Party's *zoku* ('tribes' of politicians associated with the interests of different ministries), Muramatsu concludes that 'party politicians often play more important roles in policymaking than bureaucracies' in Japan (ibid. 288).

Does this mean that Muramatsu reverses the power balance between bureaucrats and politicians outlined by Johnson and Dore? The answer is 'no', since Muramatsu concedes that bureaucrats are usually able to 'depoliticise' their activities (what he calls the 'depoliticisation rule'), that is insulate themselves from the influence of the politicians. He accordingly concludes that 'On the whole, bureaucracy governs as long as they can apply the depoliticisation rule' (289). However, in cases involving serious conflict between ministries, the bureaucracy is no longer able to depoliticise its activities and this enhances the power of politicians relative to bureaucrats. (We shall return to this argument later in connection with inter-ministerial conflicts over biotechnology.)

What can we conclude from this small (but influential) sample of views regarding the relationship between politicians and bureaucrats in Japan? We can conclude that there is some agreement that bureaucrats tend to have more influence than politicians in the making (and of course the implementing) of policy, unless the bureaucracy is internally divided by rivalry. But if, accordingly, it is the bureaucrats who tend to make policy, what is the connection between the policies they make and the business interests that are affected by these policies? In short, what is the relationship between the second part of the triad, namely between business and bureaucrats?

7.9.3 Business and Bureaucrats

There is much less agreement regarding the relationship between business and bureaucrats.

At the one end of the spectrum is Johnson (1982) who, via his notion of the Japanese 'developmental state', sees the state and its bureaucrats as being in command of both the development process and the businesses which are involved. Closer to the other end of the spectrum is Muramatsu (1991) who argues that Johnson 'plays down the role of the private sector, giving unreasonably small regard to its initiative and participation in government–industry relations' (286). In contrast, Muramatsu argues that 'industries and business enterprises act freely and independently from the government, apart from those cases where the industries are declining and demand government assistance, or [where] industries are targeted . . . to stimulate their growth' (287).

To grasp the elusive relationship between business and bureaucrats, Aoki (1988) draws on the principal–agent theory in economics, likening those parts of the ministries which have responsibility for a particular part of the business sector to the agent and their 'constituency' in the business sector to the principal. For example,

the computer industry is a jùrisdictional constituent of the Machinery and Information Industries Bureau of the Ministry of International Trade and Industry

(MITI), and the banking industry is a jurisdictional constituent of the Banking Bureau of the Ministry of Finance (MOF) (Aoki 1988, 263).

By analogy, therefore, the chemical industry, which is involved in biotechnology, is a constituent of the Basic Industries Bureau of MITI.

However, according to Aoki, while one of the bureaucracy's two roles is to represent the interests of its constituents/principals, the other role is to represent the interests of the nation as a whole. In this sense, Aoki's bureaucracy has 'two faces':

Each bureaucratic entity seems to have two faces in its operation: one is that of a delineator of public interests [i.e. national interests] in its jurisdiction, and the other is that of an agent representing the interests of its constituents vis-à-vis the other interests in the bureaucratic coordinating processes: budgetry, administrative, and planning (Aoki 1988, 263).

Aoki's 'two faces' of the bureaucracy, however, ignores a third influence on the bureaucratic decision-making process, namely the interests of the bureaucrats themselves. Aoki's analysis contrasts sharply with that of Johnson: 'Of the three broad theories of bureaucratic behavior—that state bureaucrats attempt to serve 1. the public's interests, 2. the interests of their clients, or 3. their own interests—the evidence of Japan suggests that the last has the greatest explanatory power' (Johnson 1985, 182).

Is there any way of reconciling these opposing views on the relationship between business and the bureaucracy? Any attempt at a reconciliation would have to begin from the recognition that what is missing from all of the accounts of this relationship is an analysis of the broader political process which gives sections of business, bureaucrats, and politicians their respective political power to influence decisions and resource allocations, and which constrains their political power. For example, bureaucrats may well want to act in terms of their own interests, but their ability to do so is constrained by the political power of the other groups in the society whose interests may be accordingly threatened.

To take the present discussion further in explaining the activities of various Japanese ministries in the field of biotechnology, it is useful to posit four propositions that form the basis for the explanation.

7.9.4 Some Propositions

The following four propositions are put forward:

1. While companies in different sectors of the Japanese economy have a direct relationship with the ministry or ministries with responsibilities in their areas, both companies and the bureaucrats concerned are relatively autonomous from one another.

2. The degree of autonomy enjoyed by companies and bureaucrats is contingent on their political power, which in turn depends on the broader political process.
3. Within the constraints of the broader political process, an important source of influence of a ministry and its bureaucrats lies in the companies that fall within its jurisdiction.
4. Since the 1970s, the influence of bureaucrats over companies has decreased significantly as companies have grown, strengthened their technological and marketing competencies, and improved their access to international capital markets, thus decreasing their dependenc on the Japanese state.

As will be shown in the following section, these four propositions, particularly the third, can be used to explain the role of Japanese government ministries in biotechnology.

7.10 Bureaucrats, Business and Biotechnology in Japan

7.10.1 MITI's Move into Biotechnology

There were mixed motivations behind MITI's move into biotechnology. On the one hand, as noted earlier, MITI officials had long been concerned with the relative weakness of Japanese chemicals companies and with their own apparent lack of progress in facilitating an increase in the international strength of these companies. Biotechnology, as a powerful new generic technology with wide potential application in areas such as bioprocessing, seeds and agrochemicals, pharmaceuticals, and industrial processes, held out the promise of increasing the competitiveness of Japanese chemicals companies. By aiding the diffusion of biotechnologies amongst Japanese chemicals companies, MITI hoped to achieve mutual benefit: strengthening the companies within its jurisdiction while increasing the Ministry's influence and resources. The latter would be achieved by making a strong case for additional resources from the Ministry of Finance and other sources in this new technology area with implications for Japan's competitiveness.

On the other hand, biotechnology also enabled MITI to extend its influence into other sectors of industry over which it traditionally had less influence. These sectors included pharmaceuticals under the jurisdiction of the Ministry of Health and Welfare (MHW), and food processing under the Ministry of Agriculture, Forestry, and Fisheries (MAFF). However, while biotechnology therefore offered new possibilities for MITI, the Ministry's moves in this area threatened MHW and MAFF.

7.10.2 The Response of the Ministries of Health and Agriculture

Until the advent of bioindustry in the early 1980s, the link between the Ministries of Health and Agriculture and the constituent companies under their jurisdiction revolved mainly around regulation. For example, Takeda, the largest pharmaceuticals company in Japan, had forged a close tie with MHW. As stated in Takeda's 1986 Annual Report, Yoshimasa Umemoto, the President of the company at the time,

came to Takeda in 1977 after a brilliant career that included service as Vice-Minister at the Ministry of Health and Welfare and at senior posts in the Environment Agency and the Cabinet . . . Mr Umemoto, having spent his career in public service, much of it at administrative groups that define some of the essential parameters of our market, has already been with us for nearly a decade (4).

The coming of new biotechnology, however, presented both opportunities and threats for HMW and MAFF. One of the opportunities was to enhance the influence of the ministry by extending its role beyond regulation to include industrial policy in its area of influence. At the same time, this would increase the resources under the ministry's control. This would come about by strengthening the case for additional funds from the Ministry of Finance through arguments relating to increased Japanese competitiveness, and by bringing corporate counterpart funding into cooperative research programmes established by the ministry.

However, biotechnology also presented threats, the most important of which was the spectre of the powerful MITI extending its influence through this new technology into the respective domains of MHW and MAFF. Most challenging was MITI's incorporation of companies in areas such as pharmaceuticals and food processing into its cooperative research programmes on the grounds that biotechnology was vital to the future of these companies.

Response of the ministry of health

There is a remarkable similarity in the responses of MITI, MHW, and MAFF in the field of biotechnology, suggesting that there are similar determinants of bureaucratic intervention in all three cases (summarised in the third proposition above). Specifically, each of the three ministries established new organs dealing with industrial policy in biotechnology and each set up cooperative research institutions and programmes.

Following in MITI's wake, MHW established a Lifescience Office in 1983, and a government–industry consultative committee, the Cooperation Group for Industrial Policy related to the Pharmaceutical Industry. In April 1985, on the recommendation of the Pharmaceutical Industry Policy Forum advising the Director of the Pharmaceutical Affairs Bureau of

MHW, the Japan Association for Advanced Research of Pharmaceuticals was formed.

In April 1986, this Association became the Japan Health Services Foundation (JHSF) which, according to its official literature, had two main aims: 'The first is to function as the central organisation, in cooperation with MHW, to develop the Japanese pharmaceutical and other health science-related industries by applying advanced technologies such as genetic engineering'. The second aim is 'to act as a catalyst for triangular cooperation among national research institutes, universities and private laboratories'.

In 1992, JHSF had approximately 160 company members from different sectors such as pharmaceuticals, chemicals, food, and textiles. Membership included foreign companies such as Ciba-Geigy, Du Pont, Hoechst, Pharmacia, and Upjohn. In 1991 research was supported by JHSF in three areas on a budget of Yen 1.3 billion: basic research on biotechnology, medical materials, and the immune mechanism of the human body.

MHW has also established an organisation which supports cooperative research companies in various areas that is very similar in function and organisation to the Japan Key Technology Center discussed earlier run by MITI and the Ministry of Posts and Telecommunications (MPT). The organisation is called the Research Fund for Promoting Research on Medicals. Like the Key Technology Center, the Fund provides up to 70% of the research funds with the private companies supplying the remaining 30%. In 1991, 400 million Yen was provided from the Fund. By 1992, seven cooperative research companies had been established, as shown in Table 7.6. As this table shows, through this Fund, MHW has been able to incorporate private companies which have traditionally been outside its field of influence.

Response of the ministry of agriculture

Like MHW, MAFF also followed closely in MITI's footsteps. In 1984, MAFF set up its Biotechnology Division and its government–industry consultative committee, the Cooperation Group for Promoting R&D in Biotechnology. Like MITI's Future Industries Programme, MAFF established a number of cooperative research associations. The first associations included the Bioreactor Research Association for Food Industry Biotechnology, the Research Association for Pesticides, and the Research Association for Analysing Structures Relating to Agricultural Genes.

In 1986, MAFF established the Bio-oriented Technology Research Advancement Institution (BRAIN) which is also similar in function and organisation to the Key Technology Center. BRAIN is funded largely from dividends from shares held by government in the Japan Tobacco Company and provides capital for cooperative research companies established by

Table 7.6 Comparative research projects funded by Research Foundation for Promoting Research on Medicals, Ministry of Health and Welfare

Research scheme	Company: the date of establishment	Investing companies
Targeting drug delivery system	DDS Research Institute (10 March 1988)	Asahi Chemical, Ajinomoto, Eisai, Shionogi, Daiichi Pharmaceutical, Tanabe Pharmaceutical, Meiji Seika
Medical biosensor using optoelectronics technologies	Biosensor Research Institute (17 March 1988)	Kurare, Chugai Pharmaceutical, Toso, Hamamatsu Photonics
Separation and purification technologies of proteins	Sight Signal Research Institute (9 March 1989)	Sankyo, Kirin Beer, Mitsubishi Kasei
Artificial blood vessels	Artificial Blood Vessels R&D Center (13 March 1989)	Daiichi Pharmaceutical, Sumitomo Electric
Diagnosis system of organic function	Organic Function Research Institute (28 February 1990)	Takeda Pharmaceutical, Fujisaswa, Sumitomo Heavy Machinery, Nippon Mediphysics, Tanabe Pharaceutical, Wako Junyaku, Yoshitomi Pharmaceutical
Skin and bioactive medicine administration system	Advanced Skin Research Institute (1 March 1990)	Shiseido, Chugai Pharmaceutical, Nippon Oil and Fat
Diagnosis and treatment of arteriosclerosis	Vessel Research Laboratory	Kyowa Hakko, Terumo

Source: Koseisho-Koseikagakuka, Kosei Kagaku Yoran (1992), p. 79.

representatives from the private sector, universities, and other research institutes. It supplies up to 70% of the capital required by the research company with the remaining 30% coming from the private corporate members. From 1986 to 1991, 26 cooperative research companies were funded.

In 1990 MAFF set up the Society for TechnoInnovation in Agriculture, Forestry, and Fisheries (STAFF) with around 100 corporate members from sectors such as chemicals, seeds, food and beverages, and engineering. The aim of STAFF is to help implement MAFF's policies and serve as a forum for the exchange of information between companies and government (Norinsuisangijutsukaigi, 1992).

7.10.3 Spending on R&D by MITI, MHW, and MAFF

Further perspective is provided by data on R&D spending by these three ministries. In 1991 MITI's spending was ¥256 billion while that of MHW and MAFF was ¥56 billion and ¥74 billion respectively. The Ministry of Education was the biggest spender, accounting for ¥936 billion.

7.10.4 Inter-ministry Conflict in Biotechnology

Through their attempts to extend their influence by involving private companies in their cooperative research programmes in biotechnology the ministries created conflict. As Masami Tanaka, a MITI bureaucrat who has played an important role in biotechnology and who, unusually, has also produced academic analyses of the policy-making process in Japan, has noted: 'a Ministry which may have a close relationship to a specific firm, will often be reluctant to have that firm participate in another [ministry's] programme' (Tanaka 1991, 25).

The potential for conflict can be seen by taking as an example the area of cell fusion technology, one of the major biotechnologies. In the mid-1980s, MAFF introduced a five-year programme to develop cell fusion techniques for modifying microbial and plant cells. The firms that were persuaded to cooperate in this research programme included Asahi Chemical, Hitachi, Kagome, Kikkoman, Kirin Brewery, Kubota, Kyowa Hakko, Meiji Seika, Mitsui Toatsu, the Nihon Kinoku Center, the Plantech Research Institute, Sapporo Brewery, and Suntory.

These 'constituents' reflected MAFF's jurisdiction over the food and agriculture-related industries. Thus six of these 13 firms had food as their primary business, while another five were closely related to food or agriculture. However, five of these companies, Asahi Chemical, Kirin Brewery, Kyowa Hakko, Mitsui Toatsu, and Suntory, also participated in one of the two major MITI programmes launched around the same time, namely the Future Industries Programme and PERI discussed earlier. Similarly, companies such as Takeda and Ajinomoto were involved both in these MITI programmes as well as MHW programmes.

Not only was there conflict between ministries trying to retain control over 'their' companies. Companies also expressed their opposition to attempts by ministries to pressurise them to join cooperative research programmes which frequently were in similar areas of biotechnology. As Tanaka (1991) points out, this opposition was given expression through the business federation, Keidanren, and politicians from the Liberal Democratic Party also became involved. As we saw earlier, Muramatsu (1991) has argued that in these circumstances of inter-ministerial conflict a ministry's activities become 'politicised', thus giving politicians an unusual degree of infuence in the policy-making process.

In the case of biotechnology, however, the politicians ultimately decided to avoid the minefield of inter-ministry politics, leaving it to the ministries and their constituent companies to resolve the tensions. As Tanaka puts it in a passage that may not be unduly coloured by his role as a MITI bureaucrat who played an important role in this ministry's involvement in biotechnology:

The Diet members [of the Liberal Democratic Party] realise that, in theory, politicians are the master of policy ideas and that government agencies [i.e. bureaucrats] are the master of routines and technique. They have also appreciated, however, the fact that bureaucrats are frequently capable of moulding not only techniques but also policies. Although Diet members obviously became aware of interministerial rivalries, they accepted fragmented policies initiated by [government] agencies [in the area of biotechnology]. They preferred government rivalry rather than risking Diet-induced confusion through attempted coordination. It may indeed appear to them that competition for new policy initiatives means an expansion of public expenditure. This could favour them as it may provide them with more benefits to distribute among their supporters an thus enhance their chances for re-election (Tanaka 1991, 27–8).

However, while overlapping cooperative research programmes in the same technology areas may appear wasteful, it is possible that it will also generate a variety of approaches which may be healthy from the point of view of the development of biotechnology in Japan. Furthermore, the areas of application of generic biotechnologies are different for each ministry thus further reducing the costs of overlap and duplication. The conflict between the ministries and their constituent companies may thus not be as deleterious as appears to be the case at first sight.

7.10.5 The Three Faces of the Japanese Bureaucracy

Does the present discussion of biotechnology in Japan throw any light on the theoretical debate reviewed earlier on the relationship between business and bureaucrats?

This discussion suggests that the Japanese bureaucracy has three 'faces'. First, it seems clear that to some extent the bureaucracy in the field of biotechnology has acted to further the interests of the sectors of business which it represents. Thus MITI, MHW, and MAFF have benefited chemicals, pharmaceuticals, and food companies respectively. These ministries have provided benefit through their cooperative research programmes which have subsidised research, and therefore the accumulation of competencies, in the companies. Benefit has also been provided through the information collected and analysed by the ministry and its coordination role. Evidence of benefit may be deduced from the general willingness of the companies to participate in these programmes and contribute their own resources, even if on occasion there has been complaint about the number of programmes and overlap between the programmes of different ministries. The relative autonomy of the companies, referred to in the propositions above, means that they do not have to participate in these programmes if they do not wish to.

Second, in supporting their companies and acting to increase their strength and international competitiveness through helping to diffuse new technologies to them, the bureaucrats of the different ministries have also acted in the national interest. However, where the interests of individual companies or groups of companies have conflicted with national interests, the bureaucrats have on occasion imposed the broader national interest. Examples include regulation in areas such as safety and environment and the move by MHW to decrease over time the drug prices paid to pharmaceuticals companies in the face of the government's budget deficit. Nevertheless, in the case of conflict between the first and second 'faces', between actions in the interests of constituent companies and actions in the national interest, it is not clear that the latter always dominates. A case in point is the current debate in Japan over product liability laws where critics argue that ministries have been over-lenient on companies, failing to protect the interests of consumers.

Third, the bureaucrats, through their interventions in biotechnology, have clearly also acted in their own interests. As mentioned earlier, the influence and resources of a ministry's bureaucrats are to an extent a function of the quantity, range, and size of companies that fall within their jurisdiction. By acting in the interests of these constituent companies, therefore, the bureaucrats also act in their own interests. However, bureaucrats are significantly constrained in the extent to which they can pursue their own interests. This is most notably so in the case of budgetry constraints which are subject to the overall political constraints on government expenditure and the pecking order of ministries in the allocation of government revenues. Furthermore, bureaucrats are also subject to political constraint where they attempt to further their own interests at the expense of those of their 'constituents' or other interests in the society. One example is provided by the opposition of the biotechnology-related companies to the attempts of different ministries to incorporate them in their cooperative research programmes. As we saw earlier, this opposition was expressed politically through Keidanren and the Liberal Democratic Party.

It may therefore be concluded that the bureaucracy has three faces, the relative strength of each face depending on the political process.

7.11 Universities in Japanese Biotechnology

7.11.1 Introduction

The role of universities and government institutions

Why is all knowledge not created in for-profit companies in capitalist societies? To put it slightly differently, why are not all the institutions which create knowledge for-profit companies? Why are there other forms of organisation that simultaneously specialise in the creation of knowledge?

The answer to these questions is that there are essential constraints on the ability of firms to create knowledge, and on the kind of knowledge which they create. These constraints follow from the fact that in the for-profit company knowledge is not created for knowledge's sake; rather, knowledge-creation is subordinated to value-creation. Indeed, the social value of the company stems precisely from the fact that it does not create knowledge for its own sake, but rather, in seeking profit, matches knowledge with maket-expressible need.

However, this strength of the company is also its principal weakness: knowledge which is not expected to relate to the creation of value will receive little attention from the company. However, under conditions of uncertainty, such knowledge may later turn out to have significant economic consequences. Society will, accordingly, benefit from having created this knowledge.

Furthermore, companies operate under a significant time constraint. To survive, companies must produce value now. This may leave room for companies to allocate some resources now in order to create knowledge which may produce value only in the future. But there are severe limitations on the proportional quantity of such resources. These limitations result from the pressure put on the company by competition to create value now. Accordingly, on average around 90% of the R & D of companies goes to D, with only 10% allocated to R. Similarly, most R is oriented to well-defined and relatively short-term commercial needs. Therefore, if companies were the only form of organisation specialising in the creation of knowledge, limited resources would be allocated to the generation of knowledge which only accrues in the longer term future. This would significantly limit the variety of knowledge created. And as the evolutionary approach has taught us, it is variety together with selection which is the source of economic as well as biological change.

It is for this reason that universities, which emerged before the advent of capitalism and have always been relatively autonomous from the rest of society, have remained, although in modified form, as an important part of the knowledge-creation process in modern societies. Similarly, other government-related institutions, such as government research institutes or national institutions of health in the case of biotechnology, have also played a role. Both universities and these other institutions make significant contributions to the variety of knowledge. The functionality of the co-specialisation of for-profit companies and other forms of organisation such as universities in the creation of knowledge is evident from the importance of the links that companies in some sectors (but not all) have established with these kinds of organisations.

The Japanese case

In the case of Japan, as noted in the background section above, it has been argued that universities are weak relative to their Western counterparts. But is this argument correct? Have Japanese biotechnology-related companies been disadvantaged by the quality of Japanese universities? Have they been deprived by the weakness of an important external source of knowledge?

While we have not attempted a general evaluation of the university system in Japan in biotechnology, we have tackled these questions in two ways. The first is by establishing how important Japanese universities are as a source of knowledge external to the company in six of the largest biotechnology-related companies in Japan. The second way is by analysing the company–university links that exist in the case of one of the most active biotechnology-related laboratories in the Japanese university system.

7.11.2 The Importance of Japanese Universities as a Source of Knowledge for Japanese Companies

The six companies are from the chemicals, food, and beverages sectors and are among the largest companies in these sectors. Interviews were held with senior managers from these companies in the late 1980s.

External sources of knowledge

Two main external sources of knowledge were identified: other companies and universities. Regarding companies, further distinctions were drawn between competing and non-competing companies and between Japanese and non-Japanese companies. With regard to universities, Japanese universities were distinguished from non-Japanese universities. A further distinction was drawn between two different channels of 'external knowledge transfer' to the company: joint research; defined as activities involving cooperative research between researchers from the company and the other organisation; and licensing and other forms of knowledge purchase.

Results of the study

The importance of these different external sources of knowledge for the sample firms is shown in Table 7.7.

The most important result of the study is presented in row 7 of Table 7.7, where the companies rank the significance of the six different channels of external knowledge identified. Four of the six companies reported that Japanese universities were the most important source of external knowledge in the field of new biotechnology.

The two exceptions were Firms F and B. Firm F reported that Japanese universities were the second most important source of external knowledge, the most important being non-Japanese (mainly American) universities. This firm had between 200 and 300 contracts with Japanese university researchers, about a third of which were in new biotechnology. Many of the agreements, however, involved *de facto* consulting for the firm or the sending of company researchers to the university for experience and training, rather than joint research as defined. The officials interviewed from Firm F felt strongly that the ability of Japanese universities to respond to

Table 7.7 Transfer of technology in six major Japanese biotechnology firms

External channels of technology transfer	Firms:	A	B	C	D	E	F
1. Any joint research with competing companies? (in biotechnology)		No	No	No	Yes	No	Yes
2. Any joint research with non-competing companies?		Yes	Yes	Yes	Yes	Yes	Yes
3. Any joint research with Japanese universities (or technology transfer to the company)?		Yes	Yes/No	Yes	Yes	Yes	Yes
4. Any joint research with non-Japanese universities?		No	No	Yes	Yes	Yes	Yes
5. Licensing and other technology purchase from Japanese companies?		Yes	No	No	No	Yes	No
6. Licensing and other technology purchase from non-Japanese companies?		Yes	Yes	Yes	No	Yes	Yes
7. Rank the importance of these six channels for your company		3	6	3	3	3	4
		6	2	4	2	4	3
		5	3	6	4	6	1

Source: Author's interviews.

companies' research needs was significantly constrained by the universities' inability to hire additional temporary researchers to work on company-related projects. This difficulty follows from the requirement that Japanese universities, particularly national universities, provide long-term employment for those they recruit. Western universities, it was felt, were more important than Japanese universities since they were free from this constraint.

Firm B was the most critical of the quality of Japanese university research in biotechnology. This sentiment was summarised in the following statement: 'We don't rely much on Japanese university research. Academic research is not very good in Japan [in new biotechnology]. However, we do expect to get good students from Japanese universities'. Nevertheless, this company ranked Japanese universities as the third most important source of external knowledge, out of the six sources, after licensing from non-Japanese companies and joint research with non-competing companies. This company had licenses from a number of important Western pharmaceuticals companies.

Insofar as our study is more widely representative, it suggests that Japanese universities are more important as a source of external knowledge than is generally acknowledged. This result is all the more significant since the life sciences generally have been regarded as relatively weak in Japanese universities, compared both with Western universities and with stronger fields of research in Japanese universities such as electronics-related areas like opto-electronics. This conclusion is corroborated by a recent study of Japanese scientific research based on publication citations which concluded that Japanese companies 'draw most heavily on Japanese, not foreign sources', Japanese universities being the most important Japanese source, (Hicks *et al.* 1992, 1)

Modes of knowledge transfer from Japanese universities to Japanese companies

The most important way in which knowledge is transferred from Japanese universities to Japanese companies is via the dispatch of company R&D employees to the universities. Usually this temporary transfer of staff occurs on the initiative of the company which wishes to take advantage of the knowledge that has accumulated in the university in an area that has been prioritised by the company. As Company C put it, 'We learn the principle from the university researchers and then we apply this principle in our company'.

In view of the high degree of tacitness in much of this research, it is often necessary for the company researcher to accumulate the knowledge needed through membership of the university's research group. The knowledge is transferred when the researcher returns to the company. Since there are more relevant areas of research than can be covered by the companies' limited resources, companies turn to universities for some of this research. In the case of Company C, for example, a gene producing Interleukin 6, a B-cell stimulating factor, was cloned at a Japanese medical school while the scale-up and processing was done in the company. In this way the complementary competencies of university and company are merged.

In some cases the initiative comes from the university researchers. Company A, for instance, reported that 'university researchers are pressing us to commercialise their research'. This company is involved in the genetic engineering of plants and has forged close links with a number of Japanese universities in this area.

In Japan, unlike Western countries, the recruitment of university graduates is not usually a particularly important way of acquiring university-based knowledge. The reason is that Japanese companies tend to recruit graduates with Bachelor or Masters degrees, preferring to give them advanced training in the company and therefore mould their research to the company's needs. It is often assumed that graduates with PhDs are too 'academic'. The practice of life-time employment ensures that the company is able to appropriate the return from its investment in the graduate's training and therefore the company has an incentive to train.

A contradiction?

Is there a contradiction between the widely-held belief that research in Japanese universities in the life sciences tends not to be as advanced as that in corresponding Western universities and the findings of Table 7.7 that Japanese universities are the most important source of external knowledge for Japanese companies?

The answer is 'no'. The reason is that, generally speaking, companies do not commercialise the latest frontier research, but rather are involved in developing applications of research originally done much earlier, even decades earlier. Companies therefore tend to be interested in intra-frontier rather than frontier research. And by all accounts many Japanese universities are good at intra-frontier reseach. There is, accordingly, no contradiction.

Professor Karube's laboratory at Tokyo University

In order to get a better understanding of the industry–university link in biotechnology we examined Professor Karube's laboratory at Tokyo University's Research Center for Advanced Science and Technology (RCAST). RCAST, Professor Karube, and his laboratory are by no means typical, as will become clear. However, this case is particularly useful since it indicates the kind of relationship that can be established between companies and universities in Japan under the present set of institutional practices and constraints.

RCAST was established in the late 1980s partly to break down some of the barriers to interdisciplinary research created by university departmental and faculty separations and divisions. In RCAST problem-oriented research is done in four areas: materials, devices, systems, and the socio-economic study of technology. RCAST was also created to increase university–industry interaction and the Center was the first of the national universities to be allowed by the Ministry of Education to host Endowed Chairs financed by Japanese companies.

Professor Karube's laboratory is involved in research on biosensors and bioelectronics and thus relates research in biotechnology to the other outstanding research done in RCAST in electronics-related areas. The laboratory does research in areas such as biosensors, biochips, protein engineering, biofunctional materials, and marine biology. With 66 researchers, the laboratory is the largest in Tokyo University in terms of both research staff and students.

The laboratory is also notable as a result of its close interaction with Japanese industry. In January 1993, there were 28 researchers in the laboratory from Japanese companies which included Hitachi, Ishikawajima Harima Heavy Industry, Mitsui Shipbuilding, Dainippon Printing and Toyo Engineering (Nihon Keizai Shimbun, 4 January 1993, 17). Since 1980, the laboratory has hosted 106 company researchers. Typically the company covers the costs of the laboratory work done by the researchers which they send, which usually amounts to about one million Yen per researcher per year (about $9,000 at mid-1993 exchange rates). The research done in the laboratory by the company researchers relates directly to the priorities of the company, although the topic is negotiated in advance with Professor Karube. On average, about 30 patents are produced annually by the researchers in the laboratory. Examples of research being done by company researchers in the laboratory in the area of biosensors are given in Table 7.8.

The basic costs of running the laboratory, about ¥100 million annually, are covered largely from government-initiated research projects in biotechnology funded by MITI, the Ministry of Education, the Science and Technology Agency, and so on. Since these projects frequently involved a greater degree of 'oriented-basic' research, Professor Karube is able to merge this kind of research with the more applied research done in the laboratory by the company researchers. In this way, unusual for many university research projects, an organic link is forged between more basic and more applied research, with beneficial feedback loops running in both directions between the two.

Professor Karube's laboratory, although atypical, clearly illustrates the kinds of beneficial links that may be made between Japanese companies

Table 7.8 Research conducted by company researchers in Professor Karube's laboratory, Tokyo University

TOTO	biosensors for toilets
INAX	biosensors to test urine: for toilet use
Nippon Denso	biosensors to test sweat and measure fatigue
Takenaka Construction	biosensors for pollutant
Snow Brand	biosensors to test bacteria in food
Ito Ham	biosensors to test freshness of meat
Nichirei	biosensors to test freshness of fish
Nisshin Flour	biosensors to test ripeness of fruits and food quality
Seiko Electronics	biosensors for medical examination

Source: Shukan Diamondo, 11 Jan. 1992, p. 37.

and universities under the practices and constraints currently existing in Japan. This example, therefore, further supports the result of our own survey reported above which suggests that Japanese universities are an important source of external knowledge for Japanese companies.

7.12 The Location of Biotechnology R&D in Japan

The present discussion of the role of universities in Japan raises an important question: where is the most advanced research in biotechnology being done in Japan, in universities, government research institutes, or companies? Many analysts of Japanese science and technology have argued that the most advanced research tends to be located in Japanese companies rather than universities or government research institutes. Is there evidence to support this argument?

To examine this question, we collected data on the top ten patent-holders in pharmaceuticals, the sector where biotechnology commercial applications are most advanced. With the help of experts in this field, we selected 13 pharmaceuticals products. The assumption made in analysing this data is that the quantity and quality of advanced research, and the organisational location of such research, is adequately measured by the number of patents held by the top ten organisations in these 13 products areas. The results of the patent analysis are presented in Table 7.9, and the 13 products are listed at the bottom of this table.

The striking conclusion which emerges from Table 7.9 is that while half of the top ten non-Japanese organisations were government or university-related research institutes, ALL the top ten Japanese organisations were for-profit companies. This suggests that there is indeed support for the argument that advanced research in biotechnology tends to be done in

Table 7.9 Top ten patenters, Japanese and non-Japanese

Organisation		Patents	(Monoclonal antibodies)
(a) Top ten non-Japanese patenters			
US Dept. Health		63	41
Cetus Corpn.		61	0
Genentech		47	0
Sloan-Kettering		44	36
Ins. Pasteur		39	30
Schering Corp.		35	0
Immunex Corp.		33	20
Akad Wissenschaft		33	27
CNRS		31	29
Tech Licence Co.		31	31
(b) Top ten Japanese patenters			
Green Cross	(P)[a]	125	42
Toray	(C)	78	8
Takeda	(P)	61	9
Ajinomoto	(F)	57	9
Kyowa Hakko	(C)	51	29
Teiijin	(O)	41	39
Wakunaga	(P)	34	17
Otsuka	(P)	30	8
Snow Brand Milk	(F)	29	17
Asahi Chem.	(C)	27	14

[a] C = Chemicals; O = Other; P = Therapeutics; F = Food/Beverage.

Source: Derwent Publications.
Products included:

1 = Alpha Interferon	8 = Epidermal Growth Factor
2 = Beta Interferon	9 = Superoxide Dismutase
3 = Gamma Interferon	10 = Brain Peptide
4 = Interleukin-2	11 = Human Growth Hormone
5 = Hepatitis B Vaccine	12 = Granulocyte Colony
6 = Erythropoietin	Stimulation Factor
7 = Urokinase	13 = Monoclonal Antibodies

companies in Japan (at least insofar as our assumption is correct). Note that due to the different patent regulations in different countries the figures in the two parts of the table are not comparable.

A further interesting conclusion emerging from Table 7.9 is that only four of the top ten patenters in Japan were from the pharmaceuticals sector. Three were from the chemicals, two from the food, and one from the 'other' sector. This illustrates the extent to which non-pharmaceuticals companies in Japan have diversified, on the 'back' of biotechnology, into the pharmaceuticals sector. It is likely that the government cooperative research programmes in biotechnology analysed in this paper have influenced this diversification behaviour.

7.13 Government and Globalisation in Japanese Biotechnology

How has MITI responded to the increased 'globalisation' of the Japanese innovation system which makes it increasingly diffcult to contain new science and technology within Japanese borders where it is available for the sole appropriation of Japanese companies? Has MITI abandoned what Nelson and Wright (1992), quoted earlier, refer to as 'techno-nationalist' policies, that is policies designed to facilitate the international competitiveness of Japanese companies?

In order to answer these questions it is necessary to understand that MITI has multiple objectives in pursuing its technology policy as part of its broader industry and trade policy. Among these are three important objectives. The first, as in the post-war period until the late 1980s, is to improve the performance and competitiveness of Japanese companies. The second objective, which has become increasingly important since the late 1980s, is to strengthen Japan's basic science and technology capabilities. The third, also more significant since the late 1980s, is to manage Japan's trade and international conflicts, partly by opening Japanese markets and science and technology institutions to foreign participation.

These objectives can be seen in the *Law for Consolidating Research & Development Systems Relating To Industrial Technology*, drafted by MITI bureaucrats and passed in 1988. The two aims of this law were to internationalise Japan's industrial technology and to strengthen Japan's capabilities in basic and scientific R&D. Under this legislation foreign companies from 1989 were allowed to join MITI's national R&D programmes.

The effects of these changes can be seen in the area of biotechnology. Under its R&D Programme on Basic Technologies for Future Industries (see Table 7.1) MITI introduced two new projects in 1989 and 1991, the Molecular Assemblies for Functional Protein Systems, and the Production and Utilization Technology of Complex Carbohydrates projects respectively. (The first three projects in this Future Industries programme were analysed in detail earlier in this chapter.)

Two features of these new projects are worth highlighting. The first is that while MITI regarded the original three projects in the Future Industries programme as 'catch-up' projects, the new projects are intended to make original contributions (see Karube 1992, 265). The second feature is that foreign companies participate in these new projects together with Japanese companies.

More specifically, the participants in the Molecular Assemblies project include GBF of Germany, seven Japanese companies (Chugai Pharmaceutical, Kao, Kuraray, Mitsubishi Chemical, Mitsubishi Petrochemical, Stanley Electric, and Toray Research Center), and five of MITI's national research institutes. Research is also subcontracted to Japanese universities such as Tokyo and Okayama universities. The

Complex Carbohydrates project includes the Swedish company, Pharmacia, and four Japanese companies (Asahi Chemical, Kirin Beer, Meiji Milk, and Mitsui Toatsu), in addition to several MITI national research institutes. This project is part of a broader project in the same area involving MITI, MAFF, MHW, and STA. For the further technical details on the Molecular Assemblies project and the Complex Carbohydrates project see Karube 1992.

Is there a contradiction between MITI's objectives to strengthen Japanese organisations while internationalising Japan's national technology programmes? This is suggested by Nelson and Wright 1992 quoted above who argue that the advanced industrialised countries have accumulated the capability to rapidly assimilate new science and technology no matter where it is created. The short answer is that there is no contradiction and the reason for this conclusion lies in the significant degree of tacitness in these research programmes. This tacitness means that the knowledge created under the programme cannot readily and rapidly be acquired by competitors not involved in the programme.

Furthermore, tacitness also means that the foreign participants in the Japanese programmes are unable to acquire all the knowledge that is created under the auspices of the programme. This constraint is increased where the research is not done jointly in joint research facilities, but is done within the participating organisations with only the results being reported and discussed with the other participants. In the Molecular Assemblies project, for example, most of the research is done within individual organisations and there are only two joint research projects, one between MITI's Fermentation Research Institute and Stanley Electric and the other between MITI's National Chemical Laboratory for Industry and Kuraray. (see also Fransman 1995*b*)

7.14 Conclusions

7.14.1 Companies are the Motor of the Japanese Innovation System in Biotechnology

The first conclusion is that it is companies, rather than government, that constitute the 'motor' of the Japanese innovation system in biotechnology.

The resources allocated by the Japanese government to cooperative R&D programmes in biotechnology make up only a small proportion of the R&D expenditures by Japanese companies. This can be shown by the following figures. A total of ¥9.433 billion was allocated to the three original projects in the biotechnology part of MITI's Future Industries Programme (examined in detail earlier in this paper). A further ¥17.1 billion was budgeted for PERI, MITI's 'showpiece', over the life of this project.

This makes a total of ¥26.5 billion for these four key biotechnology cooperative research projects. However, in 1992 Mitsubishi Chemical, Japan's largest chemicals company, spent a total of ¥53.4 billion on R&D. This means that the total amount spent on MITI's four key biotechnology projects over approximately 10 years came to only 50% of Mitsubishi chemical total R&D expenditure in 1992 alone.

There were a total of 24 companies which participated in these four projects, some taking part in two projects. This means that MITI's total expenditure of ¥26.5 billion came to an average of ¥1.1 billion per company over the approximately ten-year period. The latter figure is 0.021% of Mitsubishi Chemical's total R&D expenditure for 1992 alone. In 1986 Mitsubishi Chemical estimated that 47% of its total R&D expenditure was in biotechnology-related areas. If this proportion remained in 1992, Mitsubishi Chemical spent ¥25.1 billion on biotechnology-related R&D. Therefore, MITI's average expenditure of ¥1.1 billion per company for the four projects over a period of about 10 years came to 0.044% of Mitsubishi Chemical's R&D expenditure on biotechnology in 1992 alone.

These figures are sufficient to justify the conclusion that it is companies, rather than government, which take the major responsibility for biotechnology R&D in Japan. Furthermore, even where companies participate in government-initiated cooperative R&D programmes, most of the research, as we have shown, is done inside the companies using company staff and resources. It is justified, therefore, to conclude that it is companies that provide the 'motor' for innovation in Japanese biotechnology.

7.14.2 Government Plays a Major Supporting Role

While companies are the 'motor', the Japanese government plays a major supportive role. The analysis and information provided in this chapter suggests that the government has assisted Japanese companies involved in biotechnology in a number of important ways.

First, the government has encouraged companies to undertake R&D in areas where, as a result of the uncertainty, scale of investment, and time-horizon involved, less R&D would otherwise have been done. Second, the government has facilitated greater flows of knowledge between companies, particularly between competing companies, than otherwise would have occurred in the absence of government intervention. These flows have served to diffuse knowledge more rapidly to the companies participating in the programmes, thus contributing to a strengthening of the biotechnology sector as a whole.

Third, by highlighting at an early stage the implications for companies of important new technologies such as biotechnology, the government has facilitated both the entry of companies into these new technologies and the diffusion of the technologies. In this way, the government, and MITI in particular, has been able to use its efficient information-gathering network. In many cases companies, hampered by the cost of information, by their existing information channels which are not always attuned to new technologies and markets, and by their existing interpretations of information, have been able to take better advantage of new technologies more quickly as a result of the information role played by the government.

Fourth, the government has also helped companies to benefit from the other economies of cooperative research, such as avoiding duplicating research and the sharing of expensive equipment.

Fifth, by internationalising its R&D programmes, the government is providing Japanese companies with an important new input in the form of stimulation from Western companies which benefit reciprocally from what they learn from the project. This benefit to Japanese companies compensates for any leakage of knowledge that they suffer as a result of foreign participation.

For these reasons, we conclude that the Japanese government has played an important role in supporting Japanese companies in biotechnology.

7.14.3 Japanese Universities are an Important Source of Knowledge External to Japanese Companies

Evidence has been provided in this chapter which suggests that Japanese universities are more important for the performance and competitiveness of Japanese companies in the area of biotechnology than has been acknowledged. More specifically, in fields within the international frontiers of knowledge, Japanese universities frequently do research which feeds into the R&D activities of Japanese companies. In some cases, this research is of a complementary nature, for instance where gene cloning is performed in the university, and scale-up and processing is done in the company.

Japanese universities also play an important role in providing graduates with a basic traning in the life sciences who are then given firm-specific training by the company. While most large Japanese companies also have close links with foreign universities, the closer proximity of Japanese universities, the close ties between companies and some Japanese university professors, and the recruitment of university graduates through these ties, have meant that Japanese universities are often more important than foreign universities for Japanese biotechnology companies.

7.14.4 Advanced Research Tends to be Done in Japanese Companies

Although Japanese universities and government research institutes play an important role in complementing Japanese company research, advanced research in biotechnology tends to be done in Japanese companies rather than in these other organisations. This contrasts with Western countries where universities and government-related research institutes play a relatively more important role. This conclusion was supported by the analysis of patents in 13 biotechnology-related new products in pharmaceuticals.

7.14.5 *Japanese Government has Responded to Globalisation by Internationalising its R&D Programmes*

The Japanese Government, and MITI in particular, has responded to the opening of the Janpanese innovation system by internationalising its R&D programmes. Accordingly, foreign companies have been invited to join national R & D programmes and purely international programmes such as the Human Frontiers programme have been established. This internationalisation process has gone hand-in-glove with, and has been consistent with, continuing efforts on the part of the Japanese government to increase the performance and competitiveness of Japanese companies. The pursuance of internationalisation, however, also reflects other Japanese government objectives such as decreasing friction with Japan's trading partners and making a greater Japanese international contribution to science and technology (see Fransman *et al.* 1994).

REFERENCES

Abramovitz, M. (1986). 'Catching Up, Forging Ahead, and Falling Behind', *Journal of Economic History*, 46:2, 386–406.

Akerlof, G. A. (1970). 'The Market for Lemons: Qualitative Uncertainty and the Market Mechanism', *Quarterly Journal of Economics*, 84, 488–500.

Alchian, A. and Demsetz, H. (1972). 'Production, Information Costs, and Economic Organization', *The American Economic Review*, 62, 777–795.

Aoki, M. (1988). *Information, Incentives, and Bargaining in the Japanese Economy*. Cambridge: Cambridge University Press.

——(1990*a*). 'The Participatory Generation of Information Rents and the Theory of the Firm', in M. Aoki *et al.* (eds.), *The Firm as a Nexus of Treaties*. London: Sage.

——(1990*b*). 'Towards an Economic Model of the Japanese Firm', *Journal of Economic Literature*, 28, 1–27.

Archibald, G. C. (1987). 'Theory of the Firm', in *The New Palgrave: A Dictionary of Economics, Vol. 2*. London: Macmillan.

Baumol, W. J. (1986). 'Productivity Growth, Convergence, and Welfare: What the Long-run Data Show', *American Economic Review*, 76:5, 1072–1085.

——Blackman, S. A. B. and Wolff, E. N. (1989). *Productivity and American Leadership*. Cambridge, Mass: The MIT Press.

Boulding, K. (1956). *The Image*. Ann Arbor: University of Michigan Press.

Carroll, P. (1994). *Big Blues: The Unmaking of IBM*. London: Weidenfeld & Nicolson.

Chandler, A. D. (1962). *Strategy and Structure*. Cambridge, Mass: MIT Press.

——(1977). *The Visible Hand: The Managerial Revolution in American Business*. Cambridge, Mass: Harvard University Press.

——(1990*a*). *Scale and Scope: The Dynamics of Industrial Capitalism*. Cambridge, Mass: Belknap Press.

——(1990*b*). 'The Enduring Logic of Industrial Success', *Harvard Business Review*, March-April, 132–140.

Clark, K. B. and Fujimoto, T. (1991). *Product Development Performance: Strategy, Organization, and Management in the World Auto Industry*. Boston: Harvard Business School Press.

Coase, R. H. (1937). 'The Nature of the Firm', *Economica N.S.*, 4, 386–405.

——(1988). 'The Nature of the Firm: Origin', *Journal of Law, Economics, and Organization*, 4:1, 3–47.

Coopersmith, J. (1993). 'Facsimile's False Starts', *IEEE Spectrum*, Feb., 46–49.

Dertouzos, M. L., Lester, R. K., and Solow, R. M. (1989). *Made in America: Regaining the Productive Edge*. Cambridge, Mass: MIT Press.

Dibner, M. D. and White, R. S. (1989). *White Biotechnology in Japan*. New York: McGraw-Hill.

Dore, R. P. (1983). 'Goodwill and the Spirit of Market Capitalism', *The British Journal of Sociology*, 34:4, 459–482.

——(1987). *Taking Japan Seriously*. London: Athlone Press.

Dosi, G., Teece, D. J., and Winter, S. (1992). 'Towards a Theory of Corporate Coherence: Preliminary Remarks', in G. Dosi, R. Gianetti, and P. A. Toninelli (eds.) *Technology and Enterprise in a Historical Perspective*. Oxford: Clarendon Press.

Dretske, F. I. (1982). *Knowledge and the Flow of Information*. Cambridge, Mass: MIT Press.

Eliot, T. S. (1963). Choruses from 'The Rock', *Collected Poems, 1909–1962*. London: Faber & Faber.

Elster, J. (1983). *Explaining Technical Change: Studies in Rationality and Social Change*. Cambridge: Cambridge University Press.

Ferguson, C. H. and Morris, C. R. (1993). *Computer Wars: How the West Can Win in a Post-IBM World*. New York: Times Books.

Fransman, M. J. (1988). 'Corporate Strategy and Technology Transfer in Japanese Biotechnology-Creating System', in *Proceedings of the Biosymposium Tokyo '88*. Tokyo.

——(1990). *The Market and Beyond: Cooperation and Competition in Information Technology in the Japanese System*. Cambridge: Cambridge University Press.

——(1991). *Explaining the Performance of the Japanese Large Company*. JETS Paper No. 6, Institute for Japanese-European Technology Studies, University of Edinburgh.

——(1992a). 'Controlled Competition in the Japanese Telecommunications Equipment Industry: The Case of Central Office Switches', in C. Antonelli (ed.), *The Economics of Information Networks*. Amsterdam: Elsevier.

——(1992b). 'Japanese Failure in a High-Tech Industry?: The Case of Central Office Telecommunications Switches', *Telecommunications Policy*, 16:3, 259–276.

——(1992c). *Biotechnology: Generation, Diffusion and Policy*, UNU/INTECH Working Paper No. 1, Institute for New Technologies, The United Nations University, Maastricht.

——(1992d). 'The Japanese Innovation System: How It Works', *Science in Parliament*, 49/4.

——(1993). *The Market and Beyond: Information Technology in Japan*. Cambridge: Cambridge University Press.

——(1994a). 'Different Folks, Different Strokes—How IBM, AT&T and NEC Segment to Compete', *Business Strategy Review*, 5:3, 1–20.

——(1994b). 'Information, Knowledge, Vision and Theories of the Firm', *Industrial and Corporate Change*, 3:2, 1–45.

——(1994c). Knowledge Segmentation-Integration in Theory and in Japanese Companies; in Granstand, O. (Ed) Economics of Technology. Amsterdam: Elsevier.

——(1995a). *Japan's Computer and Communications Industry*. Oxford: Oxford University Press.

——(1995b). 'Is National Technology Policy Obsolete in a Globalised World?: The Japanese Response', *Cambridge Journal of Economics*, 19, 95–119.

Fransman, M. (forthcoming). 'The Problems of Decentralisation and Inter-dependence in the Diversified Large Corporation: The Reorganisations in the 1990s of IBM, AT&T, and NEC Compared', Business Strategy Review (London Business School).

——and Tanaka, S. (1995). 'The Strengths and Weaknesses of the Japanese Innovation System in Biotechnology', in M. Fransman, G. Junne, and A. Roobeek (eds.), *The Biotechnology Revolution?* Oxford: Basil Blackwell.

Freeman, C. (1990). 'Technical Innovation in the World Chemical Industry and Changes of Techno-economic Paradigm', in C. Freeman and L. Soete (eds.), *New Explorations in the Economics of Technical Change.* London: Pinter.

Fruin, W. M. (1992). *The Japanese Enterprise System: Competitive Strategies and Cooperative Structures.* Oxford: Clarendon Press.

Grupp, H. and Schnoring, T. (1992). 'Research and Development in Telecommunications: National Systems Under Pressure', *Telecommunications Policy*, 16:1, 46–66.

Hayek, F. A. (1945). 'The Uses of Knowledge in Society', *American Economic Review*, 35, 519–530.

Heller, R. (1994). *The Fate of IBM.* London: Little, Brown & Co.

Hicks, D., Ishikuza, T., Keen, P., and Sweet, S. (1992). *Japanese Corporations, Scientific Research and Globalisation.* DRC Discussion Paper No. 91, Science Policy Research Unit, University of Sussex, Brighton.

Hounshell, D. A., and Smith, J. K. (1988). *Science and Corporate Strategy: Du Pont R&D, 1902–1980.* Cambridge: Cambridge University Press.

Itami, H. (1991). *Why Is the Japanese Chemical Industry behind Other Industries?* Tokyo: NTT.

Japanese Technology Evaluation Program (JTECH) (1988). *JTECH Panel Report on the Japanese Exploratory Research for Advanced Technology (ERATO) Program.* McLean, VA: Science Application International Corporation.

Jensen, M. and Meckling, W. (1976). 'Theory of the Firm: Managerial Behavior, Agency Costs, and Ownership Structure', *Journal of Financial Economics*, 3, 305–360.

Johnson, C. (1982). *MITI and the Japanese Miracle.* Tokyo: Charles Tuttle.

——(1985). 'The Institutional Foundations of Japanese Industrial Policy', *California Management Review*, 27:4, 59–69.

Karube, M. (1992). 'Kinosei tanpakushitsu shugotai ouyogijutsu no kenkyukai-hatsu', in Tsusho Sangyo sho (ed.), *Sekaini habataku jisedai purojekuto.* Tokyo: Keigun Shuppan.

Keidanran (Federation of Economic Organisations) (1988). *Proposal for Promotion of Basic Research in Life Sciences.* Tokyo: Keidanren.

Kline, S. (1989). 'Innovation Styles in Japan and the United States: Cultural Bases; Implications for Competitiveness', Thermosciences Division, Department of Mechanical Engineering, Stanford University, mimeo.

Knight, F. (1921). *Risk, Uncertainty and Profit.* Boston: Houghton Mifflin.

Kobayashi, K. (1991). *The Rise of NEC: How the World's Greatest C&C Company is Managed.* Oxford: Basil Blackwell.

Lewis, H. W. (1984). *Biotechnology in Japan.* Washington: National Science Foundation.

Loasby, B. (1990). 'Firms, Markets, and the Principle of Continuity', in J. K. Whittaker (ed.); *Centenary Essays on Alfred Marshall.* Cambridge: Cambridge University Press.

March, J. G. (1994). *A Primer on Decision Making: How Decisions Happen*, New York: Free Press.

—— and Simon, H. A. (1958). *Organizations*. New York: Wiley.

Marshall, A. (1969). *Principles of Economics*, Macmillan, London.

Mises, L. (1949). *Human Action: A Treatise on Economics*. London: William Hodge.

——(1962). *The Ultimate Foundation of Economics Science: An Essay on Method*. Princeton, NJ: D. van Nostrand.

Molina, A. H. (1990). 'Building Technological Capabilities in Telecommunications Technologies: Development and Strategies in Public Digital Switching Systems'. Venice: Paper presented to the International Telecommunications Society Conference (Mar.).

——(1992). *Current Trends, Issues and Strategies in the Development of the Microprocessor Industry*. Programme on Information and Communication Technologies (PICT) Working Paper No. 42, University of Edinburgh.

Morita, A. (1986). *Made in Japan*. New York: Dutton.

Mowery, D. C. and Teece, D. J. (1992). 'The Changing Place of Japan in the Global Scientific and Technological Enterprise', in T. S. Arrison, C. F. Bergsten, E. M. Graham, and M. Caldwell-Harris (eds.), *Japan's Growing Technological Capability: Implications for the U.S. Economy*. Washington: National Academy Press.

Muramatsu, M. (1991). 'The "Enhancement" of the Ministry of Posts and Telecommunications to Meet the Challenge of Telecommunications Innovation', In S. Wilks and M. Wright (eds.), *The Promotion and Regulation of Industry in Japan*. London: Macmillan.

Nature (1992). 'Semiprivate Research: Best of Both Worlds', October 15, 577.

Nelson, R. R. (1990). 'The U.S. Technology Lead: Where Did It Come From and Where Did It Go?', *Research Policy*, 19, 117–132.

——(1991). 'Why do firms differ, and how does it matter', mimeo.

——(1992). 'National Innovation Systems: A Retrospective on a Study', *Industrial and Corporate Change*, 1:2, 347–374.

—— and Winter, S. G. (1977). 'In Search of a Useful Theory of Innovation', *Research Policy*, 6, 36–76.

——————— (1982). *An Evolutionary Theory of Economic Change*. Cambridge, Mass: The Belknap Press.

—— and Wright, G. (1992). 'The Rise and Fall of American Technological Leadership: The Postwar Era in Historical Perspective', *Journal of Economic Literature*, (Dec.), 1931–1964.

Noll, A. M. (1991). 'The Future of AT&T Bell Labs and Telecommunications Research', *Telecommunications Policy*, 15:2, 101–105.

Odagiri, H. and Goto, A. (1993). 'The Japanese System of Innovation: Past, Present, and Future', in R. R. Nelson (ed.), *National Innovation Systems: A Comparative Analysis*. New York: Oxford University Press.

Penrose, E. T. (1959). *The Theory of the Growth of the Firm*. Oxford: Basil Blackwell.

Pisano, G. P., Shan, W., and Teece, D. J. (1989). 'Joint Ventures and Collaboration in the Biotechnology Industry', in D. C. Mowery (ed.), *International Collaborative Ventures in U.S. Manufacturing*. Cambridge, Mass: Ballinger.

Polanyi, M. (1967). *The Tacit Dimension*. Garden City, New York: Doubleday Anchor.

Porter, M. E. (1980). *Competitive Strategy*. New York: Free Press.

——(1990). *The Competitive Advantage of Nations*. London: Macmillan.

Prahalad, C. K. and Hamel. G. (1990). The Core Competence of the Corporation, *Harvard Business Review*, May–June: 78–91.

Putterman, L. (1986). *The Economic Nature of the Firm: A Reader.* Cambridge: Cambridge University Press.

Reich, L. S. (1985). *The Making of American Industrial Research: Science and Business at GE and Bell, 1876–1926.* Cambridge: Cambridge University Press.

Richardson, G. B. (1972). 'The Organisation of Industry', *Economic Journal*, 82, 883–896.

Roberts, E. B. and Mizouchi, R. (1989). 'Inter-firm Technological Collaboration: The Case of Japanese Biotechnology', *International Journal of Technology Management*, 4:1, 43–61.

Rosenberg, N. (1982). 'Schumpeter and Marx: How Common a Vision?', in R. J. Schonberger *Japanese Manufacturing Techniques: Nine Hidden Lessons in Simplicity.* New York: Free Press.

Rudge, A. W. (1990). 'Clifford Paterson Lecture: Organization and Management of R&D in a Privatized British Telecom', *Sci. Publ. Affairs*, 4, 115–129.

Schumpeter, J. A. (1952). *Capitalism, Socialism, and Democracy.* London: Unwin.

—— (1961). *The Theory of Economic Development: An Inquiry into Profits, Capital, Credit, Interest, and the Business Cycle.* New York: Oxford University Press.

—— (1966). *Capitalism, Socialism, and Democracy.* London: Unwin. London.

—— (1986). *History of Economic Analysis.* London: Allen & Unwin.

Science and Technology Agency (1991). *White Paper on Science and Technology.* Tokyo: The Japan Information Center of Science and Technology.

Simon, H. A. (1957). *Models of Man.* New York: John Wiley & Sons.

—— (1959). 'Theories of Decision Making in Economics and Behavioral Science', *American Economic Review*, 49, 253–283.

—— (1961). *Administrative Behavior*, 2nd edn. New York: Macmillan.

—— (1976). *Administrative Behavior*, 3rd edn. New York: Macmillan.

—— (1978). 'Rationality as Process and as Product of Thought', *American Economic Review*, 68, 1–16.

—— (1981). *The Sciences of the Artificial.* Cambridge, Mass: MIT Press.

—— Egidi, M., Marris, R., and Viale, R. (1992). *Economics, Bounded Rationality and the Cognitive Revolution.* Aldershot: Edward Elgar.

Smith, A. (1910). *An Inquiry into the Nature and Causes of the Wealth of Nations.* London: J. M. Dent.

Stalk, G., Evans, P., and Shulman, L. E. (1992). Competing on Capabilities: The New Role of Corporate Strategy', *Harvard Business Review* (Mar.–Apr.), 57–69.

Tanaka, M. (1991). 'Government Policy and Biotechnology in Japan: The Pattern and Impact of Rivalry between Ministries', in S. Wilks and M. Wright (eds.), *The Promotion and Regulation of Industry in Japan.* Japan: Macmillan.

Teece, D. J. (1980). 'Economies of Scope and the Scope of an Enterprise', *Journal of Economic Behavior and Organization*, 1, 223–247.

—— (1984). 'Economic Analysis and Strategic Management', *California Management Review*, 26:3, 87–110.

—— (1986). 'Profiting from Technological Innovation', *Research Policy*, 15:6.

—— (1988). 'Technological Change and the Nature of the Firm', in G. Dosi, C. Freeman, R. Nelson, G. Silverberg, and L. Soete (eds.), *Technical Change and Economic Theory.* London: Pinter.

——Pisano, G. and Shuen, A. (1990). *Firm Capabilities, Resources and the Concept of Strategy*. CCC Working Paper No. 90–98, University of California, Berkeley.

The Economist (1991). 'An Economist Takes Tea with a Management Guru', Dec. 21, 107–9.

US Congress, Office of Technology Assessment (1984). *Commercial Biotechnology: An International Analysis*, Office of Technology Assessment, Washington.

US Department of Commerce (1985). *Biotechnology in Japan (Japanese Technology Evaluation Programme)*. Washington: US Department of Commerce.

Vallance, I. D. T. (1990). 'The Competitive Challenge in World Communications Markets', *British Telecommunications Engineering*, 9, 84–87.

Watanabe, C. (1992). 'Leading the Way to Comprehensive Transitional R&D Cooperation—NEDO's Initiative'. Chicago: Paper presented to the AAAS National Meeting.

Williamson, O. E. (1975). *Markets and Hierarchies: Analysis and Antitrust Implications. A Study in the Economics of Internal Organization*. New York: Free Press.

——(1985). *The Economic Institutions of Capitalism*, New York: Free Press.

——(1990). 'The Firm as a Nexus of Treaties: An Introduction', in M. Aoki, B. Gustafson, and O. E. Williamson (eds.), *The Firm as a Nexus of Treaties*. London: Sege.

Winter, S. G. (1988). 'On Coase, Competence and the Corporation', *Journal of Law, Economics, and Organization*, 4:1, 163–180.

Womack, J. P., Jones, D. T., and Roos, D. (1990). *The Machine that Changed the World: The Story of Lean Production*. New York: Maxwell Macmillan International.

INDEX